Hey "Cusin Zoretta"

Thank you so much for your support. Enjoy the read it's deep, but true. Any women go through this daily.

Love always
Adrianne aka A.Michelle

1

# A. MICHELLE

# STABBED TO LIFE

## THE RESILIENCE OF A DOMESTIC VIOLENCE SURVIVOR

### A. MICHELLE

# A. MICHELLE

Master Publisher: Remember To ThinkPink Publications©. Dallas, Texas

# STABBED TO LIFE

This book is dedicated to all the many Survivors and the countless victims of Domestic Violence and Sexual Assault.

This is for US.

It is my hope that I've transparently shared my journey in a way that will help people understand, the who, the what, and the why.

# A. MICHELLE

# FOREWORD

Never had I imagined editing and publishing a book would be so difficult. As I began the process of editing "Stabbed to Life" I became instantly transfixed by the candid way Author A. Michelle shared her horrific accounts of physical, mental, sexual, and spiritual abuse.

The jarring instances of Intimate Partner Violence found in this book will take readers inside the heart and mind of the victim. This book will give you an up-close look at the patterns of the abuser.

"Stabbed to Life" will not only shed light on reasons victims stay in abusive situations, but also give hope to those victims that have yet to escape.

Sharing her story in such a transparent manner will help other survivors to find their voice, and hopefully, prevent other women from going through this insidious cycle.

It is my suggestion that you grab a box of Kleenex and prepare yourself for the gripping journey of Author A. Michelle's. Her strength and resilience can be felt throughout her written words as she shares the events that nearly ended in her death.

I implore you to read this book from cover to cover and find out how a victim of domestic violence can be STABBED TO LIFE.

Happy Reading,

TiTi Ladette, Editor/Publisher

# A. MICHELLE

# STABBED TO LIFE

# PREFACE

When I was a young girl, I had many insecurities. I developed early physically, I looked like a grown woman by 5th grade. When all my other friends were still wearing training bras, I was wearing Playtex cross your heart bras from Sears with three clasps down the back. Over developed and overweight, I was teased and touched inappropriately, and I hated my body. I had no talents, no hobby's and no drive. I fought my way through everything, the boys on my block and later the men in my life. Because my self-esteem was so low, I accepted relationships that were unhealthy and very controlling, probably because I didn't think I deserved anything more. What did I really have to offer? Once I slimmed down and felt somewhat better about myself, I still got with people who took advantage of me. My primary goal was to please them and everyone else.

I was a teen mother and by the time I was 20 years old I had two children and had my tubes tied.

Married at the age of 18, I already had a toddler, and I was just doing all I could just to not further embarrass my family.

I came from a good home with two hard-working parents who ensured I had all I needed and then some. We lacked in the communication department because I grew up in the era of children were just to do as they were told. So, when I

# A. MICHELLE

was hurting, and confused with my life, everything just stayed bottled up inside.

My marriage did not last because, firstly, we were just far too young. He had a very sad up bringing that included abuse and drug addiction. The abuse he'd been exposed to as a child eventually spilled over into our relationship and my inability to communicate did not help matters. Even though I had a good example of a good marriage, I just could not do it. Eventually we ended up in a nasty divorce riddled with accusations and 30 years later a paternity test.

Both serious relationships I'd gotten into were with hidden victims of domestic violence. These men had witnessed abuse in their homes as children. They saw their mothers beat and swore they would not be that way. Sadly, they both were exactly that way.

In both my failed relationships there was a part of me that thought I could fix them. I could give them the loved they lacked, be there for there every need and I could make them all better.

I became codependent and neglected my children while trying to nurture abusive relationships.

All I ever wanted was to have what my mother and father had. No, it wasn't perfect, but they had mutual respect and there was no physical or verbal abuse.

Any goals and aspirations I had went out the door because I was dealing with jealous individuals who thought just by me smiling at someone meant we were sleeping together or had slept together at some point.

I wanted to become a nurse; an RN where I could help people at their worse. I was a care taker by nature, so I guess once I didn't pursue my nursing degree, I began to nurse my relationships.

My journey, although rough and bumpy, taught me so many life lessons. They were mainly about me and being stronger as a woman. It taught me resilience, perseverance, and courage. It taught me the importance of family and support.

I learned that I am enough. I had to learn to love me before I could properly love anyone else and even accept love from anyone else.

I certainly hope that you, my readers, will understand that my low self-esteem is what made me tolerate horrific treatment and it is my prayer that you will learn from my mistakes. There are several statistics concerning the topic of domestic violence and intimate partner violence, but it is important to know that abuse of ANY KIND is not okay.

Seeking help is important. If you or someone you know is a victim of abuse, please call:

# National Domestic Violence Hotline: 1-800-799-7233

# A. MICHELLE

# STABBED TO LIFE

# CHAPTER ONE
## THE THERAPIST

*I dreaded this day so bad, but I had made this appointment four times and had canceled every time. I was finally convinced by my mentor/friend/business partner to go, so I finally kept the appointment.*

*I was referred once again for therapy since my anxiety and panic attacks were getting progressively worse. I refused to take medication.*

*Arriving at the counseling agency, I noticed it was an average doctor's office. Nothing fancy like the ones you see in the movies where rich people and celebrities see a therapist. The décor was average; soft egg shell walls with a wood grain receptionist counter. There were some faux leather couches with  pictures of calming ocean scenery. There were also simply framed pictured that read "Inhale Exhale"*

*It was funny, because as soon as I read it…I did just that and closed my eyes. I breathed in and out for a minute, trying to gather myself, then a feeling Deja vu came over me. I felt like I had been in this very location before. I took a seat sinking into the leather couch in the waiting area. Surprisingly it was very comfortable. I looked around and noticed there was not a television in the waiting area. I would think that there would be something -a TV or*

# A. MICHELLE

*magazines to kill the time while patients waited. Most doctors' offices had those things.*

*Before I could get to comfortable the side door opened and little lady no more than 5-foot-tall walked up to me, pulling her reading glasses down to get a good look at me, and asked, "Are you Ms. Green?"*

*"Yes, that would be me…" I smiled and wondered to myself why didn't I get rid of that Green last name, HIS last name.*

*When I divorced my 1st husband, which ended being another traumatic trigger, I was painfully reminded of another failed relationship awful reminder of yet another failed relationship.*

*I hated the way my mind was starting to work. Everything that reminded me of the trauma triggered me, sometimes to the point of panic attacks. Swallowing my fear, I was determined to focus on this therapy session. I was determined to get the help that I needed for myself.*

*The lady made the appropriate small talk, asking me how I was doing and introducing herself. Looking at her notes she told me that she was happy I made it sense I'd missed several appointments.*

*A part of me wanted to come up with a long drawn out story as to why I never could make it, but instead I just said, "I'm sorry…I just wasn't ready yet…but I am ready today." We smiled at each other and she went on to introduce herself.*

*"My name is Linda Harvey I am a licensed therapist I have been in this field for over 17 years…."*

# STABBED TO LIFE

*As she talked continuing her repertoire, I looked around the office and again had the feeling that I had been in that very office before.*

*The huge window overlooked a Sizzler Restaurant and a little alley leading to the main street. All of that too seemed too familiar but I could not pin point the connection. I focused on the pictures of her family. She was an Asian lady married to a black man and she had pictures of her adult children. Her son was fine, and I do mean gorgeous.*

*She mentioned that she had been married for over 30 years. I congratulated her.*

*"Do you have any questions about me?" she asked I think she could tell I kind of' drifted off a bit.*

*"No ma'am…thanks for sharing, you have a beautiful family and a beautiful office" Actually the office was a bit cluttered, or at least her desk was. I noticed she had pictures of a house in Malibu, which appeared to be her home.*

*"You live in Malibu?" I blurted. As soon as the words left my mouth I regretted them, thinking that was a rather personal question. I was surprised when she answered, after all, she could be thinking my black ass would call my homies and come back and do a home invasion or something.*

*Apparently, she wasn't bothered at all, because she smiled and answered, "Yes I do live in Malibu."*

*"Yes, I do live in Malibu" she answered*

# A. MICHELLE

*"I could tell this was off of PCH" I pointed at a picture on the wall that overlooked Pacific Coast Highway. "Maybe a mile or two from Paradise Cove" I explained*

*"Exactly..." she smiled "You go to Malibu often?"*

*"I love the ocean and Paradise Cove is one of my favorite beach areas" I smiled, I absolutely loved that area. After my father passed I would go out there and hang out. I felt so connected to my Dad when I was there or around any body of water for that matter.*

*"Ok, Ms. Green, you are ok with me calling you Ms. Green?" she politely asked*

*"No ma'am, I'd prefer you call me Adrianne" I smiled.*

*Again, looking at her notes, she mentioned me being seen here before and asked if I recalled it.*

*"You know I felt like I had been here before, something to do with work...right?" I asked.*

*"No, you came here for marriage counseling" she explained*

*My eyes got big as it finally dawned on me. Hakeem and I had come here when I so desperately trying to save the relationship. Now he is the very person I am here to talk about today.*

*I vividly remember after one of our marriage counseling sessions we had a nasty physical fight and I ran down that very ally to get away from him. He was upset that I was sharing with the counselor about his meth use and he felt like I was telling his business.*

# STABBED TO LIFE

*He got mad and called me names, spat on me and threatened to run me over with the car. "Dear God" I said underneath my breath as I realized not only was this the same building I'd previously been to; the sessions had taken place in this very room.*

*"Ms. Harvey...did the counseling sessions take place here, in this room?" I asked as I put my shaking hand on my chest. I could feel my heart starting to race. I was having an anxiety attack right that second. She could tell, and she began to tell me to breathe through my nose and out my mouth. She came over and grabbed my hands and the tears began to roll down my face.*

*"Adrianne breathe honey..."*

*I began to calm down I could feel my heart rate normalizing; my eyes were tightly closed. When I opened them there stood my therapist, this little Asian lady who wanted desperately to help me.*

*As I sat there trying to compose myself, she sat down next to me asking if I was ok. I shook my head and told her how I remembered coming here with Hakeem, my ex-husband. At that time, we were trying to fix our relationship. I was the one who suggested marriage counseling although he was not ready or even wanted to.*

*"Ms. Harvey it seems like this was the very room the sessions took place could that be possible?" I asked*

*"This more than likely was the room Adrianne and even more crazy My Mom was your therapist" she explained "now if this is going to be too hard to continue here we can step out on the patio, it is not being used right now and we can continue there..."*

# A. MICHELLE

*"No, no, I'll be fine, your Mom was my therapist? " I chuckled a bit. How Ironic.*

*"Don't worry," she said, "All I see are her intake notes, nothing in detail due to confidentiality. The detailed notes from your previous counseling sessions are archived and securely put away, but I want to emphasize Adrianne, I can refer you to someone else if you think this room or the fact that my Mom saw you before makes you feel uncomfortable."*

*I told her that I would be fine. She seemed like a sweet lady with a lot of experience, so I decided to give her the opportunity to help me.*

*She dove right into the session asking me where the pain was coming from and if some traumatic event had happened here before.*

*I explained to Ms. Harvey about Hakeem, our marriage counseling session, and how he became combative and tried to run me over with the vehicle in this very parking lot. I shared that Hakeem was addicted to methamphetamine and how I now remembered her mother, my previous counselor, telling me that he must work on this addiction before we can work on the marriage issue. She said in so many words that if the addiction continued the marriage was doomed. I also remembered her telling me that I needed to go to Al Anon and work on my codependency issue. As I shared this with Ms. Harvey she nodded her head in agreement.*

*"So, all these years have passed Adrianne and now you are dealing with flash backs and triggers, recently right? Why do you think that is happening Adrianne, is there an*

*anniversary of something coming up, has someone reached out to you?" she asked with a concerned look.*

*"He is being released from prison, really soon..." I explained, "after a 17 to 27-year sentence for attempted murder, my emotions were just everywhere. Clearly, he is not even thinking about me and I sure hope he isn't but every day it seems like my mind goes back into vivid details of our crazy ass relationship. The things that I had even forgotten were coming up and when they came up my panic attacks began, so did my un-easiness and my racing heart. It makes me feel out of control of my emotions. It's scary," I said with a slight tremble in my voice.*

*"Adrianne, the attempted murder charge was from something he did to you?" she asked in a calm manner, but her eyes showed she was shocked and in disbelief.*

*"Yes ma'am, he tried to kill me.*

*"Oh wow, I'm sorry Adrianne, you have been through some major trauma and I don't care how long ago it was the thoughts of him out on the street again is causing you some anxious feelings that it sounds like you have been suppressing." She said this with such care as she continued, "You have got to allow yourself to properly process these emotions and not just keep them inside. Have you been prescribed medication for the panic attacks and anxiety? She asked*

*"Yes , I have but I do not want to take it. I want to work through it, hopefully with the help from you, you and I can avoid taking medication. Do you think that is possible?"*

*"Adrianne, I think it is very possible and I think you can get past it, but I'm going to need you to keep your*

*appointments. It will be a challenge, but I hope you're up for it. I really want to see you heal from this. You seem to be a nice lady, and a strong woman with a story that can help others. I know also know that you've probably only shared with me a very small portion of this near tragic event."*

*"Yes ma'am... a very small portion. I know that talking about it in depth will probably help me get through it...right?"*

*"Well in most cases, it does help to talk about it and vent and get it out...but you have to be prepared going back can be painful. It may get worse before it gets better, but eventually the power of it controlling your life will be behind you." She explained*

*"I'm ready... I thought I was over it but until being made aware he was being released soon my PTSD, anxiety and panic attacks are on overload and I am unable to sleep. I sleep like only 3-4 hours a night."*

*"Well we can get you something to sleep...*

*"No ma'am, I would like to do this all without medication, or at least try.*

*"That's right, I respect that, and Adrianne, you don't need to call me ma'am. I'm just a few years older than you. "we laughed. "So now let's get started, where would you like to begin?"*

*"Well where do you think would be best, my childhood or the relationship?" I asked*

# CHAPTER TWO

## THE MEETING

*"Since the most urgent issue is your ex being released from prison…why don't we start right there… How did you meet this man?"*

I remember like it was yesterday. It was a hot day in the desert, well over 95 degrees and I was trying really, hard to stick to my work out routine. Because of the hot weather, I was tempted to head straight home and lay across the couch to watch TV in my air-conditioned home, but I had committed to at least 3-4 days a week in the gym to try to stay fit, and I was going to do my best to honor my commitment.

Right after work was the busiest time at this 24-Hour Fitness center I used, but if I left work and went home first, there was no way I would make it back, so I always packed my duffle bag the night before. I changed at work and came ready to put in work at the gym.

I was a regular at this gym so immediately when I walked in the door, people knew me and would wave or come over and speak. This day was my Zumba class. I learned upon my arrival from one of my gym pals that our Zumba instructor was sick and was not going to show up today, so Zumba was cancelled. I was bummed because this was my favorite class. High energy -low impact, but I would sweat like crazy.

# A. MICHELLE

I had always felt like the one hour I worked out burned every calorie I consumed from that day and the day before.

Something was happening in the gym today though. There was a lot of attention and commotion going on at the row of tread mills and you could see that some people were a little upset. I was setting myself up on the lateral pull-down machine when another friend came by and shared that there was a guy on the treadmill for over an hour and would not get off even after asked by the gym staff.

I could now hear him running. You could actually hear every time his feet hit the conveyer belt. My friend pointed him out. He was a tall buff guy covered in tattoos and as I looked up he was just starting to stop the treadmill. My friend pointed him out and I nodded that I saw him. I wanted to tell her don't be pointing before he came over here tripping'.

I looked down to finish preparing for my work out and the guy looked like he was walking my way. All I could think is this fool saw her pointing and now has something to say about it. As he got closer it seemed like he was walking in slow motion. I could literally see each drop of sweat dripping off his body. He was light skinned and had a six pack and a tattoo across his stomach, around his neck, and both arms completely covered.

He took his shirt that he'd removed and wiped sweat off his head; his long legs were moving fast.

He had on gray and blue basketball shorts and was well over 6 feet, at least 6'5. As he got closer I looked down. I did not want to make eye contact with him, so I started pulling down on the weight machine. He walked right past me towards the men's locker room. Soon as he passed, I began looking again but he stopped and turned around.

"Oh shit, he is coming this way, I hope he didn't see me staring" I said to myself.

"Hey…you know you're doing that wrong…" he said in this deep voice. I almost jumped out of my skin.

"What am I doing wrong?" I responded with a bit of an attitude.

"First of all, you got too much weight on here…" he said huskily as he moved the pins "What you are doing right now is going to buff you out, you probably need to focus on slimming down first and then add some weightlifting."

He said this so aggressively and arrogantly, I immediately thought he was mean, but the entire time he talked, I was checking out his body. He was an arrogant ass hole, but he sure looked good and had some hazel eyes.

"Try it now, "he said, "and do 10 reps of 10" and walked off. When he raised up I saw he had a book tattooed on his back with the pages opened and a figure of someone praying.

He walked towards the locker room never saying bye or anything. No goodbye. No have a good workout…nothing. What a rude jerk.

I didn't go far from the men locker room area hoping to see what he looked like in his regular clothes but clearly, I must have missed him because an hour later he hadn't walked by.

# A. MICHELLE

Once I got my hour and a half work out in, I scanned the parking look still looking to see if I was going to see him. Apparently, he was long gone.

The next day would have not been my day to work out, but I had to creep through to see if I saw the big mean guy who had insulted me the day before. Sure enough, he was back on the treadmill getting on everybody's nerve.

He saw me when I came through the door and we made eye contact, but I quickly tried to look down. I went to the elliptical this time and was inputting my settings when I looked up he was standing right there in front of me.

"Hey girl, did you do what I said yesterday"

"The 10 reps of 10? Yeah I did that" I said quickly.

"Ok good, you lose about 20- 30lbs you would be in good shape…"

He kept saying something after that, but I heard nothing else after those words. How dare him insult me. Did he even know that that was hurtful? He said it so easily with no regard to my feelings? He pretty much just called me fat. Now don't get it twisted I was a little plump, but I always got major attention from guys. At this time in my life I was like a size 14 which I guess by some standards may be considered plus-size, but excuse me sir, I was in good shape.

This really set me off because I really worked hard at maintaining a size 12. As I was contemplating cursing him out, I looked up and he was staring at me with those hazel eyes and that body. Oh Lord the body! That was causing me to be weak right now. At this time, it had been 4- 5 months since I'd had sex. I was just lusting I told myself.

# STABBED TO LIFE

Here I go overlooking the nasty insults and arrogance because he is fine. Nope, not going to do it .

I grabbed my towel off the seat stood up and said, "Thank you for the advice, I really appreciate it, but I need to go pick up my kids" He gave me this smug look as if to say, "Whatever bitch, take your fat ass on, I was trying to help you." Although he didn't say that aloud I knew by the look on his face that was probably what he was thinking

My feelings were so hurt, I didn't go back to the gym the rest of that week. I ate Brussel sprouts and drank water for a week. Since childhood I had struggled with my weight and had major body image issues. His comments almost sent me back into depression.

After gaining over 80 lbs. when I was pregnant and the struggle to get it off while my husband would constantly insult me. Anytime my weight was brought up I would cringe. It got to where I weighed myself every day even after I'd lost over 100 lbs. I just did not want to be obese again. My father was already struggling with morbid obesity and I had promised myself and him that I would never have suffer through that kind of pain. I loved my Daddy, I was Daddy's little girl so watching him slowly die from complications of his obesity ripped my heart apart. The therapist stopped me abruptly.

*"Adrianne, I would like to hear more about your childhood, can you tell me a little more?"*

*I chewed nervously on my lip. I had never thought much about my childhood but tried to recall to the best of my ability, "I remember I was a very insecure kid. I was always ashamed of my body. I was overweight and developed early. This caused so much unwanted attention*

# A. MICHELLE

*from people far older than me. My father was obese, and we had terrible eating habits, I just assumed I would be overweight like he was. He was an amazing Daddy and my mother was an Angel, but they did not know how to help me. Maybe they didn't think there was a problem. But I was miserable and sad inside, they gave me all I wanted materialistically but feeling that hole of just not fitting in and not being enough they could not fix.*

*In 5<sup>th</sup> grade I looked 16. Grown woman breast, overweight and not very pretty. So early on I had to fight the boys from touching me. I got used to fighting and I became a bit bullyish. Later in my early teens when I lost weight, I started getting the guys attention even more and the moment they acted like they seriously liked me, I became promiscuous. I learned early that all attention isn't good attention.*

*This resulted in me just accepting any boy/man in my life that gave the slightest compliment. I needed validation. I wanted so bad to be like my other friends who had a boyfriend that adored them. Me, well, I accepted anyone who showed even the slightest interest. My children's father claimed he loved me and quite frankly I didn't believe him. Hell, I never knew if I even loved him. I guess I did enough for us to have had children. For the sake of the kids I tried to make it work, although he never acted like he really wanted me till I no longer wanted to be with him.*

*So early on I developed a bunch of insecurities, body image issues, low self-worth , low self-esteem and un-healthy boundaries. Other than the love I received from my parents, I didn't know what real love was. "*

# STABBED TO LIFE

*I took a deep breath and waited until she spoke to release it. I wasn't for sure what she would analyze of my childhood experiences.*

*She smiled, assuring me that this was nothing she hadn't heard before. She scribbled a few more notes and said, "Childhood issue such as those you describe like having a negative body image often leads young girls to search outside themselves for more. Thanks for sharing about your childhood. It gives me more tools to work with," she winked, and I continued...*

A week later I decided to go back to the gym, I was determined to not let the fine, arrogant man destroy my spirit and my body. I was in a good mood and happy, but I won't lie, as soon as I walked in the door I looked for him to be at the treadmill area as normal, but when I arrived I didn't see him. I was a little disappointed because my Brussel sprout and water regimen caused me to lose 5 lbs. and I was looking super cute in my matching work out gear. Of course, with these big boobs and the bouncing during the Zumba class, I always had to double up on my sports bras, but I was cute.

I could feel the stares as I walked pass the dead weight area where all the guys were hanging out.

"Stay focused A" is what I said to myself. "Get in here and get your work out on and put a beating on this Zumba class so you can burn some major calories."

I did just that too. I came out of there sweating like crazy after a full 45 minutes of dancing and having fun. My endorphins were working overtime.

# A. MICHELLE

I felt good. As I walked out…and who greeted me? The fine ass dude from the treadmill.

"As-Salaam-Alaikum Queen. I saw you were putting it down in there. That little white girl leading that class needs you in there to keep the energy up, I'm impressed, nice work" he says.

Although he'd just complimented me, I wanted to walk off and flip his ass off. That little comment didn't make up for the comments he'd made the other day.

But, me being me said, "Thank you" and smiled with all my teeth and dimple showing. I also picked up on the fact he had greeted me with an Arabic greeting that most Muslims used. I heard it often because I had friends that were in the Nation of Islam. (Black Muslims) I also thought I'd show off a little and responded to his greeting, ""Wa-Alaikum-Salaam," I said confidently.

His whole demeanor changed when I said it. It was like he transformed right in front of me. He smiled and stared at me as if he'd just seen Allah himself. I don't know why but my response touched his heart and soul. He gently grabbed my hand and kissed it. He winked and just slowly shook his head up and down. Something changed in that moment.

"Are you married?" he asked

"No, but I'm fat…" I said very sarcastically with a sly grin on my face. He chuckled and said,

"I will help you with that" he laughed. This asshole just couldn't help himself. He'd better be glad he was fine.

"I don't need your help sir," I said in a matter of fact way, rolled my eyes, and started walking off.

# STABBED TO LIFE

"I'm just playing with you… you are beautiful and thick, I like it. You see all these females looking at us right now?" He asked, "They're mad because I'm talking to you. All these women here been trying to get me to bite since I came here 2 months ago. They have been practically throwing their bodies at me. I haven't touched none of their nasty asses, but when I first seen you I liked how you carried yourself. You didn't come in here with a group of women trying to catch a man. You come in to put in work and get out. This gym is a pick-up spot, so the minute I finish my home gym I'm outta here, too many distractions." He explained.

I stood there sweating with no makeup. I could feel my hair starting to nap-up, but he looked at me as if I were an angel was standing before him. I constantly dabbed my head with the towel. I was worried I was musty and stinky, but he just kept right on talking. He was right. When I looked up several women were staring at us. It was probably because he was so damn huge though. He was well over 6 feet tall.

"You never told me your name" I asked, trying to sound sexy.

"Hakeem my Queen…" he winked and smiled. Now he was starting to seem corny and desperate, but those eyes and that body made me overlook how dumb and desperate he sounded.

He wanted THIS, but hell I was wanting him too. After my last messed up relationship I was able to have an intimate/sexual encounter with someone and not catch feelings. My divorce was brutal, and I was in no way looking for a serious relationship nor was a ready for one. I giggled quietly to myself. I was flattered by being called a Queen especially how I looked after my extreme workout.

"Hakeem how tall are you" I asked as I looked up so high it was making my neck sore.

"6'8 …and you"

"5'7" I always added a ½ an inch. I don't know why I lied, as if he would consider that to be tall. That was crazy. This dude was a giant.

"So, you're tall too? I normally deal with petite women" he grinned, and I just shook my head this dude must be retarded or something. Either he didn't realize how rude he sounded, or he was just dumb…or maybe… it was me. Maybe I was just being overly sensitive.

I shook my head and looked over at the mirror near the weight bench. I caught a glimpse of myself. Although I was sweaty and probably stinky, I looked cute so at this point I just smiled. I was not going to let this fool break me. I worked too hard to build my self-esteem.

"Let me get outta here," I said as I wiped my forehead with a few subway sandwich napkins and bent down to tie my shoe.

"No, no…let me get that for you." He bent over and tied my shoe, then reached over to make sure the other one was tight too. I looked down and took in all that I saw. His body was banging. All those tats and muscles were getting to me.

He reached for my hand again and said, "Let me walk you to your car."

As we walked he continued holding my hand. It made me feel a little uncomfortable, and of course everyone around

# STABBED TO LIFE

looked. I had parked not too far from the door and when we reached my vehicle I said, "Ok here's my car"

My blue Chevy Astro Van had chrome wheels. I had always tried to jazz up whatever car I drove. It was just instilled within me from the time I was a little girl watching my Dad. He always rolled in nice vehicles.

"Ms. Adrianne…you should let me cook you lunch one day" he said in a very soft, sexy tone.

I wondered how he knew my name. I hadn't told him.

"Hey…how did you know my name…" I asked puzzled.

"You told me" he smiled in a sneaky way.

"No, I didn't" I was shocked. Usually when I met people I always told them a fake name. Either Monique or Tanya, but never my real name in the beginning.

"Look girl, you gonna let me cook for you or what?" he asked more forcefully. Then he kissed my hand again.

"Sure…" I reached in the van and wrote my number on a Subways napkin and placed it in his big 'ole hand.

"Call me and let me know when and where…and you better tell me how you know my name…stalker" we laughed.

"Baby I don't have to stalk nobody…look at all this" he took my hand and rubbed it against his chest.

"Whatever dude…" I slowly pulled my hand away. "You are a mess…" I said rolling my eyes

"I am just playing girl…but you like it, that's why you are skinning and grinning," he teased as his mouth curled into a smile. We both laughed and for a brief second, our eyes met. His eyes were greenish/hazel and we were both the same exact complexion. We both were feeling something in that moment. He continued to stare and there was a moment of silence. I couldn't stare anymore so I turned my head.

"I'll talk to you later o.k.?" I said as I jumped into the van and put my seat belt on. He was still staring at me. I don't know what it was but we both felt it. There was a connection had just taken place between us. it was weird, and it made me feel weird too.

I thought about Hakeem the whole way home. The whole 20-minute ride home I thought about our conversation, wondering how he knew my name, and how he went from such an arrogant ass-hole to me to some tingling feeling like puppy love…ewwww, it was weird.

When I got home, my house was clean and smelled of ground beef browning, my daughter had started the meat for tacos and my son was at the table finishing up homework. My daughter was a very smart young lady so different from me at her age. She was focused on what she wanted to do with her life and she did everything necessary to meet her goals and get good grades. She was certainly Mamas little helper.

I knew that I was probably putting way too many responsibilities on her but with my chaotic life and working 2 jobs, I had to rely on her for a lot of stuff.

I told her I would take over the cooking and she could go back to her room to finish her homework. I went to the fridge to grab the tomatoes, onions and lettuce only to find that she had already cut up everything and had them securely in containers with lids. I smiled and looked in the room to thank her, but she had stopped her mission of completing her homework to assist her brother with his homework. Such an angel to just step up and help. I knew I did not tell her enough, but I appreciated all she did.

In a matter of minutes, I had fresh tacos ready to eat. We sat down at the table and ate. Even though it was family dinner time, my daughter brought along a book to continue reading while she ate. I started to stop her, but I was proud of her dedication, so I just conversed with my son who of course, was telling me about the shoes he wanted. He reminded me that I promised if he brought a grade up that I would get him those shoes. The conversation went on and on and of course Alonja was not interested what so ever. She was not a materialistic child and her focus always was her school work. She hopped up as soon as she was done and started clearing the table. Her brother and I weren't even done when she instructed us to make sure we rinsed our dishes and place them in the dishwasher when we were done, and then she headed down the hall to her room.

My son who I called "DeDe" short for Darrell Jr. was a soft-spoken kid. He was big for his age but so gentle. He had my mother's demeanor, always seeing good in people and always trying to be so helpful to others. I loved that about him and he loved his Mama. We were very close and had the same interest…shoes and shopping. Of course, his thing was sneakers and mine was heels, but we could spend hours in the mall together, window shopping most of the time when he was with me, but if he was with his Mudder and PawPaw he got everything his little heart desired.

As we are clearing our dishes the phone rang. I instantly looked at the clock and it was 8:30 pm. I figured it was my mother. She and I had a habit of calling each other before bed, so I just knew it was her, I didn't even look at the caller i.d.

"Helllllooooo…" I answered playfully as I always did with my Mama.

""As-Salaam-Alaikum Queen" the deep voice said so sensually. "You were not expecting me huh?" He asked in his sultry, sexy voice.

"No…actually I didn't, I thought this was going to be my Mom calling me to say goodnight" I explained

"Wow that's cool…you get to say good night to your Mom every night" he asked

"Yup. That's what we do. I am very close to my Mama, both my parents in fact. They are a big help to me and my kids."

I motioned to my son that I was going to head to my room, telling him to finish up the kitchen and go to bed.

With the phone to my ear, I headed to my bed room and closed the door. I fell in the center of my bed and stared into the ceiling while I listened to Hakeem. His sexy voice made me laugh and then the weird feeling I felt earlier at the gym was back.

"So how many kids do you have? He asked

"Two. I have a 10-year-old boy and a 12-year- old girl," I answered.

"I have three girls" he said proudly "and I wish I could get them from their trifling Mama"

"My kid's Daddy is not a real active participant in their lives either and I hate that because they want their Dad.

# STABBED TO LIFE

They want to have a relationship with him. When our relationship fell apart, he cut them loose too. It's really sad because they are good kids," I explained

"I don't know why these niggas think they can just make babies and not be a part of these kid's lives," he said rather angrily

"So…are you a personal trainer?" I asked trying to change the subject. It appears we started talking about kids way too soon. I was trying to get to know him. I wasn't good at this dating thing ever since me and my ex broke up. I was partying and hanging out from time to time and meeting people here and there, but I always felt things moved rather quickly in those instances. I wanted to slow this down…way down.

"No, not really but I've studied health and fitness for years and helped others get in shape" he chuckled

"I can tell you work out  a whole lot and probably eat really healthy too"

"Yeah…absolutely no pork and no beef…I'm pretty disciplined in that"

As we talked I start running my bath water to begin getting ready for bed. He continued telling me about his healthy lifestyle and why it was important to him to be healthy in a time when so many black people take their health for granted. He shared how he cooked most of his meals and that he also boxed and recently signed a contract with Don King for number of fights he was currently in training for. My eyebrows raised….like right really? I know guys lie to impress women, but he was going too far.

# A. MICHELLE

I got in the tub still holding the phone to my ear. I guess he could hear the water splashing because he asked, "Are you in the Tub?"

"Yes…" I laughed "How can you tell?"

"I see you…I'm watching you" he laughed.

"Oh see, here you go again with that stalker stuff, how did you know my name earlier? I haven't forgotten about that creepy stuff earlier," I said, teasing him.

"Your work badge was on your dash, I saw it with your picture ADR-IANNE!" he laughed "You were gonna tell me your name was something else huh?"

"Actually, I was…" I said and we both laughed

"So, you got room for me in that Tub with you…" he asked

"Anyway sir…remember your manners, you've been a gentleman up until now don't start being nasty"

"Oh…if there is one thing I picked up on you right away is that you are very nasty, but that is for a much later time, that I am already sure we will get too…, don't deny what you are feeling baby, cause I'm feeling you from the first day I met you. Allah got plans for us, but in his time. Meanwhile I'm going to tame this lust demon" he laughed

We talked till well after mid night about his goals in life, his upbringing, and his desire to get full custody of his children. He longed to be a millionaire to be able to help his family that has struggled all his life. It was good conversation and as we got ready to hang up he said "I don't ever want to push you away, so if you would be so kind as to let me know if I am being overbearing or if I say or do something inappropriate that makes you uncomfortable please let me know so I can do better. I kind of like you Adrianne, let me fix you lunch one day," He pleaded.

"Ok sure…you just let me know when."

"Sorry to have kept you up so late, can I call you tomorrow?" he asked

"Sure…it was nice talking to you."

"Very nice talking to you my Queen, now after picturing you in the tub…naked…I got to go handle my business."

"Ewwww you nasty," I said again, and we started laughing.

"Goodnight," I said sweetly as I laid across the bed and thought about our conversation. It was as if we'd known each other all our lives. He was already sharing very personal things about himself. His struggles and his previous relationships being hard. How he was raised Muslim in a very strict household where his father had him quit school to work for him pouring concrete. How he felt by boxing he could give his three daughters a much better life.

Part of me wasn't sure I believed the whole Don King boxing deal. I'd been lied to before. Brian the Detroit firemen. He was a cutie, but he was a liar and an ex drug addict. I was not easily falling for any stories, but this guy Hakeem seemed like fun. If nothing else, he could be my little boo thang and gift me up from time to time. I was going to keep my eyes open and pay attention.

I had lit a candle on the dresser while we were talking on the phone and now it was only thing illuminating my room. My room smelled of warm vanilla and the silhouette of my body covered the celling as if it were painted there. As the candle flickered, I imagined my silhouette intertwined with Hakeem's in a steamy intimate exchange. Although it would be encroached in shadows, it would be very clear what the two of us were doing. I could only blame my long period of celibacy that had me a little lustful for Hakeem. His conversation was just so cool, but I vowed right then and there before closing my eyes, I would not give him any for a while, if it even got to that…a long while.

*My therapist nodded as she continued to take notes. "So, you did detect the character flaws and the red flags early on, but you allowed the relationship to develop," she said in a matter of fact way.*

*I lowered my eyes, and she continued in a softer tone, "Don't be ashamed about that Adrianne. That narcissistic behavior is what lulls many women in and they get caught in a vicious cycle of wanting to get back the charmer they'd had glimpses of. It is quite common."*

*I took a deep breath and continued with my story….*

# CHAPTER THREE

## THE FIRST DATE

For the next few weeks I spoke with Hakeem every day. The days I went to the gym he made sure he waited till I was done with my class or he assisted me with my work out. He would always wait till he was able to walk out with me. We both thought by now we would have had a date. We thought he'd be able to make me that lunch he had promised, but we both had crazy schedules. I was working two jobs because my ex had stopped paying child support and I had to find a way to make up for that lost $800 a month. He was working out at the Boxing gym in L.A. He kept saying he wanted to be able to spend an entire day with me from morning to night, but we just couldn't make it happen.

One day while walking me to my car, as he did each time I saw him at the gym, walked up to me and said, "Come over tomorrow on your lunch hour. I will have lunch ready for you. When you arrive, and we can talk, and you can get back to work on time."

Keep in mind during this 3-4-week period that I'd known him we had not even kissed. Well, not an intimate kiss. He would kiss me on my hand, as he often did or on my cheek, but not a long sensual tongue kiss. He would hug me and often I would feel a full-on erection against me, but he would rush and back away. I found that to be weird because most guys, if that happened, would try to get some even if it had to go down in the parking lot in my van.

His will power was to resist the temptation was amazing to me. It reminded me of a virgin, like he was afraid to have sex. He later explained that his trainer told him absolutely no sex before a fight. He had a Golden Gloves match coming up and he needed to be able to really demonstrate his talent.

Regarding going over to his place for lunch, I agreed. When I said yes, he was so excited. He acted like a little boy with his first crush. He told me how to get to his place and told me to be there right at 12. I told that I had to leave work at twelve,  but I could be there by 12:10.

He was not very far from my job, and to be honest, I was excited too. I tried picturing his place when I would talk to him every evening. It sounded rather big and hollow, almost as if it was an unfurnished place. Apparently, his house had  hardwood floors and high ceilings because sometimes his words would echo.

He didn't ask me what I wanted or what I had a taste for.

He told me that I would like what he cooked but assured me that we'd still talk later that night.

"OK," I said with a smile.

He went over to his car and realized he didn't exit in his normal manner. He ran back over to me with long extremely tall self and put his whole upper torso in my van and kissed me on the cheek "Peace to a Queen, I talk to you later baby…"

# STABBED TO LIFE

Baby? Now that was new one. Because he was so "different" than anyone I had ever dealt with, I picked up on everything he did. He was certainly a creature of habit and I had already begun to pick up on some of them.

That evening we talked before I headed to bed and he was very upbeat. Normally he was relaxed, and I could always tell when he laid in his bed. He usually talked like he was comfortable. This night, though, it was almost as if he was full of nervous energy. Our conversation was brief this night although normally we'd easily talk until midnight; until the Jerry Springer Show went off, then we'd say our goodbyes. But tonight, he ended the conversation early saying, "I'm going to let you get your rest and I will see you tomorrow a little after 12"

"I'll be there," I said happily.

The next day was a bright sunny day, not too hot. I thought I'd wear a sun dress that wasn't too skimpy and work appropriate. I wore a cardigan on top of it so that my arms and shoulders weren't exposed I had the cutest sandals on. They had small wedge heels. Even with the heels I was still nowhere near his 6'8" frame. This would be the first time Hakeem was going to see me in a dress and in regular clothes. He had always saw me in my gym clothes and sweaty with my hair pulled back in a pony tail. I got extra cute this day and 12:00 noon could not come fast enough. I kept watching the clock at 11:55 I snuck out the door and headed to Hakeem's house. Of course, I ran into every light but still managed to pull in front of his house at 12:05.

I checked to make sure it was the correct address. I pulled up in front of a very simple, old-style duplex with a porch. Even the screen door was old. It reminded me of the screen door on the front of Mister's house on the movie Color Purple. Hakeem was so excited the other day I thought for sure he would be waiting at the door. I looked at my face one more time in the rear-view mirror.

I had a very light lip gloss on just in case I was going to get a sensual tongue lashing after lunch. I also had plenty of watermelon Trident in my purse.

As I approached the door the smell of incents hit me. I recognized the smell. I think it was called black magic. There was a lady named Ella at work that sold oils and incents, and this is a smell that everyone loved.

When I got to the door, I instantly rang the doorbell, but I didn't hear anything but his music. Frankie Beverly and Maze was playing "That's the Golden Time of Day."

I knocked on the screen door, and finally I could hear feet coming towards the door. When I walked in it was just as I thought; hard wood floors that were shiny and clean enough to eat off.

"Hey, hey pretty lady…" He said, standing there, all 6'8 of him wearing nothing but basketball shorts and tattoos. I don't even think he had on drawers under those shorts either…Oh boy.

"Well Hello there…I put on a dress to come see you and you in workout clothes" we laughed

"Oh, you don't like it?" He asked in his sexy voice.

"Hmmm, I like it, but it's inappropriate for a 1st date Hakeem, I thought you were trying to stay celibate" I said in a slightly scolding voice.

# STABBED TO LIFE

"See you nasty…I'm trying to stay cool in this hot ass desert just finish cooking all this food…Never mind that, look at you. You are looking like a fresh Summer Breeze, I love this dress."


Hakeem had a kitchen towel in his hand. He reached over near his stereo and picked up the remote control, switched the song to "Never Let you down" and then grabbed my purse and sat it down.

He threw the kitchen towel on the table and pulled me close to him and slow danced with me the entire song. Every time Frankie Beverly said "I'll never let you down" he whispered it in my ear. By the end of the song I was damn near in tears. I had been let down and treated so poorly by my kids' father, that these lyrics made me melt into his arms. Even when the song was over he just held me my head against his big chest and rocked me from side to side. He gently grabbed my face and made me look him in the eyes,

"I will never make you cry tears of sadness baby…only tears of joy…I promise, you hear me?" he said as he kissed me on the lips and then on my neck and whispered in my ear "You are going to be my wife one day"

My eyes got big as he said, "I felt that the first day I walked you to your car at the gym, it was feeling like I had never experienced with anyone like Allah was connecting us." He explained "Tell me you didn't feel it, because I know you did we were stuck for about 30 seconds"

"Yes, I do remember that, and it scared the shit out of me. I want to believe it was a positive thing and not some type of

# A. MICHELLE

warning. Hakeem, I just went through the nastiest divorce, some other crazy relationships, and just the thought of loving someone again scares me" I explained sadly.

"I'm not going to' hurt you baby…and we can take as much time as you need for you believe in me. I just know that you were sent to me by Allah and I am not going to stop going after you." He said all this such a matter of fact way.

"Now come in here and eat this meal I cooked you, I don't want you to be late going back to work." he said.

The kitchen was so cute. It was very clean and quaint. The table and chair were like those at café bistro. Those high chairs and high tables. He had matching place mats and when I sat down, he placed a cloth napkin in my lap. The pictures on the walls were black and white pictures of civil rights movements. I would have not thought it matched with the other kitchen accents, but he made it work well. There were a lot of black and green colors throughout the entire house. It was small, but it was very cute and very clean

"Here you go babe," he said as he brought over a plate of steaming hot vegetables and something that looked like Kung Pau Chicken. It had peanuts in it and some type of thick noodles. He sat across from me with the same thing and we ate. The food was delicious.

"You like it?" he asked.

"It's delicious, thank you so much, you can cook for me anytime." I said looking at the clock. I noticed it was 12:45 and I had to be back at work at 1:00 pm. I got up and put my plate in the sink and I asked one more time for clarity "So you cooked that entire meal?"

"Yes babe, all of it" he said, but I'd caught a glimpse of some items in the trash. There were Chinese/Thai takeout containers.

"Maybe that was from the night before," I thought to myself, "No. I knew all the food spots around here and those were clearly from the Dragon Garden restaurant around the corner." I did not want to embarrass him, so I just left it alone. I didn't want to make a big deal out of that.

"Before you go let me show you around my little spot," he suggested. You could tell he was proud.

First stop was the bathroom. It had the old-style tub with legs. I looked up and noticed the light had to be turned on by a long string hanging down, and there was a window that was off to the side of the toilet that overlooked the alley.

He had live plants; the easy ones to take care of. The floor was a faux tile / linoleum but shiny and clean and the bathroom smelled of Pine-Sol. To me, this was a sign of a clean house, when you can smell the Pine-Sol. Fabuloso, or Bleach. The tub was clean and just for a moment I pictured his long body covered in bubbles laying back in that old beautiful tub.

He walked me over to his bedroom that was filled with Black art. Directly in front of his bed a picture of Malcolm X hung. Over to the right of the bed, a beautiful black and white sketch of Mohamed Ali. On his end table was the open Quran, the Muslim equivalent of a Bible.

# A. MICHELLE

His bed was huge and filled the small room completely up. It was a King size, sexy canopy bed draped with shear green panels. Everything was neat and organized. His shoes were all neatly lined up and at least three of them were boxing shoes. The others were Nike running shoes and a pair of dress shoes.

I was impressed with how clean and organized his little place was. While he explained the pieces of art, I could not help but pick up in his explanation that he had more art pieces at his "other place."

I didn't want to complicate things by asking him to elaborate, because I didn't want to seem nosey. So, I just nodded my head. I looked over at the clock. Now I only had about 5 minutes to make it back to work on time.

"Nice place," I said honestly, "but I better get back to work. Thank you so much for lunch you are an excellent cook"

I said that even though I had seen the take-out containers in the trash. Not sure why he felt it necessary to lie about something so unimportant, but it was ok. I guess it wasn't that big of a deal, right? He looked at me with a slight grin and grabbed my hand and pulled me really close into him.

"See what you did?" He asked as he pulled me closer so that I could feel his erection against me. "You sure you got to go back to work?" he asked.

With my head on his chest, he looked down at me with those hazel eyes and went for my lips. I knew if I went there with a sensual kiss I would not be returning to work, so I took a deep breath, kissed him on the lips with my lips tightly smashed together. He grabbed my bottom lip with

# STABBED TO LIFE

his teeth very softly as if he knew I was trying to avoid the kiss to avoid doing something nasty.

He hugged me and whispered in my ear "You're going to be my wife…"

I giggled, but it was a little disappointing. I didn't want to hear about being someone's wife in the least.

I had just finally made it through a nasty divorce with my children's father. He was very abusive, controlling and jealous, and blamed the relationship failing on me. It was awful. What was even worse my ex nor his family had anything to do with my children. I didn't understand that. Ok, so he and I didn't work out, but he was their father and he and his entire family abandoned them completely. That hurt, and I was still very angry about that. I vowed I would never marry again, nor would I have more children, which is why I had my tubes tied at the age of 20. That man had hurt me so much.

Hakeem walked me out to my car, opened the door and kissed me one more time on my cheek before closing the door. He was a hot mess. He stood there in his basketball shorts - no shirt,  and purposely placed his hands at his side so that I could see the huge imprint of his extremely large manly part. "Wow!" I thought to myself. He blew me a kiss and  I drove off one last wink.

When I arrived back to work I played the whole hour I'd spent at Hakeem's repeatedly in my head. A couple of times my co-workers caught me smiling and were laughing and teasing me. I had been sharing with them about this dude I met at the gym. I had shared that I was going to have lunch with him today, so they were just clowning me. I was really starting to catch feelings for this dude. Yes, he was arrogant. a little rude, and nasty. I liked the nasty part, so maybe again these feelings were just lusting. I was certainly on a long period of abstinence, so maybe these feelings were just from being horny.

I didn't like the fact that he only shared bits and pieces of his life. Like his living arrangements. Besides the home he had invited me to, there appeared to be another residence he had access to, then again maybe it was too early in this dating process for me to expect all that. "Slow down Adrianne," I told myself. "You haven't shared very much either." I reminded myself. "Just slow down girl."

I figured if I just wanted to have sex with him and not catch feelings, I could do that. I could just remain single and he'd just be my "friend" right? There was so much stuff going through my head.

The rest of the day seemed to drag. I wanted to get to the gym. I wanted to get my work out on, and I couldn't lie, I wanted to see Hakeem. As soon as 5:00 pm hit, I went to the rest room to change into my gym clothes so that I get to the gym. When I arrived, I'd normally see Hakeem on the treadmills, but he was not there. I went on with my routine and began my Zumba class. Even after my Zumba class Hakeem would usually be standing outside of the doors to greet me. That had happened since day one, a little over month ago.

I guessed something happened. I tried to play it off like I wasn't too concerned, but I was. I had just seen him a few hours ago, and he hadn't mentioned that he wasn't going to the gym. Wow. I was acting like this man was MY MAN. Nonetheless, I guzzled down a bottle of water and headed to my vehicle. When I got to my car there was a card on my windshield held by my wipers. I pulled it off and opened it. It had a beautiful picture of an African Queen and it read:

*"You deserve the world and I want to give it to you...you deserve love and I have it to give, if only you will allow me to treat you like you deserve to be treated... My Queen I am sorry I missed you tonight, but I had a meeting with my manager and promoter, I hope you like what I got you...call me later"*

I began looking around. I didn't see anything. I looked the other side of the van-nothing. I was puzzled and confused. Just as I got in the van, one of the ladies that worked in the office came running out with a huge bouquet of flowers.

"OMG, I almost missed you. I'm so sorry these are for you…from Hakeem" she said breathlessly. "He really likes you…just be careful" she looked so serious for a minute.

Be careful? What did that mean? I was happy with my gift though. So very thoughtful and sweet. I thanked her and placed the flowers in the van and drove carefully all the way home, trying to avoid them turning over.

When I arrived home my children had already eaten and cleaned up. My daughter told me she left some food in the microwave for me. I wasn't hungry, so I sat and chat with them for a while then headed for my bedroom. My daughter was so sweet. She had even vacuumed my room. Before I left this morning, I'd changed clothes at least 10 times before I decided what to wear. Finally, I chose the sundress that Hakeem liked so much. She'd put everything back in my closet and straightened up my room. "Thanks Lon" I yelled to her. This girl was like the Mama when I was away. She did a great job of looking after her brother and taking care of the house when I was away.

'You're welcome Mom…good night" she hollered back.

Once they were both in their rooms. I went out to the car and brought the flowers in, I am not sure why I felt the need to sneak them in, but I did. I placed them on my dresser. They smelled so good and looked so beautiful. I read the card over and over, and then the phone rang. I knew his number now and soon as it showed up on the caller ID, I smiled.

"Hello?" I answered the phone sweetly.

"Hey My love… I wanted to catch you before you went to bed, did you like your gift"

"I loved it…so thoughtful…Thank you so much," I said blushing.

"I'm getting closer and closer to getting me some huh?"

"Real close…" I laughed

"I believe I could have got some earlier today, you were all on me" he laughed "You wanted Daddy?"

"Boy stop… I'm good I will not be having sex with you, we are just friends," I laughed

"Girl…them flowers weren't cheap, I got something coming for that at least," he joked. He was too funny. He made me laugh. He had already made me cry. Were really vibing.

"I want to bring you down to L.A. and meet some of my business folks. I know you probably don't believe I'm really boxing," he said sardonically. "So, do you think you can come down and watch me spar a little?" he asked.

# STABBED TO LIFE

"Ooooo are you sure? ,I don't think I can bear to watch you get your ass whooped, that would just break my heart sweetie" I said cracking up.

"You see, I got to let you see how the Champ get down," he said confidently.

"I guess I'll go… when?" I asked

"This weekend, you can spend the entire weekend with me in L.A."

"Where will we stay?"

"Just come. I won't have you sleeping in the car, you'll be fine" he said. I could imagine his wink and then those puppy dog eyes.

"Okay. It's a date," I said pretending reluctance.

The week went by fast. I worked both of my jobs every day then went to the gym at least 4 times a week even though I knew Hakeem would not be there. I would come home in the evening and talk to him at least 20 to 30 minutes before he went to bed. His trainer had him in the gym from 7 am to 7 pm everyday which started with a 7-mile run in some very hilly areas in Los Angeles.

Hakeem was from the Inland Empire which was like San Bernardino and Riverside area, so he e wasn't familiar with his surroundings. When he would try to tell me where he was when he ran, he would always describe land marks or by food spots and freeway signs. He was so funny, and he always made a point to ask me how my day was too. I thought that was so awesome because my ex never cared about my feelings or my interest, he was selfish and careless. Not this dude. Hakeem would ask often what I

# A. MICHELLE

wanted to do with my life. I never had an answer. All my life I believed I was not good at anything. The only things that stood out the most about me were my big boobs and the fact I was good in bed.

I was told that often, so I began to feel like that was my only talent. Oh, and that I had good penmanship, but no one used calligraphy anymore, so there wasn't a market for that.

Being a Mom and working for the County was about the best thing I had going for myself. Pretty sad and pathetic, I know, but my self-esteem was low since I was a young girl, and I certainly carried that into my adult hood.

I had planned all week for my kids to have a place to stay for the weekend as I planned to spend the entire time with Hakeem. DeDe, my son, was going to be staying with his friend Sid and Alonja would be staying with her best friend Christina.

That Friday evening, I dropped both off at their destinations and let them know to call me if there was a problem. The parents of both teens were both cool. They knew I worked a lot, and both families encouraged my little get away. They assured me they would take good care of my kids. I was so pleased! Excited; yet, a bit nervous. It had been a while since I had been out, and I was concerned about the sleeping arrangements.

Hakeem was very religious, so I didn't think it would become intimate, but I certainly wanted to be prepared just in case. I packed some slutty lingerie, condoms, and sex toys. I giggled to myself. I knew I was doing way too much, but a lady had to be prepared, right? You never know.

# STABBED TO LIFE

At exactly 7pm, I pulled up to Hakeem's house as he had instructed me to do. It was dark and looked like no one was there, but there was a 500sec Benz in the driveway. This was certainly not the car I would see him drive at the gym. At the gym, he drove an old model Cadillac. It was clean and all original. The car in the driveway did not look familiar at all. I was a little scared. With my ex-husband stalking me from time to time, an eerie feeling came over me.

You couldn't see through the dark-black tinted windows of the Benz, not even the glow from the radio, but I knew it was on because I could hear it.

A small gentleman stepped out "Are you Adriana?" he asked people always wanted to make my name Spanish. "Yes, I am Adrianne, who are you, where is Hakeem?"

"I am going to take you to him" the driver explained.

"Wait...I don't know about that, I don't know you..." I said looking around still trying to figure out what's going on.

"Look," he said rather impatiently. "I'll call him on the phone right now."

I made sure to watch the little dude. He was short and petite, if it was appropriate to call men petite.

As I was pondering this thought, the driver handed me the phone and Hakeem's voice was on the other end of the line.

"As-Salaam-Alaikum Queen. That little guy there to pick you up is my brother Sol, he's ok, I promise you. I would not put you in harm's way baby... he is going to bring you to me and by then I will be dressed and ready to go. My damn trainer, this Nigga! I been telling him all week I had something planned and he worked me right up till 7, so I am just getting done."

"So, my bother Sol will get you to me safely. If you want I will stay on the phone with you the whole time." He continued.

"Maaaaaan...I was freaking out. I got on heels and I thought I might have to fight this little dude," I tried to say that part low, so Mr. Sol would not hear me. "Ok Hakeem, I'm going with this stranger," I told him locking up my car and grabbing my purse.

"I'm going to head to my house and take a shower...I'll see you in about an hour... ok?"

"Ok...see you soon"

Mr. Sol came over and opened the door. He looked as if he were checking me out. I had to admit, I was looking mighty fly, so I couldn't blame him. When he opened the door there was a huge bouquet of flowers lying on the seat and a card.

"This is a gift for you  from my brother..." I opened the card, *" I hope you are ready for a great weekend"* the card read.

The flowers were beautiful. The brightest colors were the yellow sunflowers and orange gladiolas and white daffodils wrapped nicely with burlap and twine. It was big at least 70-100 flowers. I have never seen a bouquet this big except for the other one he gave me. I now noticed Mr. Hakeem does things big.

# STABBED TO LIFE

"My brother is very fond of you Adrianne…he speaks of you often and I just gotta be really honest with you. For him to get this money in the Boxing game, he really cannot have a serious relationship.

He has a contract he has to fulfill." Seeing the look on my face, he asked, "Do you feel ok sitting in the front with me? If not, I am ok with you in the back.

"No, I am good to sit in the front," I answered quickly. I was looking a little puzzled because I felt like he just checked me about something.   I felt like I needed to show him I wasn't scared or anything, so I sat right up front.

The car was new. It still smelled like the new-leather smell. It was apparent that every piece of leather had been rubbed down with the best leather conditioner. I was a car buff and I knew quality stuff; my Daddy was into cars and so was my ex-husband, so I was very knowledgeable on cars from body work to interiors and motors. Everything. I knew that the care we were rolling in about to get on this Highway 14 was easily almost $100, 000 vehicle, and it just floated on that highway.

"So, what do you do Adrianne?" Sol asked. "My brother,  I am sure, told you he signed this contract and got a huge upfront bonus?" he asked with an attitude.

"Mr. Sol let me be really honest, I have known Hakeem a little over a month, in that time we have been in each other presence 5-6 times and most of that has been at the gym. We are just friends. I find him very charming, extremely handsome and hella funny. I am not trying to get anything from him.  I think that's awesome that you are looking out for him and have his best interest, but I am certainly not looking for anything other than his friendship" I explained.

# A. MICHELLE

"I can tell you that for him, he is looking for more than a friendship Ms. Adrianne, and really likes you," he said quietly.

I smiled because I knew that, and I was liking him quite a bit too. I was excited to be spending the entire weekend with him and to see what he had planned for us.

Sol asked questions about where I grew up and shared how of a dedicated Muslim he and Hakeem were. He told me that because of their back grounds they were really trying to do something positive.

BACKGROUND? I wanted to ask what he meant by that, but I didn't. I just did not want to pry, so for the rest of the ride we talked about cars. He was really impressed that I knew so much about cars especially classic Chevy's. He was all into that conversation and talked about how he and Hakeem had once restored a 59 Chevy. Our conversation was so good that we were both surprised that pulled up at our destination so quickly.

We were somewhere near downtown L.A. on Pico at a Boxing gym. We pulled in the parking lot and there standing as handsome as ever was Hakeem. His goatee was lined up nice and neatly and his gleaming white smile made him look like a black god.

When the car stopped, Sol looked back and said, "There's your man lady. Make sure you treat my boy right, if you do right by him, you are going to have every woman jealous. He is going to be able to give you the world. He is going to be the next Heavy weight champion...watch"

"Thanks Sol...nice meeting you, awesome conversation," I said.

# STABBED TO LIFE

I could not keep my eyes off Hakeem though. I was holding my flowers and walked over to him and before I could get close I could smell his sultry scent. He smelled of Drakar or CK, whichever it was, it was something very subtle but sexy.

Hakeem reached for me and grabbed my free hand, twirling me around.

"Mmmmm…" he moaned "Look at all that Thickness" he kissed me on my chick then thanked Sol for getting me there safely.

Sol assured him I was a good woman and definitely a winner.

I smiled and said, "Thank you."

I was blushing. I had to admit, though, I did look fly. I had on some really form fitting jeans that made my stomach look flat and a blouse that one side fell off the shoulder and of course my signature strappy heels. I wore very light make up and my hair was fresh from the shop bouncy and flowing.

"Damn baby…you look good…" Hakeem said.

Sol threw Hakeem the keys and he jumped in a fixed-up Chevy Silverado all back with chrome wheels. I'm thinking oh boy this is Hakeem's 500 Benz. Maybe he does have a little change. Hmmm…

"Those shoes may not work for what I have planned for us later, did you bring some other shoes? Oh, looking at those feet though, I may have some you can fit" he laughed…I laughed too

"Ok, you got jokes…" I giggled.

# A. MICHELLE

He grabbed my hand and this time he interlocked it between my fingers, I don't know why, but for some reason that meant something to me. It meant that we were moving to another level and it felt kind of good. I was still holding on to my huge bundle of flowers and honestly, I did not want to let them go I felt like a bride being walked around the old, funky gym. He was so proud of this place even though it was almost completely empty. It smelled like sweat and funk was embedded in the walls and floor. The wall was sprawled with pictures of boxers, mostly Hispanic and Black boxers; a few white ones too. I did recognize a few: De la Hoya, Sugar Ray Leonard, Shane Mosely, Holyfield, Foreman, just to name a few. Of course, he began quizzing me and was quite surprised I knew so many legendary boxers. He walked me around and pointed out some pictures of him on the wall as well.

I did think he was a little tall for a boxer, but all the pictures showed fighters just as big as he was. By now it was going on 9:00 pm and neither of us had eaten. His tour took a little over 20 minutes and the entire time, he never let my hand go. He was such a gentleman; assisting me down stairs and over the lifted linoleum. It was crappy in this raggedy ass place that he absolutely adored.

"You hungry? " he asked. I wanted to yell "hell yeah" but since he always joked about my weight, I dared not say anything.

Instead, I replied, "A little bit...not too bad," sweetly flashing my little, innocent smile.

"Let's go," he said.

Still walking hand in hand, he said his goodbyes to the few people that were still in the gym and we headed out to the car. He walked me to the passenger side and helped me in. This time he even put my seat belt on and planted a sweet kiss on my lips.

 As soon as he got in the car he looked over at me and smiled and said, "Um Um Um… girl, you are going to' get me in trouble."

He kept looking  me up and down. I thought to myself how I was the fat girl he'd met in the gym. I guess he starting to like this chunkiness.

As we drove he still insisted on holding my hand only letting it when it was necessary to use both hands to turn or park. We pulled up to Maestros Steak House in Beverly Hills. He had the car valeted and we were seated immediately.

The restaurant closed at 11 pm and it was almost 10 o'clock when we arrived. Surprisingly, he was recognized by a few people who yelled out "Hey Champ" or greeted him "As-Salaam-Alaikum."

The restaurant wasn't too busy, so we were waited on immediately. I asked for just water and Hakeem ordered Perrier. He already knew what he wanted to order. I saw a French onion soup and salad I wanted. He ordered shrimp and oysters.

 While we waited on our food Hakeem asked, "So how are you feeling about me so far?"

His straightforwardness caught me off guard. Before I could answer, he spoke again, " "I try to give you your space, and I am working on being a little less tacky with my comments. I never want to hurt your feelings," He said softly. "I haven't tried to get them drawers, but that may change tonight though" he laughed. "I really like you lady…and I know you will one day be my wife because I prayed for you," he explained.

I thought to myself how sweet this guy was. It was apparent he was trying so hard to impress me. I really was feeling him, and I really got a kick out of seeing how romantic he was. The slow dances and the holding hands, the opening of doors, and the beautiful flowers pampered me.

It was nice to get this kind of treatment when all you've ever known was to be treated like shit in relationships.

I thought intensely about my reply. I wanted to make sure my answer was honest, but not too forward that he would feel  as though he already had me. It had been my experience that when you let your guard down and let men think they've won you over, all that nice stuff stops.

I took a deep breath and answered, "Hakeem…you are a sweetheart. I appreciate how kind you are to me. I cannot help but be attracted to you physically because you are extremely handsome. More than that, you go to all these lengths to allow me in your world. Like today when you shared with me your passion to box. Although that makes me nervous in thinking of you getting hurt or suffering some type of injury, I understand your desire and commitment. I know we still have a lot to learn about each other, but I like you a whole lot sir." I revealed.

Hakeem gently took my hand and kissed it saying, "I want to make you happy, you deserve someone to treat you like the Queen you are, and I know Allah sent you to me, so I have to treat you with love and respect."

# STABBED TO LIFE

When we finished our meal, we got into a deep conversation. I could tell that he was starting to feel comfortable with me. He told me about his previous relationship and his children. He has 3 little girls that live in the Inland Empire all have beautiful Muslim names.

He shared that he and the ex-wife did not work out because of their difference in their religious beliefs. The ex-wife was a devoted Christian and wanted to raise her children that way, and of course, he wanted his girls to be Muslimas and study Islam. He shared how he was raised by a father who made him work at a very early age pouring and finishing concrete instead of going to school. He also shared how he witnessed abuse in the home.

His father beat his mother throughout his childhood. You could tell when he talked about it, how much that hurt him. He shared his love for Islam and how he was first in the Nation of Islam and then was later converted to Sunni Muslim. He said this was why he admired Muhamad Ali and how the sport of boxing helped him take good care of him and all his daughters.

He went on to say that he made salat (prayed) 5 times a day and all he ever wanted was a real Muslim woman, modest and covered only for her man. I tugged on my blouse to make sure no cleavage was showing. I didn't interrupt or stop him because he sounded like he needed to vent and just get some stuff off his chest.

When he told me how he and his father stayed on bad terms because of the way he mistreated his mother, always cheating and putting other women before her. I noticed that he mentioned his father's abusiveness several times.

# A. MICHELLE

You could tell that he loved his mother, but maybe he felt he had disappointed her in some way. From the way he spoke of his past, something had happened and whatever it was he felt bad about it.

He said that boxing was going to put him in a position to better care for his daughters who had suffered because he said the mom was "trifling,

He said she was smart, but she was nasty and was a poor example of a woman for his girls. He talked about her poor hygiene and lack of taking proper care for herself like grooming and keeping the house clean.

"I just want them to have a better life than me and be a better Daddy to my girls than what my father was to me. I don't want them to struggle like I did," his voice cracked, and it almost seemed like he was about to cry.

I reached over and touched his hand. I didn't know what to say. I couldn't relate to anything he was sharing. My life was not like his at all. Clearly, we came from two totally different back grounds, but that did not change how I felt about him one bit.

The restaurant had closed, and the wait staff was cleaning up. The kitchen staff was rattling pots and pans, I'm sure not just cleaning up-they were probably hinting to us to go home.

"Let's go baby," he said as helped me up and pulled me into him. He hugged me tightly and just held me for a long time. He looked at me deep in my eyes and stared so long, that I became uncomfortable and had to turn away.

# STABBED TO LIFE

"You got something to hide?" he asked, "You know you can tell me anything, just don't hurt me baby, because I'm falling, and I don't want to get up."

"Actually, that's my worry. You have a lot of attention on you Hakeem. You are at places where women are going to throw themselves at you and love all this body and height. Especially those hazel eyes…" I said, unsure if I could handle that.

"You ain't got to worry about me sweetie, if I roll with you…I roll with you good bad or indifferent," he said solidly.

Hakeem and I walked to the parking lot hand in hand. The restaurant manager had to come unlock the door to let us out, and with attitude I might add. They were not happy that we over stayed our welcome. Hakeem slid him $50 extra dollars and Thanked him for everything. He was such a polite gentleman.

Then he looked over at me and said playfully, "This pretty lady is very long-winded, and I kept trying to tell her let's go, but she just kept talking and talking…"

Of course, he had everyone laughing.

"Whatever." I replied sarcastically, glad that he was charming in public.

I was still walking in my heels. My feet did not hurt, but he says to me.

"Next stop you are going to come out of those shoes"

"Where are we going?" I asked with excitement

# A. MICHELLE

"We going to get wet" and he made this little nasty seductive face and started laughing.

We headed off and again while we drove and sang songs on the radio, he held my hand the whole time. We sang oldies till we arrived 20 minutes later at Santa Monica Beach. By then it was well after midnight and most parts of the beach was shut down, but Hakeem was determined to walk on the beach or whatever else he may have had planned. He parked, then came over to my side to let me out He didn't let me out immediately. Before letting me out, he reached down to my feet and began unbuckling my sandals. Once they were off he popped the trunk and got a pair of socks out of his gym bag. He put the socks on me and then assisted me out of the car.

He towered over me now. 5'7 and 6'8. I don't know why but that really turned me on. The smell of the ocean breeze hit me and the sound of the waves coming ashore sounded so peaceful. Hakeem had a small little blanket draped across his arm for us to sit on once we found the perfect spot. As we walked he asked me at least 5 times if I was cold.

I assured him I was not. I was rather hot; this place was so romantic, and my body was yearning for him. He stopped abruptly and looked around and tosses the blanket down. We were in a very dark spot, but light was illuminating from the pier.

The stores along the shore kept it from being too scary, but shoot I was with a big handsome boxer who would protect me. I sat Indian style on the blanket. It was a little tough in my tight ass jeans, but I managed to make it happen. Hakeem laid all the way down flat in his back his head facing the stars and moon. He was so long though only his head and torso were on the blanket, the rest of his legs and feet were in the sand. He motioned for me to lay down next to him the same way so that we both stared into the sky. There were no clouds, just dark sky and sliver of the moon. We were so close to one another I could hear his every breath.

"Damn I love this…I've missed the beach," he said wistfully.

"When was the last time you been out here? I asked.

"Hmmm… maybe six years ago."

"Oh wow…well I am glad to have this experience with you," I said, and I meant it.

He grabbed my hand and kissed it. You could tell he wanted to say something, but he hesitated. I tried not to make a big deal about it, but then he began to speak.

"I was in Prison," He said quickly. " I did four years for some bullshit and I am on high security parole. That shit is behind me now, and I am in a better place. I am trying hard to be a good Muslim, trying hard to be a good father to my children, but this bitch won't let me"

I started releasing his hand, not instantly, but because the conversation had become so serious and intimate, that I became so relaxed my hand just slid from his grip, but he grabbed it back, and clinched it tighter by interlocking our fingers. I thought that was a little rough, but I guess his emotions had the best of him.

# A. MICHELLE

"She feels like we have to be together to care for the children and I don't want to be with her any longer. She's having a hard time excepting that." He explained

"Hakeem was she down with you while you were away?" I asked reluctantly

"Hell no, that's the point. She wouldn't bring my children to see me either. They're girls but she always had them raggedy and shit, looking homeless." He had begun to raise his voice, so I started talking a little lower to calm him down. It was not like there was people around that could hear but I just wanted to bring his level of anger down.

"Well was she struggling once you were gone, who supported her while you were away ?" I asked curiously.

"My Mama, her Mama, she was on welfare and she worked, at a fish market but at least she did work. I always got word back that she was not taking good care of my children, and when I received pictures they were looking raggedy as fuck"

"Hakeem, I am not trying to be on her side but when you go to jail babe you've got to understand the dynamics change. A woman feels abandoned she feels all kind of ways and automatically goes into survivor mode. I don't know you all's history, but I know from having boyfriends locked up it's hard to support a dude locked up. It's very emotional, what is the current arrangement for the children?" I pushed for more information.

"There is no arrangement. I have been out 5 months and I have seen my kids 4 or 5 times," he said sadly.

"Was she expecting you guys to be back together once you got home?

# STABBED TO LIFE

"I am not sure how she could have thought that, she left me for dead. She didn't except my calls, she never came and visited… Allah forgive me, but I can't stand that bitch or her family," he said bitterly. "It's all good cause I got me a good woman now." He looked at me and winked one of those beautiful hazel eyes of his, and my heart just melted. I think it was because he talked about how bad he wanted to see his children and I had a ex who acted as if he didn't give a shit about his kids. I am sure he never told anyone how bad he wanted to see his kids. Man, this guy was pulling me in more and more.

As we sat there the tide started coming in and was getting closer to our blanket. Hakeem stood up with his long, self and reached down to help me to my feet. We walked right at the edge of the water hand in hand. The socks he'd put on me were covered in sand. He hugged me and said, "I think I am falling love with you Adrianne."

He pulled me close to him and for the first time since we met he planted the most intimate, sensual kiss on my lips. Gently and slowly entering his tongue in my mouth. I think he had hesitated with that before because he knew where it would go and because he had been training so hard. The trainers stressed to him no sex before a fight, but tonight he was trying to go somewhere. He was feeling something. He grabbed my butt and kissed me on my neck and licked me in my ear.

I wanted to slow things down because the entire week that he trained, he kept emphasizing he had to be ready for this fight that was less than a week away. He started unbuckling my belt and normally I would have done the same to him, but I just stood there and let him have his way with me. I whispered in his ear:

# A. MICHELLE

"Are you sure you should do this? " I pleaded

"Do you want me to stop??? " he asked

"No… not really but…"

"Shhhhhh…"

Even though we had walked away from our original spot, we were still out of view of anyone and the beach was pitch black and deserted. It was almost 2:00 am.

By now my jeans were at my ankles and he had touched me everywhere inside and out. He laid the blanket back out and he sat on it and sat me in his lap facing him. I could feel he was ready, and there was no turning back at this point. I wanted him, and he wanted me. Even though there was a cool ocean breeze his body was hot, and his forehead was sweating. He didn't pull his pants down but managed to pull his penis out.

He lifted me up…way up, to be able to insert himself inside me. I cringed a bit because he was long and thick, and plus I had been celibate for well over 6 months, so my vagina was in shock to be having such bigness inside it. But she handled it like a Champ.

I shifted my hips around and around, kissing his neck and grabbing his entire head and his ears. He lifted my butt up and down to make sure I felt all of him., pulling my breast out and licking my nipples. If someone had been filming or watching this, they were getting a real show. It wasn't distasteful at all. It was truly two people who cared about one another and wanted each other…bad. He still sat down but turned me where my back was against his chest and while he was still deep inside me, he leaned me back and whispered "I need you in my life lady… I LOVE YOU."

# STABBED TO LIFE

I didn't respond even though I heard him, I could not say it back, not yet. I really started giving it to him then, so he could hurry and be done. I had gotten mine. A sound like a grizzly bear came from his mouth as he spilled his hot juices in me. I tried to get up. We had not used a condom, and I wasn't sure why I wasn't thinking. I needed to wipe myself off some way. He wouldn't let me up. He held me and laid me on my side, and just stayed inside me till his penis went all the way soft.

He helped me sit up and began to literally dress me. He helped me back in my panties and shook out the sand off my jeans. He straightened my blouse and helped me stuff my breast back in my bra. Once we were both dressed he helped me up and he kissed me over and over as we walked to the car. I was a little mad at myself that I had unprotected sex with him. I knew he was fuckin his baby Mama or I had a strong suspicion about it. Based on what had just experienced I could see why she had an attitude, it's hard to leave good dick alone.

Once we made the long hike to the car it was covered in dew. He leaned me up against the car and began kissing me again. I could tell he was ready to go again. He took my hand and made me touch it. Now I could see it good.

"Mmmmm, boy you ain't ready for no more of this" I said and smiled

"Don't I look ready?" he smirked

"Let's Go Hakeem, I need a shower" I pleaded

"Okay, okay," He said sounding like a disappointed kid.

It was a rather quiet ride on our way wherever we were going. I thought we were headed to his place since he said

# A. MICHELLE

he had a place in L.A., but instead we pulled up to a swank hotel that was about 15 minutes from our love making spot on the beaches of Santa Monica.

We were both kind of tired, but once we got in the room that he had clearly checked into earlier that day, we took a long hot shower together and helped rinse off the sand that had seeped into some hard to reach areas.

More sex happened in the shower and once we cuddled in the bed it started again there too. I guess we were making up for the time that we'd both been sexless for months. Or so he said.

When we finally woke up around 11 am, he was hungry and ordered in some food. We ate and talked. We laughed and replayed the whole beach scene over and over to each other. If there was no other attraction, it certainly was some major sexual chemistry. But that was not going to make this a healthy relationship, would it?

*The therapist immediately chimed in, "No, it doesn't make it a healthy relationship. Often there is a strong sexual attraction in abusive relationships. It can eventually lead to sexual abuse and other controlling sexual behaviors."*

*"That's nothing, let me tell you this part," I said, ready to get it all out.*

# STABBED TO LIFE

# CHAPTER FOUR
## THE BABY MAMA DRAMA

The trainers claimed that they could tell by how Hakeem was fighting and sparing that he'd been sexually active. He told them no, but they did not believe it. I was spending a lot of time at his house on the weekend, but my schedule was crazy. It was probably best because we were always all over each other every chance we got. His fight was coming up. According to them we needed to really cut back on any sexual activities.

His children's mother was being more consistent in bringing the children to see him. She would bring them to his apartment in L.A. and she would allow them to stay the weekend. He would take them back on Sunday evenings. I had finally got to see pictures of them. They were beautiful little girls, very close in age. Just as Hakeem said some of the photos they did appear to be a little unkept. Their hair would not be combed, and their clothes looked a little tattered, but they looked happy and well fed and that was what was important. They had beautiful Muslim names and smiles like little angels. I kept my distance and respected their Mom, we had never been formally introduced, but Hakeem said she knew about me. He said that he talked about me often and shared how much he loves me.

One Saturday evening Hakeem had told me to meet him at his house. The plan was we to meet there and then head out to the movies and dinner. Now I was told to be there a 6:30

and it was almost 7. I pulled up slowly and Hakeem was walking what appeared to be his children to a car and a lady was there too. I assumed this to be their Mom. He had not mentioned to me that they were visiting and before I let my mind wonder or risk the chance of starting a commotion in front of the children, I just stayed a little further down the so that neither of them could see me. I figured one she was gone I would pull up.

Clearly Hakeem was nervous. You could see it all over his face as he looked up and down the street expecting me to pull up any minute. I chilled.

Once the woman had the children securely in the car, she reached over and kissed Hakeem. On the lips. Part of me wanted to swoop up, but their kids were there, and I just didn't want to be "that" girl.

I prided myself on my new classy approach to issues and I wanted to remain in that space. As soon as I no longer saw the vehicle in sight and Hakeem was in the house, I pulled up.

Before I got out I looked to heaven and said, "God please help me approach this in a calm manner."

I thought we were exclusive. I did not agree to an open relationship, and he did not tell me he was still seeing her. As a matter of fact, he talked so badly about her, the kiss they shared made no sense at all.

I knocked on the door and I stood there in my heels and purse in hand with the fakest smile ever.

"Hey babe," he said lightly as he went in for a kiss. I turned my head quickly and gave him my cheek.

# STABBED TO LIFE

"Hi. The movie starts at 7:45 and you're not even dressed, what have you been doing?" I asked with a slight hint of an attitude.

"Had my kids today...they wore me out," he sighed with exhaustion

"Oh cool. That's great, they were here?" I asked feigning ignorance.

"Yes, Sherry just came and picked them up," he said slowly.

"Here?" I could hear the attitude entering my voice, so I took a deep breath.

"Yeah, her trifling ass just left."

You could tell he felt a little uncomfortable. He was fidgeting and moving around.

"Trifling? Why do you call her names? That's not cool. She obviously ain't too trifling sweetie you were kissing her on the lips" I said in the calmest, classiest way I could muster.

"What do you mean baby? You are spying on me now?"

"No, I was pulling up and you kissed her, on the lips Hakeem...the very lips you just tried to kiss me on the lips with. No, I'm not with that sir," I said firmly, then asked "Are y'all still fucking?" Even then I asked calmly and collectively.

He sighed and came over to me, really close to my face.

"Girl, I don't want her, I am trying to play nice, so she brings my girls to see me. It wasn't a passionate kiss..."

# A. MICHELLE

"It was on the lip," I said pointedly. "Maybe I just need clarity on what we are doing. Do we have an open relationship, are we seeing other people? Please let me know so I can stop turning all these dudes away that are trying to get at me"

"Don't do that Adrianne, don't do that, that will really cause things to get ugly" he said and then he got serious. "First of all, baby I'm gonna do whatever I gotta do to see my kids, if a kiss on the lips is what makes that happen then that's what I'll be doing. You also need to remember I am Muslim, and I can have multiple wives."

Wait, what did this Nigga just say? He can have multiple wives?? I remained calm and let him finish. I was waiting for the laugh or the giggle. The hee-hee-ha-ha or something. He was serious? So was I.  I most-definitely had to say something.

"Let's be clear Hakeem.  I am all for a man being a father to his children and this is possible without you having a relationship with their mother. Maybe you want a relationship with her other than just co-parenting. If that is the case, I will gladly step aside for that to happen. I don't want to do anything to come between you and your children. Oh, and that multiple wife's thing, that will never ever happen with me."

"Hey, calm down, look at me," he pleaded.  He got so close to my face I thought he was going to kiss me, but he grabbed my cheeks with his hand, rather forcefully I may add, then said distinctly, "You ain't going nowhere. It's me and you baby, for life, so we gotta work this shit out. How do you suggest I do this?"

# STABBED TO LIFE

I shrugged my shoulders and flopped down on the coach. He went to the back room to get dressed. I looked around the house to see if I saw any evidence of her staying there.

 I stuck my hands in the pillows and side of the coach thinking I'd pull out a pair of panties or something. There was not so much as a lint ball or a coin. This dude was such a clean freak he would never slip and leave anything behind. As I waited I took a glimpse of myself in the mirror. I was cute. I was classy. I did not have to deal with this foolishness.

I figured I would just get what I wanted from him. I refused to pursue a serious relationship, because this fool clearly had no respect for me. Multiple wives??? Nigga please. When Hakeem came out dressed, he looked good and smelled good, and he was smiling from ear to ear.

He picked up the remote control to his stereo and pushed play. A song by Stephanie Mills and Teddy Pendergrass "Two Hearts" played. He pulled me up from the coach and started to dance with me. His long arms wrapped around me like a straightjacket. So very tight but loving. He was not a singer but every lyric he sang it in my ear especially ones like:

*You Came into my life a stranger*
*You captured my heart*
*Now I've got to face the danger I'm ready to start*
*Thought that I could make it on my own*
*All alone I tried so hard to fake it*
*Now the truth must be known*
*Two hearts are always better*
*Together forever*
*Two hearts are always better*

# A. MICHELLE

*True romance we'll treasure*
*You've given me so much of yourself*
*Till I don't need nobody else*
*And with each passing day*
*My love for grows strong in every way*
*You are my life...*

He let the entire song play and at the end he said, "I love you baby. That kiss didn't mean shit...I say and do what I do to see my kids, if that's too much I will figure something else out ok?"

I just shook my head yes and never uttered a word about it again. He could tell though by my body language and my lack of conversation I was a little upset with him. The whole dancing thing, as cute and romantic as it was, I knew he was just trying to deflect from what had happened. I was slow, but I wasn't stupid.

"Let' go somewhere my Queen, let me show my woman off with your fine self," he said hopefully.

Normally he would get a little bashful giggle out of me. Not today, the things he had just said were still stuck in my head. He no longer wanted to discuss the kiss. He did not deny it, just simply made it seem as if it were something he needed to do to be allowed to see his kids.

We were too late for the movie, so he had a taste for Olive Garden. I was not very hungry and had salad and bread sticks. He ordered a bunch of stuff. The conversation started of dry, but I gradually began to talk to him.

"You staying the night with me?" he asked while he scarfed down the last of his food. He often ate like he was still in prison; like he was on time limits. It was disgusting.

# STABBED TO LIFE

I would have normally said, "Babe slow down," but I was still mad with him, so I just let him look like a savage.

"Nope. Not tonight" I said sarcastically "I need to spend some time with my kid. Alonja has a game tomorrow."

I had initially planned on staying the night with him and getting up extra early and going home. Fuck that and him. I was the type of person that once you did something foul, it was hard to let that shit go. What he said and what he did was still right in my craw.

He picked his napkin up from his lap and looked at me with one eye brow raised like he was about cuss me out. Come on with it nigga. That was something I was good at. Please say something smart and threatening so I can go off on your ass.

"Baby…I would love for you to stay the night, I haven't seen you all week. When we get back to my spot we will call Sherry and work out something together with these kids ok? They need to meet you anyway and she needs to know how serious we are. Hey…you ok?"

I was looking down playing with the salad I had barely eaten. I didn't want to look him in the face.

"I am sorry ok?" He pleaded and motioned for me to come and sit next to him on his side of the booth. He scooted over and hung that long arm around me and kissed me on the cheek.

"I guess kisses on the lips are over all together now?" he asked trying to be funny.

"Yup…till I see you brush your teeth, tongue and lips and gargle with alcohol" I said very seriously.

# A. MICHELLE

"But I didn't even…" he started to explain

"Don't play with me" I said cutting him off. We both had to laugh.

The drive home was nearly back to normal. We laughed and for the first time, we talked about me a little. My upbringing. My parents, my brother. I grew up way differently than him. I did not want for much. Both my parents had decent jobs that they'd been on 20 plus years. I even took the time to invite him to my mother's 50th birthday party. I would be 30 in July and my Mom 50 in November. She was already in the planning stages and it was going to be a grand affair.

Just as Hakeem said, as soon as we got in the house he called Sherry and put her on speaker.:

"As-Salaam-Alaikum, I just wanted to thank you for bringing the babies over here," he said. I could tell he was trying to be cordial.

"No problem," she said quickly.

"We will need to work out a new arrangement because I think I am sending mixed signals. My actions today were probably confusing because I kissed you, and I shouldn't have done that." He said gingerly.

"What do you mean?" She asked hotly.

"Sherry I am in a new relationship. I've told you about that, and I know you are open to us all being married together but she is not with that."

I was on the couch shaking my head, thinking she had to be stupid to be ok with that shit. I felt sorry for her.

# STABBED TO LIFE

"So, what are you saying, you don't want to see the kids anymore?" She asked pathetically.

"No…I am simply saying we need to work it out where I pick them up and all that," He said sharply.

"You'll have to take me to court and they will take my side because you have 2 strikes" she said and began yelling.

"So, you would rather I pretend to like you just so that I can see my children? Bitch you got me fucked up!" He screamed.

They began to start arguing in earnest; cursing and calling each other names. It got so ugly that I wanted to intervene, but I was trying to stay in my lane.

"I was ok for you when you were broke, but now that you have a little money, those are the kind of girls you like, the ones with high heels and fake hair," she said sounding angry and desperate.

I scoffed at her remark. Although I did wear heels, most of the time I wore my own real hair. How dare she.

"Look we are not getting anywhere. I want to see my kids at least once a week and by next weekend I would like it if we could sit down like responsible people and work out a plan." Hakeem pleaded.

You could tell he loved his kids. His eyes filled with tears. "Drop them off at my Mama's house and I will pick them up there or visit them there."

"No." she said and hung up the phone.

"You see Adrianne? You see what the fuck I am dealing with?? I have been away from my kids for 6 years and this raggedy bitch will not let me have a relationship with my kids unless it is totally on her terms!" He yelled, still angry.

"I'm sorry. There is a way Hakeem. Fathers have rights too. Of course, if your background is that bad, they will probably favor her over you for custodial parent, but they cannot stop you from seeing your children," I said knowledgeably.

"I want to take a bubble bath…can you wash my back?" he asked with a grin. He was trying to change the subject and get back to us.

I thought for sure he was going to blame me for his argument with Sherry over me making a big deal out of the kiss, but he seemed fine. I had a baby daddy who was here free on the streets and barely saw his children. Yet here was a guy who, although had his run ins with the law, still wanted to be involved in his children's life. That heffa wouldn't even let him unless, of course, they were together.

I had paid close attention to what she had said while they argued. She said he had 2 strikes. So, based on that statement I figured he must have already been to prison prior to the last six years he only told me about. I had some questions that needed answers, but for now I was going to enjoy this bath and the nakedness before me.

Hakeem had no shame or problem getting out of his clothes. He was out of them before the tub filled. I sat on the toilet holding his towel while he made sure the water was just right, and he had adequate bubbles.

Even without an erection he was flopping and plopping around, about to hurt someone with that thing. Purposely getting close to my face.

# STABBED TO LIFE

"Um you need to get in this water before it gets cold…nasty" I said playfully and we both laughed. When he got into the antique large tub with the clawed feet at the bottom, his long 6'8 legs had to hang out.

"Soap me up girlll," he said playfully.

I lathered the towel and started washing his shoulders and back and we talked. I needed answers.

"So, Hakeem, Sherry said you have 2 strikes…" my voice trailed off so that he could elaborate.

"Yes…that is correct. I was going to tell you but since it's out there I better address it. Ok so the first one was I beat up this white boy who was talking shit, so based on how bad I beat him up, I took a deal because they were trying to give me like 9 years for what they claimed was an assault. This dude was calling me all kinds of niggas and I got mad and I served him a 3 piece. They claim he almost died. I didn't want to do that much time so my "public pretender" suggested I take the deal, so that also gave me a strike. The second one was when I was working at…hey is that my phone ringing? Can you go answer it?

"No , but I will go get it for you"…the caller id read *Sherry Lakes* He answered, "As-Salaam-Alaikum."

I could tell she was asking a bunch of questions. He gave one-word answers; no, uh huh, yep. I wasn't sure of what was being said on the other end, but looking at his facial expression, he did not look pleased. He sat there holding the phone for 5-minutes just listening. It was well after midnight. I bet she was trying to see if I was there.

He suddenly said, "Ok, Sherry. I am going to put you on speaker, so my lady can hear."

# A. MICHELLE

I shook my head no frantically. This was not my business and it was inappropriate for him to involve me in his baby mama shenanigans.

I decided to speak up, "Look Sherry…I really do not feel it necessary that I be a part of discussion pertaining to you and your children. This is something you and Hakeem really need to work out. If I can help as far as transporting is concerned I am willing, but that is all I care to help with," I explained.

"I need to know what your role with my children is?" she asked all tough.

I wanted check her on how she was coming at me. But I am very protective of my children too, so I get it.

"There is no role as of right now. I have not even met the children but first and foremost I respect them, and I respect you Sherry, as their Mom. If they are ever in my presence, I would take on one role for sure and that would be to protect them. I have children too."

I didn't know what this woman expected from me. She probably thought I would act all ghetto and cuss or talk shit, but that's not how I get down. Especially regarding children. But don't get it twisted, I can go there if she comes at me wrong, so far, she was trying to be respectful.

"You do realize you are sleeping with a married man?" She says very condescending. My eyes got big and I looked over at Hakeem and he held his head down in shame. This asshole. The more I stay around him, the more secrets are revealed.

"Hmmmm no ma'am, I had no idea," I said, looking at Hakeem with piercing eyes.

# STABBED TO LIFE

"Well we are not officially divorced yet" she says so sarcastically that Hakeem yelled, "We were divorced the minute you left me for dead for four years and wouldn't bring my children to see me. You were already seeing some other man bitch...fuck you."

I looked at him and rolled my eyes and I moved my lips to make sure he could read them *STOP CALLING HER NAMES*... In my opinion, he was the one who went to jail she didn't. Her life shouldn't stop because his ass fucked up and went to jail. I didn't say that but that was certainly what I was thinking.

"Sherry look, it sounds like I need to step aside and allow you two, to figure out what you guys are going to do about these kids; that is priority. Besides, they haven't had their Daddy in their lives for a long time, and he wants to be a part of theirs. Honestly, our relationship is hindering that. For whatever reason, you are not able to accept that he has moved on or maybe he has not moved on, I just know I am not going to be in the middle of thissssss mess, it was nice talking to you," I said abruptly, and handed the phone back to Hakeem.

He was still in the tub when I handed him the phone. He immediately told her before he hung up, "You are not going to ruin this for me!"

I acted as if nothing just happened. I added some more water hot water to his bath and told him to stand up, so I could wash his body as he asked me to. With a smirk on my face and an idea in my head. I soaped him from head to toe. Washing every part of his sexy ass body, I giggled to myself as I washed and rubbed on him; he had to have problems in prison because he had an ass like a girl all plump and big. When I finished washing it, I slapped it.

"Hey…don't be doing that gay shit…" he laughed as I rinsed him off and dried him off just like a baby.

He cleaned out the tub and then it was time for him to wash me. He ran the water and added bubbles as he washed me all over. Of course,  he paid more attention to his favorite spots.

"Hey. You missed my neck and shoulders." I said playfully.

It was weird after talking to Sherry. I felt like I had to fuck him good since I was "sleeping with a married man" as she claimed. I wanted to say yeah, "I AM like 15 or 20 times. I was mad at him, but I had to do have revenge sex with him-then leave his lying ass alone.

He pulled me up from the tub and I was completely covered in bubbles. I tried to rub them off, but he pulled my hand away saying no. I guess he had some sort of fantasy with bubbles. It was crazy how dudes that had been in and out of prison always had some sort of weird fetish they came home with.

He led me to the bed and laid me down and drug that anaconda of a penis all over my lower torso until the big snake awoke from his sleep. He played with my boobs and kissed me all over. He then led his snake into the warm but moist den of my center.

I let him get a few strokes in and then took the lead and led us to the promise land. I changed ever-so often into every position we loved. Our favorite was the "scissors" and the other when I laid completely flat on my stomach.

# STABBED TO LIFE

It wasn't exactly doggie style, but he did enter me from behind. That was his other favorite. I gave it to him like I was getting paid. When it was all over, he curled up like a little baby in a fetal position. The only thing that was missing from this picture was his thumb in his mouth. Bahahaha…I looked at him, kissed him on the cheek, then took a real bath got dressed.

When I snuck out the door he was snoring like a fat, full, baby. I loved this man, I couldn't lie, but I needed a break. I needed for him to make his kids a priority and learn to be honest. I especially needed to learn to take care of some of my own business.

I started realizing that I always put more focus on the man I was with than I was with my own life and priorities. I figured the plan of action should be that we'd come back together once we were both straight, because my divorce was not final either. The only thing, I was honest with him about that. I knew that this was how it had to be.

Before I'd made it to the freeway, Hakeem started blowing me up. I wouldn't answer the phone because I knew if he found exactly where I lived, he would be there in the blink of an eye.

When I got home, I played Nintendo with my kids and cooked them dinner. Afterward, we watched my bootlegged copy of "Men in Black" together. It was a bad copy too. You could see people in the audience stand up to get popcorn in the movie. I enjoyed spending time with my babies. Talking to Sherry just made me realize how I had been neglecting my own children.

The next day was spent with my kids.

# A. MICHELLE

I called off on my extra job on Sunday and went to Alonja's game  After her game, the three of us rode bikes and hung out in the park. We had a full day of fun, and then made cookies that evening. I missed my kids. After such a full day, I was tired. Once they were in bed, I took a long, relaxing bubble bath and just sat there thinking- then praying- then missing Hakeem.

Oh, how I wanted to call him. I noticed that he had called while I was in the tub and left a message that said, "Baby…you have every reason to be mad at me. I have not been honest for a whole lot of reasons, one is that you are such a classy woman and  I felt if I told you too much of my past. it would result in just what happened."

I could hear the sadness in his voice as he continued, "You trying to leave me. I love you and I know you love me girl. I am going to let you have this break but I ain't giving up on us. I'm at the gym in L.A. all next week, but I am going to call you every day until you answer this phone. The only thing I ask of you is that you don't give my pussy away …you hear…"

The answering machine then cut him off because his message was too long. I could not lie. I wanted to talk to him so badly, but I am going to be strong. This break was very necessary.

The next day was a Monday and I woke up at 5 am as usual. I did some Pilates off a workout video I'd purchased from a late-night infomercial. I had always done this every day as well as hit the gym for an hour in the evening after work. No sooner than I was done working out that morning, my phone rung. It was awfully early. My kids were still asleep, I normally woke them up at 6:00 am.

# STABBED TO LIFE

I looked at the caller id : *Sherry Lake*.  I started not to answer it, but I had to see what the hell she wanted and have the audacity to call my house before 6:00 am.

"Hello"

"Hello Andrea"

"Hello Sherry. My actual name is Adrianne, you know like Rocky's wife…the boxer?" I thought that was rather funny, but she didn't laugh.

"Oh well Adrianne. I am calling you because I just wanted to let you know that me and Hakeem-our relationship has been over. It has been for a very long time. He called me and went off on me saying our conversation last night made you not want to deal with him."

"That conversation Sherry made me realize that the both of you need to come up with a better way to co-parent your children. I do not want to get in the way of that," I said gently.

"Well that is what I want too. I also need to let you know, God put it on my heart to warn you that Hakeem can be very violent. He used to hit on me, especially when he was on drugs"

"Drugs?" I asked shocked that she'd said it like that. "You mean like smokes weed?"

"No, he used to use Methamphetamine, crack, he would self-medicate when he doesn't take his meds for his bi-polar condition"

"Bi-Polar?" I asked in disbelief. My heart sank. I didn't want Sherry to hear, but I was crying.

# A. MICHELLE

So, 2 strikes as a felon, a drug addict and bi-polar? Wow I was in definite shock. This big sweetheart of a man, such a gentleman, had a drug problem and mental illness. I knew now I really couldn't do this. My kids' father was not diagnosed crazy, but he was, and I could not deal with another crazy man.

"Yes, he was diagnosed his last trip to prison. He has been in and out of jail all his life, but he says when he takes it, he does not like the way it makes him feel." Sherry explained

"Well I appreciate the information" I said rather abruptly and hung up.

At this point I rushed her off the phone because I did not want to hear anything else. Bottom line, this bitch was hating on the fact that he loved me, and she wanted to destroy our relationship any kind of way she could. She was not looking out for me and how did I know any of this shit she was even saying was true.

Part of me was angry and part of me was sad with what was just shared with me, but I was still going to stick with my initial plan, and that was to give this relationship thing a break. I wanted to call Hakeem and ask him about the information shared with me, but it was time to get myself ready for work and my kids ready for school.

My children and I made it to our destinations as planned and on time. The kids to school and me work. My work day was rather busy as Monday's were at the welfare office. I worked reception, so I saw crazy stuff daily. I even saw many fights and would even get cussed out from time to time when trying to help a person fill out their paperwork.

# STABBED TO LIFE

I assisted clients that could not read or write and believe me it was several. I was really close to the security desk where an armed security guard sat. We had metal detectors that each of the clients were required to go through to gain access to the building. This was the building where people who signed up for either food stamps, Medi-Cal or cash assistance. My job was to get them ready to see the eligibility worker by screening them and educating them on the process.

What I loved about my job was that it was super busy and that always made the day go by fast. Lunch approached quickly on this day, and as usual I had lunch with either Mag or Wendy, the best work buddies ever. I had vaguely shared with them about Hakeem, but not too much. If they knew they would certainly insist that I leave him alone. So, I only spoke about the good stuff. I loved these ladies. One was religious and could give me a scripture and spiritual insight in a heartbeat the other one was a rida'…she was down to fight and beat a bitches ass, so both these ladies were very important in my life.

When I arrived back from lunch, there was a huge bouquet of flowers on my desk with Hakeem's signature.

The card read: *"**You are my Queen…from now to eternity. Allah sent you to me and I promise to treat you like the precious diamond you are. I love you, Hakeem**"*

Everyone was in awe of the huge bouquet. The vase was nearly 3 ft. tall and the variety of flowers were amazing. Pink and purple tulips, red and white roses, white and yellow lilies, it looked like something that would be placed as a centerpiece for a wedding reception, it was huge.

# A. MICHELLE

All day someone would enter the room and say, "damn that man loves you." I thought to myself that maybe he did, but that man had a whole lot of issues.

At the end of the day, I decided rather than haul it home I would let it stay in the office so that we all could enjoy it. I called him knowing he would be training, and I left a message thanking him for the beautiful arrangement.

On the ride to the gym I thought of Hakeem and even though it had only been two days I missed him like crazy. I went over and over in my head what Sherry had told me. The taped in my head played again and again, and I just hoped and prayed she was making this stuff up. I needed to ask Hakeem about it, but I couldn't right now.

My work out at the gym was quick. People who knew him asked how he was. I would just smiled and said he was fine and training down below. This is what we called L.A. when you lived in the Antelope Valley. "Down-below."

I still had not been to his spot in L.A. For all I knew he could possibly have another woman staying there and didn't want me over there. My head was all over the place about this man.

When I got home, right away I checked my caller id and noticed Sherry had called 4 times. I didn't know what the heck she could have wanted, so I jumped in the shower and prepared to get ready for bed. Once I reviewed their homework and made sure my babies had eaten, I put a load of clothes in the washer, and got them off to bed.

I laid across the bed and stared into the ceiling. The tears rolled down my face. It was probably best I did not continue this relationship with Hakeem.

# STABBED TO LIFE

My gut feeling was saying that I should leave him alone, but I loved him.

Just as I was going to get under the comforter the phone rang, I saw it was Hakeem. I hesitated at first, but I had to hear his voice:

"Hello?" I said, answering the phone with a quiet voice.

"Masha Allah, I am so glad you picked up. Why you do me like that baby? I prayed to Allah to please let you answer this time and he did just that," he said earnestly.

I remained quiet, but I must admit, his excitement just from me answering meant so much.

"You there…???" his voice cracked

"Yes… I am here," I said, not sure of what to say at this point.

"I am sorry for upsetting you, for hurting you, whatever I did wrong baby forgive me ok?" He pleaded.

"You know your wife called me again," I accused.

"My wife… ok now she's my wife?" He asked sarcastically.

"She shared more stuff with me…Hakeem you need to be honest with me even if we're just going to be friends. I am not going to go into all she said because quite frankly I was hurt by it and I really do not want to believe it. I hope she is lying," I said, close to tears.

"Adrianne, I want to go over there, you and me, so you can meet my babies. We can talk face to face with her and work out something"

# A. MICHELLE

"I don't want to be involved Hakeem," I said quickly. I wasn't getting involved in some polygamous love triangle.

"Come on, once we get past this shit we can move forward with our life," he said, darn near begging. "Let me call her back and see if she is cool with that, depending on where her head is, maybe we can try and have a conversation." He continued, "Can I just say this??? I am willing to do whatever you feel is best so that you are satisfied and happy with this situation."

"Hakeem! I should not matter! Those are your kids at risk and you two grown ass people need to figure out something like adults for the wellbeing of your children," I scolded.

"You right, but you have to remember Sherry is not normal," he said convincingly.

Not forgetting everything Sherry had told me, I took a deep breath and said, "According to her baby, neither are you…so stop all the name calling and try talking like adults."

We talked a little while longer. He shared how he had been going really hard in the gym and after his fight on Friday night, he wanted to spend the weekend with me. He sounded so remorseful, so sincere in his conversation that I really didn't know how to feel.

I can't lie my feelings for him went deep . They were deep even for these children I hardly knew anything about. I had only seen their pictures. Their little faces were embedded in my brain.

I agreed to see him the weekend and before we hung up, he said how grateful he was to have me in his life.

# STABBED TO LIFE

He begged me to please be patient with him, because he was going to "tie-up all the loose ends" soon so that we could live happily ever after.

As soon as I hung up with him I called Sherry. I told her that I had spoken with Hakeem and he wanted to see if we could meet up soon. I told her that maybe we could put our heads together so that the children had a set schedule to see their Dad.

She was open to the idea and suggested Saturday at her house. I was a little hesitant at first, but I agreed as long as Hakeem was open to it. I felt like a mediator and something in my head said this is the job of Family Law and the courts, but I was pulled into it now. In the meantime, at least until they went to court, it would be nice for the kids' sake that they have their Dad in their life.

I had two kids at home whose dad made no effort whatsoever to be involved in their lives. My kids were the best kids ever. Those little girls of Hakeem and Sherry were stuck in the middle of their parents bullshit feuding. It was going to affect them negatively further down the road if someone did not stand up and advocate for them.

The week seemed to go by so slow. I did talk to Hakeem every evening before he went to bed for only five or ten minutes just to hear his voice. He had the nerve to ask if we could move in together after his fight. My children had not even met him. They may have answered the phone when he called or may have heard me say his name while giggling on the phone, but that was the extent of it. I told him straight up I was not ready for anything like that. It was way too soon.

# A. MICHELLE

When Friday came, although he had invited me to the fight, I was so hesitant to go. Even watching him spar killed me and that was with head gear and stomach/groin protection. He was a heavy weight and they hit hard. I sucked it up and went anyway. I was placed ringside and saw some very famous people.

It was not a huge fight just a debut like the Golden gloves. The idea was to get his name out there. I managed to see him very briefly before he went out. He was in his zone. He barely said a word to me, but he did give me his signature wink while they were taping up his hands. I took my seat and right next to Sol, who was also his trainer and manager. He whispered to me

"I really need to talk to you when this is all over" he said very seriously.

"Ok… no problem." I said slowly. The look on his face was a little concerning.

I cheered my man on. He was doing a great job. He was really a talented boxer with major potential. He was going toe -to- toe with his opponent who was a much more experienced boxer, but Hakeem was smashing on him.

He was holding his own and I was proud. Judging by Sol's reaction, he was pleased as well. There was a point where the opponent was dazed and confused, but he didn't fall. The last round was a POUND FEST. They were banging on each other. Unfortunately, it came down to a decision and Hakeem did not win, but the promotors, the trainers and the mangers were pleased.

Sol leans over to me and mumbled, "If he can stay focused and stay running and, in the gym,-and you know the rest-no sexual activity, he will go far. He has another fight in 30 days Adrianne. I need him focused, and you need to check that bitch Sherry, so this nigga will be back in jail behind her."

"We are supposed to be going over there tomorrow to talk with her," I explained

"Aww shit, good luck with that, the girl has got major issues," he said gingerly. "Hey, let's congratulate your man, I'm sure he wants you in the ring with him."

We walked up, and Sol helped me climb in the ring, Hakeem reached out for me and kissed me.

"How did I do?" He asked like a little kid.

He always looked for my approval as if he had never been praised as a child. Like no one had ever told him he was good at anything.

"You did good baby," I said, "You looked really good. I am proud of you," I said, kissing him and wiping sweat from his forehead. I could tell that tomorrow the little minor scratches and contusions on his forehead would look a little different, but my honey did look good in that ring. He had on his custom-tailored robe that someone had made for him and his matching trunks had his initials on it.

I was proud and could tell by his performance he really had been in that gym going hard for the last few weeks. I was sure with all that went on Sherry, his kids, and I- that added stress probably didn't help or maybe it did.

He draped his long arm around me and off to the locker room we went. There was a little area right outside the showers that I stayed till he showered and got dresses. As

# A. MICHELLE

soon as he walked out, he was interviewed by a local cable sports channel and a guy from a boxing magazine. I didn't mind waiting. I sat there in awe. Even though he did not win this fight, it was good publicity for him and each interviewer spoke on how impressed they were with his performance. He consistently thanked Allah his trainers and team, and in one interview, expressed an actual thanks to me. I smiled from ear to ear.

Once all the interviews and pictures were done, we gathered up our things to go. I felt special because I had the opportunity to be in a few of those pictures. I reminded Hakeem that we needed to be at Sherry's the next day at around noon, so we'd better get to bed. Everyone else was going out to celebrate but I could tell he was ready to go. He was tired and needed to rest.

My kids were visiting with my Mom, so the promotors put us up in a hotel. Once we arrived he took a long hot bath and soaked in the jacuzzi tub. He even tried to get some, but I encouraged him to get some sleep. He slept like a baby snoring and drooling. However, when the alarm when off at 7 am, he was all over me.

He wanted to make love and I welcomed it. I missed his gentle touch and seeing his nicely chiseled body. I missed the grizzly bear sound he made when he reached his orgasm. I giggled.

"You like that huh…" he said with this little smile. He went underneath the cover and bit me. The initial bite hurt, probably the second one too, but the rest after that was so erotic and passionate. He bit me as many as 12 times, all over. My shoulders, my back, my inner thigh, and even my butt cheeks. As sick as it sounds it was amazing.

# STABBED TO LIFE

I glanced over at the clock and noticed it was a quarter to 9 am. We needed to have breakfast, shower and get dressed. I just wanted to respect Sherry's time since she was allowing me in her home. The least we could do was be on time. I got Hakeem moving but he wouldn't keep his hand off me. He insisted we shower together, but I made sure we got in and got out. While we dried off, he pulled the curtains open in the dimly lit room and everywhere he'd bitten me earlier were his teeth marks. They were sprawled all over my body.

"Oh my God...look what you did to me...you freak!" I said, I could not believe it. It hurt only a little, but dang, I had no idea he'd left marks.

"Well now everyone will know you are spoken for and that's my shit," he said in a very commanding tone. He was taking ownership of me. I was his woman and as sick as it probably sounds, I liked that. That made me feel like he loved me. Knowing we were going around Sherry made me feel like he wanted her to know that as well.

"Maaaaan...get dressed!" I shouted

I threw him his pants, shirt and kufi (Muslim cap). He wanted to wear the kufi because it would cover the small bruising on his head from the fight, and because he liked dressing in his Islamic clothing. Although, as in most religions, sex with a woman that you are not married to is frowned upon.

Hakeem still tried hard in other areas to compensate and be a good Muslim. He prayed 5xs a day, ate halal food, and tried to refrain from talking bad, but like for everyone else, living right is sometimes the biggest struggle.

# A. MICHELLE

We were finally dressed and ready for our day. We had breakfast via room service and was ready to hit the road. I had to admit, when we stood in the mirror side by side, we were a cute couple. I could comfortably wear any size heel and not worry about being taller than him. I loved that. I loved that whenever we were out we were constantly complimented on how good we looked together.

I tried to coordinate with his beige linen shirt and pants, so I wore a beige sun dress that was a little low cut, but since we would be around his kids, I was sure to wear a light sweater.

I offered to drive since Hakeem was still a bit exhausted from his fight and this was finally a day of rest from running and training. I was pleasantly surprised that we didn't hit any traffic seeing as how we had taken the 405 to the 91. These were two very busy freeways, but we managed to make it on time. When we pulled up to the apartment complex , we saw there were children everywhere, and people were listening to loud music in the parking lot.

As we walked up the stairs, I noticed how a lot of the apartments didn't even have screens on their windows. There were several open windows throughout the complex and you could see several curtains blowing in and out the windows.

One little girl walked near us and said "Yo shoes are cute lady."

I smiled and said, "Thank you baby."

The smell of weed lurked in the court yard that you could tell was once a play area. You could see where jungle gyms and slides used to be but now it was nothing but patches of grass growing where the sand should have been. The kids were still playing with balls and remote-control cars. It was a busy complex full of happy children. Hakeem looked a bit nervous. Usually he'd hold my hand tightly, but now he held it loosely and it was sweating.

We got to the door and I took a deep breath. Looked over at Hakeem and he smiled. He did his wink as if to say, "Here we go..." and knocked on the door.

When Sherry came to the door, I spoke first hoping that I didn't sound too chipper. She spoke back, but her tone was dry, even when she acknowledged Hakeem.

The kids quickly ran to their Dad, and they were all over him. I watched their interaction and it seemed like the youngest one was the most excited to see him. The other two were a little stand off-ish. Other them Hakeem seemed happy talking to the kids and laughing. There was no communication between me and Sherry, so I finally said something.

"Soooo I'm Adrianne, and I know this is just as awkward for you has it is for me, but I do appreciate you allowing me to come today." I said.

"Well I guess you seem to think it will be best for my daughters to build a relationship with their Dad, who just goes back n forth to jail, and received all this money and hasn't sent anything to help me with these kids" she said angrily.

"Nothing???" I asked

"Not one dime," she answered firmly.

# A. MICHELLE

By then Hakeem had walked to the children's room. He was in there for a very brief time before he came out and said angrily, "Their room smells like shit Sherry, you know why? Because it a trash can full of dirty fuckin diapers. Yo ass is trifling."

I gave Hakeem a look as if to say cut it out. In my opinion he should have never been out of these kids' lives for all this time. Now he wanted to come here and call shots?

Shut up. I pressed my lips together tightly and said, "Why don't we just take it out."

I said this in the most calming voice I could muster. He grabbed the trash and had the girls show him where the dumpster was outside. Sherry and I were in the house alone. She still had not given me permission to sit down, so I remained standing. She didn't have much to say.

"So how often would you be willing to allow Hakeem to have the kids?"

"I am not sure. He goes back and forth between wanting to be with me, then he wants to be with you," she said.

"Yeah, I understand, well we need to get some clarity once in for all, so when he gets back we need to get an understanding and please know Sherry, I will gladly leave this situation alone if he says he wants to work things out with you and be here for his kids," I said that and I meant that.

I do not fight over men. There are too many out there and if that's what he wants that is exactly what he will get.

# STABBED TO LIFE

Hakeem walked back in with the trash can in one hand and his daughters all linked together in his other hand. He was smiling, and they looked so cute too.

"Maybe we should have the kids go in the other room," I suggested, "So we can talk."

The fact that neither of them thought to remove their kids from the discussion let me know these two didn't have a fuckin clue.

Sherry walked them in their room and closed the door. When she was out of our view, he looked around the house and rolls his eyes in disgust. I knew he wanted to say something negative about their living conditions.

Sherry came back in the room. I was still standing really close to the kitchen table and chairs, but still standing until Hakeem said, "sit down babe."

"Sherry is it ok if I sit here at the table?" I asked very politely.

I was trying hard to remain cordial. Not to be mean but this little apartment reminded me of the old TV show "Good Times."

It was somewhat clean and was decorated with mismatched items. Even all the chairs at the table were different. Her couch was broken down and Hakeem literally looked as if he was sitting on the floor. I shook my head. This may have been the best she could do and part of this was clearly Hakeem's fault too. How could he allow his kids to live in these horrible conditions? Yet he was driving Benz's and had two places to live that were fully furnished.

# A. MICHELLE

"What are we going to do Sherry? You have my kids living foul. All I asked was that you let me help you and see my kids, at least once a week to start. Like I suggested earlier, I can drop them off at my mother's and I will visit them over there."

"Why not here, are you scared we may end up in bed together like we always do?" she questioned hotly.

Then I took a good look at this chick. Her hair wasn't combed, her kid's hair was barely combed (even knowing their dad was coming) and she had on some dingy stretch pants and a T-shirt with grease spots on it. I knew that some women let themselves go after they have a bunch of kids. It's overwhelming and a lot of those women go into a depression. I wasn't trying to diagnose her, but this looked to be the case.

"Look, that's a good question Hakeem," he knew I was pissed as I continued, "I shared with Sherry if you want to be with her and raise these beautiful little girls together, I can handle that, I can step away, no love loss. I can go on about my business." I am sure I sounded a lot stronger than I felt.

"Hell no. We have tried this over and over and she does the same old shit, calling the police on me, won't clean up, and doesn't take care of my girls. I'm not with that. We came here to work out a schedule. That's it. Now let's do this and get out of here," He said very sternly.

"Ok Adrianne, I guess he's made his mind up, let me get the girls so they can say goodbye," she said and then she walked to their room. As soon as she walked in the room with the kids, Sherry and Hakeem started arguing.

# STABBED TO LIFE

"Sherry, can you just do what I asked and have my kids go to my Moms?" he pleaded

"No, take me to court!" Sherry yelled.

While they continued to argue back and forth the smallest girl came over to me and tapped my thigh and said, "My Daddy is the devil."

My eyes got big and I said, "Well sweetie that's not very nice."

I knew this little girl could have only heard her Mama say things like that. This child was much too young to come up with something like that on her own, right?

I was shocked. They continued to go back and forth, and I kept giving Hakeem the eye. I wanted him to calm the hell down, the kids were getting scared. One by one they trickled out of the room.

Before I knew it, Sherry was right behind me. Since I was at the kitchen table I just assumed she was going in the refrigerator or doing something at the sink. Before I knew it, she grabbed my hair. I reached up and grabbed her arms to toss this bitch to the floor. I got my balance, grabbed her wrist away from my hair, and pushed her towards the couch where Hakeem stood. He grabbed her by her throat and began strangling her. The kids were screaming as he tossed her to the coach and squeezed her neck with all his might. She could no longer scream, and she was losing consciousness. She couldn't breathe. Her eyes were big at first and now they were closing. She was dying.

"Stop!" I yelled. "Let her go!"

# A. MICHELLE

I had to literally pry each finger from around her throat. His eyes were bulging in rage.

"Fuckin let her go right now!" I yelled. By then I had managed to get his other hand loose.

I heard Sherry coughing until she nearly threw up.

"Let's go!" He shouted. "Give me the keys!"

I tossed them to him. When I got out the door, I ran in my four-inch heels like they were track shoes. Sherry was yelling for people to call 911, while chasing us, and I could still hear those little girls screaming and crying.

We jumped in the car and before I could close the door good, Hakeem was hauling ass toward the freeway. All I could think of is that we would be on tv for being in a high-speed car chase.

"Why you didn't let me kill that bitch?" he screamed.

We were flying through Riverside trying to get on the freeway. I couldn't even answer, just watched this fool drive had me scared. He was so angry.

"Hakeem…calm down and slow down please," I begged

"Are you ok?" he asked.

"I'm fine, I cannot believe she just walked over to me and grabbed my hair like that."

"She is just jealous babe, you see her?"

"Yeah, I see her but according to her y'all are still having intimate relations-you know…fucking," I spat. I was mad.

"She was just trying to make you mad."

# STABBED TO LIFE

"You know why I am mad?" I screamed. "I'm pissed that those little babies are struggling like that, but you are living good. That shit is not cool. Even if she is not letting you see them, you need to send them some money. Or at least purchase stuff and have it sent down there." I finished angrily.

"Yeah, you right. I need your help Adrianne. I appreciate you so much. I didn't get taught regular shit like this during my childhood, it was fucked up," he said with a crack in his voice. "You are so right; my girls are suffering."

The rest of the drive home was quiet. I think we were both just thinking about what had happened, and how that whole incident could have landed him back in jail or the children could have been hurt. Just so much. My thoughts were focused on how short this dude's fuse was. His anger was out of control. Maybe what she said about him being violent was true. Maybe he was abusive.

*"Adrianne, there is no doubt he was abusive. You witnessed him assaulting another woman, and not only did you leave with him, you didn't stop to get her help. My observations are in no way meant to bring you down. I want to help you recognize some of the signs and symptoms of abuse so that you never have to experience this again. Continue dear."*

# CHAPTER FIVE

## THE MOVE IN

It had been a month since the hair pulling incident, and although Hakeem was sending the girls money, cloths and toys on a weekly basis, he still wasn't visiting them enough. Part of the reason was because his mother was not cooperating with the arrangement and on several occasions, she was too busy. Ironically, Sherry called me the day after that craziness and apologized and thanked me for saving her life. I told her I just broke up their fight. I let her know Hakeem was out of line but so was she. I also warned her if she ever touched me again I would beat her ass. She apologized again saying all she could think of is how I was destroying her family.

By now, my kids had met Hakeem several time. We would all go to the movies together. He'd come over and show my son how to hit the heavy bag. I started cooking Muslim dishes. and we had just about eliminated all pork from our diet. We all felt better and good about the dietary changes.

I had started making Salat (praying) with him. I just wanted to learn the prayers so whenever he stayed over I could get up and do Wudhu, which is the ritual of washing performed by Muslims before prayer. Muslims must be clean and wear good clothes before they present themselves before God. Muslims start in the name of God, and begin by washing the right, and then the left hand three times. Water is breathed in gently through the nose three times.

# STABBED TO LIFE

Then we would make Salat, the ritual prayer of Muslims, performed five times daily. I was enjoying learning about the religion and at this time he kept saying it was no pressure for me to convert my religion. I grew up Christian all my life and Islam was way different, but I found it very interesting,

My kids began greeting Hakeem with the Muslim greeting, and he would share stuff with them he learned in prison. He taught them how to play spades and dominoes and a few other card games. It was beginning to feel that he was a part of our family. He didn't live with us full time and at this point would only come and stay on some weekends. He still had his place in L.A. and he had his place in Lancaster. He talked about moving in, but the conversation ceased for a while when he found out my ex-husband was cop. I felt we needed to wait anyway.

It was getting close to my 30$^{th}$ birthday and a few friends of mine had planned a get together at a fancy restaurant in Granada Hills called the Odyssey, The Odyssey sat on a huge hill overlooking the 5 and 405 freeways. The view was beautiful and although we were scheduled to arrive at 7:00 pm, for some reason Hakeem chose to have us arrive an hour early. It was awesome too because the sun was just about to set as we sat in the parking lot. He wanted to walk around before everyone arrived.

"You have been the downest female I've ever met. I have never had no one stick by me and believe in me like you have," he said looking deeply into my eyes. "I also never had a chick who checks me when I'm fuckin up, but who also has my back when I am gone out of town. I trust you, you've never given me a reason to doubt you. You are just a real woman. In the past, I have been with little girls."

# A. MICHELLE

You know our childhoods were different, but you never mind teaching me things. I have learned so much from you. I'm trying to be the man you need for me to be. Please be patient with me."

He smiled with a twinkle in his eyes and reached into his pocket.

"I got a birthday present for you," he continued. At first, I was going to give it to you in front of all your friends, but I didn't want to be embarrassed if you said no." When I saw the black velvet box, my heart sank.

"Oh boy…" I said in a soft quivering voice.

"At some point, like I told you from day 1, I wanted you to be my wife, so I am asking you my Love, My Queen…Will you marry me?"

He handed me this ring that was so big with so many diamonds. I had never seen anything like it before in my life. I was shaking, and he was shaking. I was crying, he was trying not to cry.

"I needed to get a big ass ring, so I can keep these dudes up off of you, I see them looking at my baby, and you're mine forever," he said sternly. Then he repeated himself, "FOREVER! So, what's it gone be Adrianne?" he smiled. Before I uttered a word, I couldn't help but think about how much this ring cost and how his kids were over there in the projects barely making it.

"Of course, YES…I love you Thank you so much," I said emotionally.

I dried my tears fixed my lip gloss and eye liner. I was no longer wearing a lot of make-up now. Hakeem insisted that

# STABBED TO LIFE

I just wear lip gloss because I had such a natural beauty. Oh, and those sexy outfits I used to wear, those super tight jeans and shirts that showed a little cleavage or the imprint of my nipples, he'd kindly tell me, "Classy ladies and Muslima's do not dress like that."

He also reminded me on several occasions that we should move in together since we were practically engaged. But until I saw divorce papers between he and Sherry, I said no. He made sure that he saw mine though, especially after finding out my ex was a policeman.

The dinner went well. Everyone brought me nice birthday gifts, and my favorite cake. Some of them were meeting Hakeem for the first time. Like everyone else had said, they thought we were the cutest couple ever. They also thought he was such a gentleman and very funny.

Hakeem was weird around my friends sometimes, because he was used to saying he was a "felon" or a two-time loser; a jailbird, he didn't want to slip and say this in front of my friends and embarrass me. I don't even think it was obvious to anyone that he was an ex-con, and at this point I really didn't care. Not everyone gets caught doing bad, he just happened to be one who got busted, but now he'd done his time. He was trying hard to stay free and on the streets for me and his children.

As the night ended, he was nice enough to walk all the ladies to their cars who'd come by themselves. We also waited until everyone took off safely then headed to my place. There was only one person noticed my ring and as she was leaving she said, "Hey girl, I seen that big rock on your finger! Did you get engaged?"

# A. MICHELLE

Hakeem and I both and nodded our heads yes. She gave me a "thumbs up" and headed to her car.

The ride home was quick. We talked about our future and our current living arrangements. This was a topic that was still a little scary for me. I had not let my kids know he would be completely moving in, and I felt I owed them an explanation or maybe even their permission or approval before making such a big decision.

Once back in the Antelope Valley we ended up staying at his little house in Lancaster. He thought it would be better to have some wild birthday fun without traumatizing my kids. So, as always, when we were alone, it was a wild night. He said he was going to give me a "Pancake Massage"

I asked what the heck that was and explained it to be a massage while on your stomach and then you turn over and massage your front, head to toe. He did all that and so much more.

When it was all over, he ran me his famous bubble bath and talked to me while I soaked in the tub. This time he put some oils in it that smelled so good and he dropped rose pedals in the water too. It was so relaxing. I started thinking about me being 30 years old and the fact that I hadn't accomplished much. I'd just made it through a bad relationship and now I had Hakeem, with his fine ass. I was so blessed… I thought.

The rest of the evening was spent lying in bed. The illuminated the dark room and the windows were open. It was a beautiful, warm night. You could hear dogs barking and the next-door neighbors arguing. We'd been laughing, clowning and talking about our plans to move in together,

# STABBED TO LIFE

but the couple arguing next door changed the mood and things suddenly became serious.

"I hate the sound of fighting like that" Hakeem said "My mother and father fought, and my father use to beat on my Mama. I hated that shit" he said bitterly.

I wanted to know more about why they fought, and Hakeem explained that his father was just abusive and that his mother would try to protect

"Why would they fight?" I asked

"Dumb shit…honestly I really don't know…my mother tried to protect me from my father a lot., I'd get in trouble and then he would want to fight me like a grown ass man, just cause I was taller than him, but I was a kid…" he explained I'm telling you babe, my life was fucked up…it messed me up."

I could tell the conversation was taking him to a dark place so, I tried to make things a little lighter, his mood had just drastically changed.

"Well your life is going to be great from now on, ok?" I said as I grabbed his face and kissed him.

"So where is all this boxing equipment going to go when you move in? This junk is not going in my house." I said laughingly

He had heavy bags, free weights, speed bags, and so much other stuff. I was scared to make this move because I had not told my children, or my parents. They didn't even know we were engaged. Since me and my children's father divorced, they knew I was dating and had met one other person, but they knew very little about Hakeem.

# A. MICHELLE

My kids knew it was serious because he did spend the night occasionally and I'd never brought people around them.

"I'm going to have you working out on all this stuff. Boxing is good exercise and you probably need to sharpen up on your fighting techniques since you let that bitch Sherry grab you in the head," he laughed

"Oh, you got jokes! I got her up off me, I had no clue she was coming for me," I said exasperated.

"She wants your man," he laughed, but I didn't find that funny at all.

"Just know this sweetheart, I don't fight over men. I know you don't think so but plenty of men want me honey and those men don't have baby-mama-drama," I laughed sarcastically.

"Yeah…they may want you, but they will never have you…see that ring…look at it…you mine girl, you understand?" he asked gruffly.

I couldn't tell if he was playing or not, he sounded very serious.

He took the sheet and covered my head…"Don't end up like this" and he forced the sheet down over my head as if to say, dead with a sheet over me.

He pulled me close into him, my back against his big chest and kissed me on my ear. "I love you…" He whispered.

We stayed in that position for what seemed like hours talking and watching the curtains sway from the gentle breeze outside. Listening to the humming of the old fan was even relaxing and calming and it was completely quiet outside. The arguing couple either went to sleep or left.

# STABBED TO LIFE

Hakeem dozed off first because I could now hear him snoring, very lightly but he was clearly knocked out. There were somethings about this man that puzzled me, his obsession with me was flattering but intimidating . My ex-husband was jealous and controlling but in a different way. This  man Hakeem just loved me…a whole lot…and I loved him.

The next morning, I woke up to the smell of breakfast but also the call of adhan. This was when Hakeem pulled out his prayer rug and did his morning prayer. I was beginning to memorize it. That was so beautiful to me. This man's commitment to his religion was so attractive to me. I laid there and just listened until he was done. The only thing my ex was committed to was his cars. He was a very self-centered man and his family came second to his vehicles and his friends.

Hakeem came in the room once he was done and greeted me. I was lying there in his long t-shirt and no panties. I got up and brushed my teeth and while I was doing that he came behind me.

After brushing my teeth, I go into the kitchen to see he had a light little breakfast of beef sausage, cantaloupe, honey dew & strawberries, eggs and wheat toast prepared. It was great. There was hardly any conversation that morning.

Hakeem was rushing me off because he needed to be in L.A. and I needed to go to home and chill. My kids were still at my parents and they had plans, so I was going home to prepare for the move. We agreed it would be on July 15, so I had a few days to make room for him and tell my children the good news.

# A. MICHELLE

I was ready to leave and Hakeem when Hakeem let know he would be in L.A. a couple of days and to have my phone on me because he was going to be checking in on me. I thought to myself "whatever dude" he already had the attitude that the ring he placed on my finger makes him my owner. Never will I go down that possessive, crazy jealous rode as I had done with my children's father. No way.

I gave him a smirk and shook my head as if to say, "you are ridiculous." He hugged and held me like I was going across seas never ever to see him again. He kissed me and then pulled my hair up off my neck and bit me, yes bit me. He had done this when we were having sex before, but this time we were fully clothed and were just saying our goodbyes. It was a bit sensual, I guess, but it hurt, and it felt like he'd ripped the skin. Before he pulled off I said.

"Ouch, that hurt!"

"You know you like that shit," he said in his sexy voice

It even stung a bit, so I said in a slightly irritated voice, "You are so rough and nasty Hakeem, damn."

"Now you don't like it…quit acting like a punk. I was thinking we should go get some tattoos when I come back. That is going to be another birthday present from me. Think about where you want my name," he laughed.

He walked me to the car and planted his last kiss on me, told me he loved me, then promised me that we were going to have a beautiful life together.

I drove home with my neck still stinging and sore, but I was smiling because I loved that crazy ass man. I loved him so much. I had this goofy grin on my face the entire ride home. When I arrived, the house was quiet.

# STABBED TO LIFE

It was hot inside because the air was off, so I opened some windows, and turned on some music while I got started on re-organizing. He had made it very clear that my bed would have to go, and we would keep his bed. He didn't want me to keep mine because he felt uncomfortable being in a bed that I had slept with my ex in. It was crazy, because I didn't know who all had slept in the bed with him.

Rather than go back in forth about it with him, I didn't say anything. Plus, I did like his bed. It was a cute, sexy canopy bed. The area I needed to mostly make room in was the garage. That's where all his work out equipment would be. He had newer furniture than me, but both of our stuff was nice. I still had stuff in boxes in my garage because when I moved to this house it was from a 4 bedroom much larger home, so all my stuff would not fit. To be fair I wanted some of my stuff and some of his stuff too.

I also was thinking of my children and what their reaction was going to be when they were told Hakeem was moving in. I felt bad that I should have talked about with them at first. I knew they were going to let their Dad know, so I knew there was going to be major back lash from him and my family. I couldn't worry about that right now. I felt like it was my turn to be happy. I had spent almost 10 miserable years in a very controlling relationship with a very self-centered person. Here was someone who was all about my happiness.

It was hot in the garage. I'd spent a good two and a half hours out there and was sweating like I'd worked out. I had done a good job organizing and placing boxes in the rafters. The entire garage was roomy enough now for whatever he needed to put out there. When I came back in to take a break, the phone rang. I ran to catch it to hear my babies on the line singing Happy Birthday to me and asking all sorts of questions about what I did for my special day.

I almost told them that me and Hakeem were engaged but chose not to. Alonja told me that they had been to the mall and went swimming. They had been hanging out at the park up the street. My parents were great with making sure they took them places, and although their father was not really involved in their lives, my dad did good stepping in as father and he was an awesome grandfather. Thank God for wonderful parents.

We talked a little longer and then my mother got on the phone and emphasized to me to enjoy my free time without the kids. She encouraged me to get out and do something fun. If she only knew I was preparing for her soon to be son-in-law to move in.

Just as I hung up with my Mom and my kids, the phone rang again, but this time it was Hakeem. When I answered the phone, he didn't say a word just played Mary J. Blige's song "Share My World." He knew Mary was one of my favorite artists, and this was a song I loved:

*Share my world*
*Don't you leave*
*Promise I'll be here*
*Whenever you need me near*
*Share my world*
*Don't you leave*
*Promise I'll be here*
*So baby don't you have no fear*

He almost let the entire song play and just before the end he says.

# STABBED TO LIFE

"I know you like that song babe, and every time I hear it, I think of you"

"Awwww yes honey that is my song…what you are doing?"

"Got this whole place packed up and ready to go." He explained.

I had only been to this place 2 or 3 times but had never once been inside. When I pulled up, he was outside waiting for me. This was a small area in a very old part of Los Angles, called Silverlake, it was on Descanso Drive. His place was ancient. It had an old fire escape and the building was brick on the outside and in the inside. It had old hard wood floors and the sink was a pedestal sink with antique fixtures. The place looked weathered and old and was rather spooky.

"Well I have room for all your stuff now, took me just 2 hours but I organized and cleared out the garage.

He shared that he was going to take the truck and head back to Lancaster and in the morning to start packing up that house also. He explained he then had some business to take care of with his manager, Sol and his trainer. He did not volunteer any information, so I did not ask. He said he would probably be moving in on the 14th.

He never once asked if I had talk to my kids or family. I started to feel bad about the fact that it didn't seem to faze him one bit. I honestly thought we should have both sat them down and asked them how they felt about it.

Then again, maybe I was doing too much. I was the parent and what I said should go anyway, right? No matter how I rationalized it, the fact that he showed no concern just did not sit well with me.

My head was everywhere by then, but it was too late to turn back. He had already prepared to come. I sat with the phone to my ear totally doubting my decision to do this, trying to convince myself it was the right thing to do. My gut feeling was saying no, my heart and my body was saying yes.

"Hey baby…you still there "Hakeem asked breaking my reverie. I hadn't heard a word he said.

"Yes, I am here…"

"You are probably tired and hopefully excited your man is coming home soon, our home," he said confidently.

"Yes…I am really excited." I said

He told me he would see me Monday for lunch, that he loved me, and we got off the phone. I laid there across my bed for a while, beating myself over this decision. Something, whatever it was,  just did not feel right about it.

Monday came along, and I met up with Hakeem, and he seemed even more excited. I met him at his other place in Lancaster. He was leaving the place shining like new money. Nothing was left in there except his prayer rug and his Quran. We sat on the floor and ate salads he'd picked up from our very favorite café. The people there knew us. It was so good to see his handsome face. It had only been two days, but I was missing him. It was going to be nice to wake up to him every day.

"Hey babe, I was thinking, it seems like the kids like me and are ok with me coming. I saw your son watching me make salat (prayer), you think he might be interested in learning about Islam?"

"I am not sure…" I said quickly. I was not forcing anything like that on my children. "We'll have to see."

"So how did your meeting go with Sol and everyone?" I asked to quickly change the topic

"Not well, these Niggas are trying to play me out of money, all they kept saying is we are under contract…we are under contract. I said fuck that contract I only get 33 and 1/3 of any purse and they get the rest."

"Did you read the contract before you signed it?" I asked very calmly and concerned.

"I did, then I had a lawyer read it over for me, but the lawyer worked for them, then they dropped that lure on me… over $100 thousand cash to seal the deal, of course a broke nigga like me fresh out the penitentiary jumped on it, this is a vicious game. Then they want to be in all my personal business, I think Sol was fuckin Sherry while I was gone too"

"Really?" I couldn't imagine that, but I mean it's possible." I said hopefully.

"Look baby…I am starting my life fresh with you. I got money in the bank, I am debating if I will keep boxing. The last fight had me pissing blood, and you have made me realize I need to be there for my kids. I also realize I need your guidance. You down with yo man?"

"I'm with you baby," I said honestly.

Sounded like he was ready to hang the boxing up Now my question was what would he do if he doesn't box? I was not one to have some man just laying up in my house. I hoped this wasn't the plan all along and now that I have rearranged my life, he is springing unemployment on me.

"When I move in I will pay everything the rent and utilities and your money will be just for groceries and taking care of the home," He explained almost as if he'd read my mind.

It sounded like a great plan to me.

"Either way I have a concrete finishing job lined up if I decide to no longer box." He explained

It seemed as if he had thought this whole thing all the way through, I liked that.

It was time for me to get back to work, so he helped me up off the floor, gave me a great big hug, and said how he couldn't wait to be able to hold me every night in his arms and wake up to me every morning. I was so excited, but worried at the same time. I was praying for the best.

The day of the 14th I called off work so that I could help Hakeem. Our plan was to have everything in and settled by the time my children came home. Before he brought his things in, he mopped the entire floor. I just let him take the lead and place things where they needed to be placed

When we unpacked everything, I noticed that his things were practically new. We took out my little country style table and chairs and replaced them with his more ultra-modern bistro style from his place in Lancaster. He had some cute clocks and pictures that we found places for throughout the house. We also pulled my old bedroom set out and replaced it with his nicer newer stuff. As I mentioned, he had an issue with my bed because me and my ex-husband use to sleep in it. Whatever... We started

# STABBED TO LIFE

taking stuff off the truck at 8:30 am and we were finished by 5 pm with everything in its proper place. The only things left to do was to set up his home gym in the garage and that would be a great task, because he had accumulated so much stuff since he had been training.

We went hard on the house and it looked great, very neat and organized and very clean. We had not stopped for lunch, just a few water and bathroom breaks, so we were rather exhausted. We ordered a pizza (cheese pizza because Hakeem didn't eat pork) and once the pizza arrived, we sat in our new remodeled kitchen and had a bite to eat. You could see in his face the excitement. I was excited as well but my children's reaction to all this was in the back of my head. I hope they were going to be ok with all this. There was silence while we ate, we were both so exhausted. When we were done eating, Hakeem looked up and winked at me, "this is our beginning babe" He walked over and kissed my forehead. "Let's go look at this room."

Hakeem now had his side of the bathroom; all his colognes and deodorants were on his side. It had been a long time since I had seen that. It felt good looking in the closet and seeing men's clothing and a row of men sneakers amongst my hundreds of pairs of stilettos. I couldn't help but smile and reflect on how we met and how arrogant I thought he was, and he turned out to be a good guy. Not flawless but very sweet.

I laid across the bed while he finished putting a few things away he came over and laid across the bed, next to me.

When he told me he needed to tell me something, my mind started racing wondering what now? I figured he would say he wanted his kids to come and live with us, or heaven forbid, Sherry.

Whatever it was, judging by the sound of his voice, it was serious.

He told me that since he was on parole, he had to report his change of address and his new parole officer would have to come inspect the house and could possibly once a month, searching through our personal items, including the kids' things.

"I know you were not prepared for all this but, it won't be that bad I promise," he finished.

"When are they coming?" I asked disappointed.

"Probably tomorrow…" he said softly

I was not happy about this. What a major violation of my privacy and of my children's privacy. He went to prison-I didn't. He went on to explain that because he had paroled to L.A. County and now he was living in Kern County a different set of parole rules applied. I was confused. He told me that because had mandatory drug testing, I could be asked to change the feminine products I used. This was not cool. I didn't sign up for this. I bet he waited till he was nicely moved and then dropped all this on me on purpose so then it would be too late to change my mind.

"Damn Hakeem," I said, clearly bothered.

"I know babe… and you know I have to protect my family and you are my family now, so I want you to know that I will protect y'all no matter what. You know a felon cannot have a firearm, right? So, I do have some heat that I cannot have legally, but these niggas ain't gonna catch me

# STABBED TO LIFE

slipping. I will have it in a place in the backyard. I won't even tell you where I put it I don't want that stress on you." He explained.

He unfolded a blanket and unwrapped a tightly snuggled AK 47 Assault Rifle and an extra magazine that held thirty rounds. I was not scared of guns, because my ex was a cop. I had been around guns as a child and my father always had shot guns, but this was an assault rifle. One which the person who owned it had already displayed issues with his anger. I can't lie, it made me a little uncomfortable. He must have seen the uneasiness in my face.

"Hey, it's going to be ok. Shit what you expect me to have a 22 or something? I need to lay a nigga down that come and fuck with me or my family" he said defiantly.

"What about my kids? Had you given that any thought Hakeem?" I asked angrily

He stared at me long and hard, almost like he wanted to go off, he took a deep breath and said

"Baby...I will leave the gun at Sol's house. I am just trying to make sure you guys are safe that's all. I would never put you or your kids in an unsafe situation. You have to trust me babe." He wrapped the gun back up and stood there holding it like it was a baby.

I did not feel comfortable at all, after witnessing him choking Sherry, and had I not been there, I am clear he would have killed her. This gun just made me feel that he'd have one of his angry episodes and hurt me.

"Just make sure it's left outside Hakeem," I said curtly and walked off.

# A. MICHELLE

The house smelled so good. He had cleaned the carpet and mopped the floors, and the chairs were placed on top of the tables, so he wouldn't miss one area of the floor. It reminded me of the way my mother cleaned.

At the front door, there was a shoe rack. Because he made salat and prayed on the floor, everything needed to be clean and their shoes removed to keep from tracking dirt and outside evils. Certain pictures had to be removed from the walls and other adjustments had to be made to accommodate Hakeem; his parole, his religion, but I rolled with it. After all, he was my fiancé, so I tried to keep the peace. This was only day one and I was already having a few regrets and second guessing myself and the relationship, but I trusted him. He said we would be safe, and I believed that.

My children were due back home in a week, so I figured every time I talked to them, I would share a little more with them on the changes in our house, so they would not be shocked when they got here. Every time they called I mentioned the no shoe policy, the prayer room, the new kitchen table, my new bedroom, and how things looked way different from when they left. I needed to share with them the new chore rules Hakeem and I had come up with. Whoever's night it was to do the kitchen had to also mop. Before they would just have to sweep but Hakeem said they need to mop every night. He would give them $10 a week if they followed the rule.

The Parole agent came by and it went well. Hakeem had the gift of gab and he had the agent laughing and they talked like they were good friends. He looked at me strangely when Hakeem introduced him to me as his fiancée. He had this disgusted look on his face.

# STABBED TO LIFE

I just smiled and stayed in my lane. We walked him out and while standing in the driveway Hakeem remembered there was paper he needed him to sign allowing him to travel to Vegas for a fight. When Hakeem ran inside the house to get the form, the agent asked me, "Ma'am...with all due respect this guy has a dangerous past, you need to be very careful. I know it looks like he's changed but this guy is a very shady character, I spent 3 hours reading his file." He shook his head, pulled out his business card and handed it to me. "You cannot fix him" the agent said.

Hakeem came out with the form to travel and the agent signed it. The agent told him when he returned he must call in ASAP, to report in. Hakeem agreed, shook the agent's hand and sent him on his way.

I could tell that the agent was going to be monitoring him very closely. The P.O. from L.A. County was due to show up too. This was the agent Hakeem had been dealing with since he had been released from prison. They were familiar with each other. I was hoping this process was not going to take too long because I told my job I was just going to be late, not miss the entire day. The phone rang, and it was the P.O. he was getting off the freeway and would be here in 5 minutes. Once he arrived he did a very similar inspection, just this guy was a bit more thorough in terms in writing things down for his report. I imagine L.A. County was a bit tighter in keeping up with their parolees.

The agent's name was Myers he was an African American guy who looked about our age and he also looked very familiar. I later realized I recognized him from being at Hakeem's last fight. This P.O. unlike the Kern county gentleman was very serious, there was no laughter and he was very serious. He asked the both of us many questions.

# A. MICHELLE

He wanted to know about my children how often they would be left there alone with him, if ever. I told him if ever it would only be occasionally after school. Hakeem was getting a little agitated and told the agent none of his charges ever involved harm to children of any nature. Agent Myers explained this was a routine question and he showed him on the paper the list of questions that he was required to ask.

I had to help keep Hakeem calm during this process. I knew the man was only doing his job. He asked repeatedly if there were any guns in the house. Hakeem said no immediately, then looked at me to answer as well.

It was hard for me to say no sir when we'd already discussed the AK. I didn't like lying, especially about something so serious. Hakeem squeezed my hand as if to say thank you. He even asked about the cars we drove and then went in the kitchen and pointed out which knifes had to be out of the house because they exceeded in length to what was acceptable for a high security parolee. Agent Myers then said something that really was to help me.

"Hakeem you stated you all are getting married and I have right here in my notes from the visit we had on our initial inspection in Riverside that the Sherry woman was your wife, and apparently she provided something to the prison as a marriage certificate, so make sure you get a divorce before you marry this lady. Or you will be violated for bigamy" he explained

"Myers, you know I will do that, I ain't trying to go back to prison man," he said sarcastically. I could tell he was pissed.

# STABBED TO LIFE

"Ma'am, thank you for allowing me to inspect your home, sadly I will be back in about 30 days, next time, unannounced. We will do this all over again, but again, these are the terms of his parole. Please feel free to contact me if either of you have any questions." He said all while looking at me.

I thanked him, and we walked him out, Hakeem did not even wait till the car pulled off good before he started it in.

"Did you see that babe? That nigga was looking at you like he wanted you. His job ain't to tell you all that, he didn't say that shit to Sherry. I think this nigga was flirting with you. See these fools got me by the balls, got me kissing ass. They know though…they know what I am capable of," He said angrily.

"Baby don't trip, you just do what you supposed to and eventually you will be off paper with them and can go on with your life," I said in the most calming way I could.

"I would have preferred you not smiled showing your dimple and shit, that made that nigga think he had action at you. You think he look good?" he asked escalating.

"No, I wasn't looking at the man like that, I was only trying to be polite…damn!" I said. I didn't know why he was tripping.

"Look, I know how these dudes work baby, I am sorry I Am not trying to be an asshole, you've proven time and time again you got me and are down with me, I appreciate that, just don't get chummy with these cats they will try to turn you against me," He explained and came over and kissed me.

# A. MICHELLE

He apologized over and over but assured me that we were going to make it through it. He sent me off to work promising to take me to the movies

I called Hakeem several times in between the busy periods at work and he didn't answer. When I took my last break I tried calling again, no answer. He was probably still working on the house and didn't hear the phone. When 5:00 rolled around, I could not wait to get home and see my man. I ended up sitting in the parking lot for 20 minutes talking to some very close friends/ coworkers. They were saying how happy they were for me, and happy that I had found love. They also loved the ring. I could not stop smiling, yet I knew I'd better head home and see about Hakeem and why was he not answering.

Soon as I hit the corner I saw Hakeem's car in the driveway, I could hear music coming out of the garage and he and some older white man was sitting there on patio chairs, looks like they were drinking alcohol and the smell of weed was in the air.

"Hey babe this is our neighbor Willie, lives right there across the street" he pointed at the house that had an actual flag pole in his yard flying the United States flag. The old man was holding the cutest pit bull puppy and handed it to me, telling me it was a welcome to the neighborhood gift. He explained that their dog had a litter and Hakeem told him to check with me to see if we could have one.

This man had to be 60 or 70 years old. He was wearing a Vietnam Vet hat and some dirty shirts, with a long, white, beard and every other tooth missing. He smelled of alcohol, like it was coming out of his pores.

# STABBED TO LIFE

I sat my purse down and grabbed the little puppy which was so cute. I could even smell his little puppy scent through the stench of the old man. He was cute, and I know my kids would love him. I just could not get past that I smelled weed, saw liquor and the P.O. was here less than 5 hours ago. We needed to talk. I was able to calm myself down. Hakeem told Mr. Willie goodbye and let the garage down.

"Uh oh…you mad at me huh" Hakeem said sounding intoxicated.

"I am…what are you thinking Hakeem your parole officer was here earlier and now you are drinking, and smoking weed? Tell me I am wrong, please tell me just the old man was doing that right?" I asked

"I was doing it too, I was trying to be neighborly, he came over and introduced himself and offered me a dog, weed, and a beer…I didn't want to be mean and tell him to get his old ass back across the street and I thought your kids would like the dog."

"I thought we were going to the movies, and I see your project of getting the garage in order and all that in place didn't get to happen either, this is so not like you Hakeem." I knew sounded like his Mama or something.

"Baby I will finish up tomorrow, let's go to the movies, I promised you, so let's do it." He was trying to be nice.

"That's ok…I'm going to take me shower and watch Martin," I said.

"Come on baby you wanted to go see Cable Guy with Jim Carey…let's go get our laugh on," he pleaded.

# A. MICHELLE

I did want to see that movie, and after all, the kids would be back soon, and my focus would be them. Before Hakeem, if I wanted to spend quality time with my children, I would have to quit my extra job at Mervyn's.

Hakeem told me to quit. The extra money wouldn't be necessary. I was happy about that. I could breathe again.

While I showered and got dressed, I could hear Hakeem playing loud music. He had on his romantic oldies. I soon realized that it was beginning to be a pattern. Every time he thought I was upset with him, he would play slow, dancing music, and then want me to dance with him.

I only had my panties and blouse on when he came and grabbed me by my hand and pulled me in the middle of the living room. The song that was playing was Mid-Night Star's- "Slow Jam." It was hard staying mad at his ass! I swear! He whispered in my ear, "I love you my Queen, don't be mad at me…it won't happen again."

He held me close and while the song played he whispered the lyrics:

*I asked her for her hand*
*Said, "Would you like to dance?*
*So pleased that I had asked*
*She quickly took my hand*
*And we danced and fell in love*
*On a slow jam yeah, yeah*

*Play another slow jam, this time make it sweet*
*On a slow jam, for my baby and for me ooh*
*Play another slow jam this time make it sweet*
*On a slow jam (a slow jam, yeah)*

# STABBED TO LIFE

It was a sweet gesture and would have been better had he not smelled of puppy, liquor and weed. Major turn off.

He got in the shower and once he was out we had a real heart to heart conversation. I needed to set some rules before my children got home.

"Hakeem I just want you to know I love you and I want to be supportive of you but with my kids coming home I cannot have what I witnessed today ok. I just really do not want that around my kids," I explained emphatically.

"I understand, I will not do that again, especially once they are home," he said contritely.

I asked if smoking and drinking would interfere with his healthy lifestyle and training, and he snapped on me.

"Look…I said it won't happen again baby…let it go, stop that nagging shit," he said sternly.

I could have said something else, but this was the second time he talked crazy to me I didn't feel like creating a scene, so I just walked back into the bedroom and finished putting my clothes on. Once I was dressed I stuck my head in the bathroom where he was finishing his shaving and asked him if we were still going.

He tried to lighten the mood by suggesting we skip the movie if I just wanted him to sex me down.

"No…I'm good" I said softly

"No, you ain't …. Come here…."

He still had shaving cream on one side of his face. He took off the towel he had wrapped around his waist and wiped the shaving cream with it. I had on tight jeans, but he managed to get them down quickly.

"Daddy gone make it all better..." he laughed

Grudgingly I just went with it and afterwards we laid right there cuddled up and watched Martin. No movies tonight. He probably apologized 10 more times before I started laughing and playing with him again. I clowned him because he forgot to shave the other side of his face and he was all up in my face trying to be romantic. So, I nicknamed him Smooth and Scruffy. We laughed and talked he asked me to make salat with him in the morning, I had been telling him I would, and I almost knew the prayer by heart just from listening and watching him.

We talked about his children and his desire to be more active not just sending money like he claimed he'd been doing. At first, I was getting the money orders, but he said he would do it going forward, so I got myself back in my lane and minded my own business.

All I could think about was my kids returning in a few days and their reaction when they finally realized he moved in. Every time I talked with them over the phone I hinted around but they never really said anything, I think they were too into what my Mom and Dad had them doing, which was usually a whole lot.

Ugh! I loved this man, but my gut feeling was telling me this was all wrong. Just as that thought entered my head he got out of the bed butt-naked, body banging, motioning me to come take a shower with him. I swear this fool could read my mind. Every single time a negative thought entered my head about him, he either stood up naked, wanted to dance or kiss me or something intimate. He knew how to

# STABBED TO LIFE

keep me in his good graces and I fell for the okey-doke every time.

The rest of the week Hakeem got up every morning super early and insisted I make salat with him, then he ran a minimum of 5 miles before the sun came up. He would then get dressed and go to his boxing gym in L.A. for more working out. He would head back up the hill before rush hour traffic and do it all again the next day.

I tried to stay out of his business deals with the boxing thing, although some things just seemed strange, but he kept his promise of paying the bills and that my money could go toward the household necessities.

The next day after finishing his routine, when he came back from running he asked me to come step on the scale. He wanted to see how much I weighed. I hesitated because I so self-conscious of my weight and my body, I did it. I weighed 172 and I know that sounds like and awful lot but honestly, I was cute, thick and proportioned.

He told me if I got to 175, he was going to make me start running with him. I laughed and told him I could run with him tomorrow. He reminded me of his preference for petite women.

He was insulting, even if he was joking, so I made sure to let him know that if I was too big for him, he could go find his petite girl because a lot of men that would love this thickness.

There was a huge moment of silence. He took a deep breath and got close to my face; real close. Me not being the type to not back down, stood firmly planted and did not move. I made a promise to myself after the way my children's father always had me cowering down that I would never allow another man to make me scared. I would not act nervous or all passive. He started speaking almost in a whisper…

"I told you about raising your voice Adrianne…I don't like that shit and trust me sweet heart ain't no nigga ever gone have you but me, so I don't care what they like. You. Are. Mine. All of you. So, don't say that shit again, you have one of these niggas come up missing Remember I already got 2 strikes, whatever I go back for I will get 25 to life, so let one of these muthafuckas get stupid if they want too. You probably ought a let them know," He said through clenched teeth.
 I nervously swallowed hard and rolled my eyes at him.

"Come on let's go pray" he said as if nothing just happened. He really looked like he wanted to hit me just then. His forehead was all wrinkled and the vein on the side bulging. I know I was a little mouthy at times, but hell I was still hurting and recovering from that last brutal relationship. Just getting away from another very controlling jealous man, my kids' father. So, I was very defensive.

After prayer, we didn't say much to each other but when he left for L.A. he made sure to come and give me a kiss goodbye and say have a great day. I responded, "you too."

When I got ready to leave for work Mr. Willie from across the street came over and said to me that the puppy was now 6 weeks old, and if I still wanted him to come and pick him up when I got home from work that day. I thought my kids would really like the dog too and maybe then they would not be so mad when they found out Hakeem had moved in.

# STABBED TO LIFE

I told Mr. Willie as soon as I got home I would come over and get the little dog.

On my lunch break I would be sure to get all the stuff he would need and then prepare for yet another move-in. I had called to confirm with my "fiancée" Hakeem to make sure he was ok still with the idea. He had been intoxicated when he said yes last time, and he was still ok with it today. He was happy that I called and asked his permission. He was cocky like that. No matter what he'd said, I was going to keep the dog anyway.

When I arrived home, Mr. Willie was sitting in his same area in his drive way surrounded by empty beer cans and the same nasty shorts with no shirt. Before I could get the bags out of the van he walked across the street with the dog. I scooped him up and quickly brought him into my nose to smell that sweet puppy smell. Ahh he still had it.

"Thank you so much…I will take good care of him." I said

"Where is your husband? " he asked, so abruptly

"He's training today…" I said

"Training for what?"

"He's a boxer." I explained

"Boxer? Boxer my ass…the only person he's going to be boxing is you," he said sarcastically.

"Excuse me…why do you say that?" I asked very seriously

"Lady your husband is a dope fiend he's just like me, fighting demons from his life from his child hood that has his mind going crazy. The war fucked me up, something else fucked him up.

# A. MICHELLE

You'll end up leaving him like my family did me. My demons came back over and over and the only thing that helps me deal with it is this," he held up the beer can, "and dope…just like your old man."

I stood there with my mouth hanging open. How did he know anything about Hakeem? Had they talked that much? Was the old man just crazy and talking shit? If I said something to Hakeem about this, he would probably do something to Mr. Willie.

I took a deep breath and thanked him for the dog. I got the dog settled in a box from the garage lined with newspaper and an old baby blanket. The dog warmed my heart as I played with it, but I couldn't stop thinking about all Mr. Willie just shared. He was a stranger, so first, why would he warn me as if he were trying to protect me? Who was I fooling? This man was a weird old vet probably with PTSD and didn't know shit. He probably just made all that up, but…how would he know all that?

I could hear the garage door going up, Hakeem was home. My thought was to mention to him what Mr. Willie said, but our last few days had been chaotic. I just wanted to have some peace and quiet and get along before my children got home; which was in two days. The little puppy who we hadn't named yet was snuggled asleep in his little box. He was a good little dog that never whimpered. At least not yet.

"Salem Alikum…" Hakeem said, as he walked through the door duffle bag in hand.

"Walikum Salem," I replied giving him a light peck on the lips. "How was your day?" I asked

# STABBED TO LIFE

"Not too good, me and Sol got into again, I really need to cut ties with this fool because he is going to make me do something to him…where is the puppy?" he smiled

I pointed to the side of the bed and the box.

We debated over what we should name him, and finally he named him.

"AK," he said softly.

"AK? Like the assault rifle?" I asked in humorous disbelief?

"Yeah…this muthafucka gon' be hard as hell," he smiled and made little goo-goo noises to the dog.

I warmed up lamb chops and mac and cheese while I listened to him vent about Sol owing him money from a previous fight. Sol said Hakeem owed him some of it for the trainer and equipment they had purchased. Although the previous fight Hakeem lost he was still supposed to get $20,000, Sol only wanted to give him $8,000, so they were at an impasse.

Hakeem refused to return to the gym until they paid him the money. While we talked, someone was blowing up his cell phone, but he would not answer it.

While I finished getting his dinner together, he walked in the room to take his shower but yelled for me to come in there, so he could finish telling me this long drawn out story. He talked as he showered, and I said an occasional uh huh, yeah, and What? The shower turned off.

"Ain't that some shit baby?" He asked, clearly pissed.

"Wow, Sol seemed so cool," I said reflexively.

# A. MICHELLE

"So cool…? What the fuck does that mean? He tried to get at you that night he drove you down to L.A. for me?" He asked. You could tell his anger was rising.

"Nooooo…he was very respectful, a gentleman" I explained, trying to soothe him, "but I'd seen a change in his demeanor take place lately.

Hakeem dried himself off and continued staring me up and down.

"So, you think that little nigga looks good?" he accused.

"No! He's not my type! I cannot believe you asking me this shit Hakeem, what the fuck is wrong with you? Whatever issue y'all having why are you pulling me in it?" I asked incredulously.

"Your food is ready?" I said flatly and walked back to the kitchen.

He started yelling at me to come back because he wasn't finished talking to me. I started talking to myself *"Adrianne don't say anything don't yell don't say anything. This dude is crazy."* I realized he was upset with Sol, but he just turned it all back on me, what the hell? I turned around to go back to the room and we met in the hall way. He walked so close that my face was smack dead in the middle of his chest. He grabbed me by my ponytail and pulled it down so that my face was looking up at him.

"You want that sorry ass nigga…huh?" he pulled my hair harder, but I didn't flinch, and I think that made him angrier.

"What are you talking about?" I asked in a whisper.

# STABBED TO LIFE

I was trying so hard to keep a straight face and not cry, but a tear rolled down my cheek. I could feel the tenseness in his body relax. He kissed my face and let out a long sigh and let me go. I went to the room and laid across the bed crying very quietly. I could hear the fork clinging on the plate as he ate his dinner. Other than the noise from him eating the house was completely silent. Then suddenly, I heard a whimper and movement from the puppy's box. I guess the commotion woke him. I picked him up and cuddled him until he fell back to sleep. I quickly jumped in the shower, because by the time Hakeem was done, I wanted to be in the bed asleep. When I got out the shower he was sitting on the edge of the bed, staring at the ceiling.

"I'm sorry," he said calmly.

"Ok," I said quickly and got in the bed, pulled the covers up to my neck, then rolled into a little ball, shutting my eyes as tight as I could.

He turned on the tv and I fell asleep. I woke hours later to him right against me, "spooning" as my back was to his chest and his long arms were wrapped tightly around me. The tv was still on, and I had to use the bathroom, but the slightest move was sure to wake up the unpredictable giant. So, I just slowly tried to slide out of the bed, the moment I moved he tightened his grip and whispered in my ear:

"I love you baby…where are you going"

"I have to use the bathroom," I rolled my eyes, he couldn't see me, but he loosened his hold and allowed me to get up. I went to the bathroom in the dark seeing only by the light from the tv. I sat on the toilet and thought, *"Here I go again. What have I done?"* My babies were due home in 2 days. I planned to go shopping with them to get them a few

# A. MICHELLE

things, figuring the puppy and a few gifts would make our new house guest a little easier to accept.

When I got back in bed, he was turned over on his side, with his mouth slightly hanging open, wearing nothing but a sheet. I swear this man was so sexy, but clearly, he was crazy as hell. Maybe his trips to prison had messed him up. I don't know, but I knew the next time he came at me wrong, I will let him have it. I looked over at the clock and it was 3:15 am. I still could get some more sleep before my alarm sounded. No sooner than I laid my head on the pillow the alarm went off. I had slept so hard the time flew by. Hakeem was already up, and his side of the bed was already pulled together and neatly tucked. I heard the garage going up and then going down. The phone rang and it's him calling from his car telling me he was getting breakfast. When I answered, the first thing he asked was, "Hey Beautiful…you up? as if last night didn't even happen. Clearly, I was up, I answered the phone, didn't I?

But said, "Hi, yes I'm up," instead. When he asked if I wanted anything to eat, I declined, telling him I was good. One minute he was complaining about my weight, now he wanted me to eat.

"I will get something low calorie babe," he said, ever so mindful of my weight, of course.

"Ok but I have to leave for work in an hour" I explained

"I will be there in 15 minutes to fix you something"

While I was getting dressed I heard him come back and begin cooking. He yelled that breakfast was ready. He had fixed me a beautiful veggie omelet made with egg whites. It was delicious.

# STABBED TO LIFE

I was fully dressed and as soon as I was done I rushed off to get to work on time. Only thing I needed to do was put my shoes on in the car, because again, shoes weren't allowed in the house. I was still a little nervous as to how my children will feel about this new rule.

As I bolted for the door, I reminded him that my kids were due home tomorrow and to please remember to shampoo their carpet and get the dog's shots. He was staying home today, and I wanted to make sure he was going to stay busy and not be hanging out with Mr. Willie.

Of course, I called almost every hour on the hour with a reminder and another chore I needed done. His attitude was good, and he was willing. I could hear music playing in the back ground, and that was fine. I knew he loved him music especially his Tu PAC and oldies.

The day went by fast. I had talked to my kids several times and surprisingly they were ready to come home. They loved being with Mudder and Paw-Paw, because they spoiled them to death and they always came home with new clothes video games and expensive stuff. I was so grateful for my parents, even when I didn't deserve it they were there for me.

As soon as 5:00 came, I bolted to the car and rushed home. I pulled up and saw the yard was neat, the house smelled clean, and the puppy playing on the clean carpet was clean, but no signs of Hakeem. I called him on the cell and he didn't answer. He wasn't with Mr. Willie because he was sitting in a lawn chair in front of his garage.

A few minutes later, I heard the garage door go up and a happy Hakeem walked in.

# A. MICHELLE

"As-Salaam-Alaikum baby…I did everything you asked of me and I went grocery shopping, I want the kids to be happy when they come home," he explained. "I got their favorite things even though some of it is pork, and you know how I feel about that. Help me get the stuff out of the car."

He had a trunk full of food and the back seat was packed. He had to have spent well over $250. Now after our visit to his kids home and to see how his children are living, I felt bad that he did all this. I planned on telling him he needed to go down there and take them some food or at least send them some money.

I helped bring all the bags in the house, he had cookies and cereals, meat for sandwiches, soda, drink boxes, everything you could think of. He also got lots of fruits and vegetables. I thought he did a really good job. Together we put everything away, of course he asked me to fix him something to eat. He sat there at the table while I made him a steak and baked potatoes with mixed vegetables. He was a happy camper. He deserved it, I thought to myself, he did everything I had asked. He helped me clean the kitchen and we went in the room to watch a movie and he suggested we get our freak on one last time before the kids came home the next day.

I really didn't feel like it. I was nervous about the kids coming home, but not wanting to rock the boat after such a good day, I gave in.

That man knew how to put a smile on my face, and he was right, after what we had just done, that could not go on when the kids were back in the house. We'd done it on the kitchen counter, the couch, the patio-all those areas would be off limits and we would be confined to our room. I could not deny, I was in love with this man, and although he had displayed some very concerning things with his anger and aggression. I just figured it was associated to him being in prison and once he got use to me, knowing I was down with him no matter what, he would let his guard down and ease up a bit.

The next day I woke up early and although I knew my Mom had fed them before putting them on the train, but I still wanted to have their breakfast fixed when they got home. I fixed some batter for waffles and cooked some sausage then when I returned home with them I would just need to cook their eggs and waffles. I'd gotten the dog a new little collar and leash. He was all fresh and clean. I knew they would love him.

I arrived at the train station 30 minutes before they were to arrive, and I left Hakeem at the house so that I could have this moment to explain our new permanent house guest. I played back in my mind the many men I had dated since their Dad, none of them serious like Hakeem. After my marriage ended, I went through a phase of getting used to my new-found freedom. I dated a lot and was even a little wild, but now I had a religious, hardworking man who was going to be good for us all, so I was ready to settle down again.

I'd never had someone who was willing to step up to the role of father, especially since their father wasn't being much of a father. He never kept the court ordered visits and barely payed child support. Eventually I had to have his wages garnished. Even with Hakeem's back ground. I felt he'd be good for us and a great addition to our family.

# A. MICHELLE

The train pulled up and I instantly got butterflies in my stomach.

I wasn't so worried about De-De, but Alonja was like a little grown woman. She was so smart, and her expression would tell it all if she wasn't cool with it.

They were loaded down with bags; much more than they left with. They had Foot Locker bags, Nordstrom's and Game Stop. I was surprised they didn't get jacked. Their duffle bags stuffed full of their clothes and I am sure a bunch of new stuff my parents had purchased. I loved my parents and they loved their grand kids. I helped them with all the bags and stuffed them in the van. They were happy to see me, and we hugged and kissed.

"Hey guys…have I got a surprise for you when we get home" I said

"Really???...what?" Dede asked all excited.

"Hmmmm what Mom?" Alonja said, I swear this girl did not trust me.

"We will see when we get home…" I said smiling from ear to ear. I knew they would like the dog.

"I have something else I need to tell you, I've had the carpet cleaned and we will no longer come in the house with our shoes on ok? All those nasty stains in the entry are gone. So that we can keep that clean that area clean, we have a rack at the door to leave your shoes. Hakeem cleaned the carpet really nice, so we want to keep it that way." I explained as pleasantly as possible.

"He lives there huh?" Alonja said with a little attitude.

# STABBED TO LIFE

"Why do you say that Lon?" this girl was no dummy, she was smart as a whip.

"I called the house one day, and he answered the phone and it just seemed like it. I know you like him a whole lot, it's whatever Mom, you don't need my permission, right?" She asked coolly.

"Well I want to know how you feel about it…"

"Mom, Hakeem is cool, he can stay with us" De-De said and smiled at me.

"You only like him De because he bought you that game!" Alonja laughed then continued, "I don't care Mom, he ain't my Daddy so I am not calling him Daddy or nothing like that," Alonja explained.

"Nooooo, you don't have to call him anything other than his name, he is not there to be your Daddy. You have a Daddy," I said quickly.

"Really Mama? our Daddy don't do nothing for us! Mudder and PawPaw, and you, that's all we got!" She said angrily.

"Your Dad will do better," I said this only because I couldn't think of anything else to say. I really tried not to bad mouth him, but it was hard.

"So, what's the surprise" DeDe asked again

"Yeah Mom, what is it?" His kids live there too?" she laughed but looked at me to make sure that was not the case.

"We're almost home, you'll see when we get there," I said, amused by their suspense.

# A. MICHELLE

The rest of the way home they told me all the fun things they did with my Mom and Dad. They went to church of course, got to visit other family and friends, and went shopping. They also got to eat out a lot, visit Mulligans, the miniature golf spot and arcade, went fishing, and bowling. They did a whole lot and I was so happy they had a good time.

When we pulled up Hakeem walked out with the dog in his arms. They rushed to get out the car and ran to see the dog. He playfully jumped around them licking and yelping. They loved each other instantly.

"Hi Hakeem" De-De said as he rubbed the puppy.

"Hey man" Hakeem said, and handed him the dog. "Hi Lon," he said to Alonja

"Hello" she responded, "I love the puppy," she said happily.

She and De-De played with the dog, talking baby-talk to it.

Hakeem and I carried their many bags in the house, I reminded them to remove their shoes and bring the dog inside.

"Can we name him Buddy" De-De asked

"His name is AK," I explained.

"AK? what kind of name is that, what does it mean?" Alonja asked.

Before I could explain she carried AK like a baby into her room. She was so excited at how pretty it looked. She had a new comforter and bedding that was so cute. It was purple; her favorite color and she had a desk in there now, so she didn't have to do her homework at the kitchen table any longer.

"Thank you, Mom, I love my room," she smiled and came over and hugged me, while still holding on to the dog.

So far things were going ok. DeDe was happy with the dog he seemed fine with Hakeem there. Alonja, was willing to accept it also at least for now.

Even though it was close to noon, I still fixed the breakfast I had planned and for the first time we all sat down at the table and ate dinner including Hakeem who led the prayer in Arabic. While we ate they asked Hakeem about Islam and he gladly shared with them about him praying 5 times a day, facing the East when making salat and not eating pork. They were warming up to him and it looked as though we could be one happy family.

*"So, what happened next Adrianne," the therapist asked, truly interested in what I had to say.*

# CHAPTER SIX

## THE NEW JOB

Everyone was back in their routine; school, practices, homework, and me working just one job now. Hakeem had still been working out hard boxing and training, however, the trainers, promoters, and managers were having some disagreements about pay. Hakeem had had another fight and was doing well, or at least that what he'd said. The last fight he would not allow me to attend.

He had once again started some paranoid stuff about Sol looking at me thinking he and I were messing around. Really weird stuff. I tried to convince him that Sol was 5'5, and that alone hardly made him my type, but he was so jealous. He told me that Sol always liked girls with big boobs, so because of that he thought he was looking at me. I learned to ignore that crazy stuff even though it bothered me.

One day Hakeem arrived home furious and said he was having them to buy him out of his contract and they were using him and not being truthful. He spent a whole night arguing over the phone with his boxing team about payments he was owed and them explaining what he owed them. I stayed out of it, even when he asked my opinion, I just nodded in agreement with him even when it made no sense.

# STABBED TO LIFE

I was tired of arguing, but I kept reminding myself that Hakeem was not always like this. Once he was mad though, or felt lied to, he would rant and rave all night.

On this night, I asked him to lower his voice and not wake my kids, but because he was already upset with the issues with his boxing folks, he became enraged with me.

"I pay all the muthafuckin bills in this bitch, I'll talk as loud as I want too!" he yelled.

"My kids are sleep Hakeem, please lower your voice" I whispered and plead with him.

"I'm sick of people thinking they can use me, I'm taking care of you and your kids and I don't even get to see my own seeds!" he continued yelling.

"This is something you insisted on Hakeem, I can take care of mine just fine and I suggest you take care of yours! I have insisted you do that all along, so don't come at me with that shit!" I countered.

"If it wasn't for me you'd still be over in that house your ex-husband allowed you to lose, and he don't do shit for his kids!" His veins bulged as he roared.

"You helped me, but if not you my family would have helped me!" I screamed back, close to tears.

"Or some nigga huh? Another nigga would have gotten sprung on that pussy and went broke behind it, lost everything because of it like me!" He spat.

"Wow really Hakeem? I never asked you for shit," I said. My feelings were truly hurt.

# A. MICHELLE

"Bitch…I was doing good when I was by myself focused on my boxing and then you come along distracting me!" He got so close to my face, I could feel his breath.

"Bitch? Oh, now I'm a bitch, I'm to blame for your boxing thing being all fucked up, that's my fault?" I was determined not to back down.

"Yeah bitch! I was fine before you. I was focused," he said cruelly.

"Please don't call me out of my name again Hakeem, you are being really disrespectful," I said flatly.

"Bitch fuck you!" he said in slow motion pronouncing every syllable.

My response was, "Yo Mamas a bitch!"

Before I knew it, his hand was around my throat. I pulled back and he punched me in my jaw. Knocking me out cold for a few seconds. The room was silent. Everything seemed like it was happening in slow motion. I tried to get up from the floor, but I was dizzy, and it literally felt like I was in the cartoons when the birds are flying around your head. I got to my feet and it was if the room was spinning. When my eyes were finally able to focus I could see him just standing there no expression, no remorse, and didn't budge to help me.

"See what you made me do." He said in a much softer voice, either that or I could no longer hear, it seemed very low and muffled

I stood there with my fist clenched ready to fight, but I still couldn't see straight. I heard him grab his keys and he left the room. I fell across the bed holding my head and jaw. I could not believe what had just happened. He punched me. It was not a slap. It was punch like he was trying to break my jaw. Every time I tried to open my mouth my jaw made a clicking noise and I could barely open it. I stood up to look at it in the mirror. Luckily there was no knot, no bruise or scar. I was sure in the morning it would be very noticeable. I rushed to check on my kids, but they were sound asleep or at least pretended to be. There is no way they could have slept through Hakeem yelling like he did. I slowly closed the doors to their rooms and headed back down the hallway to my room. Still in shock I looked over at the clock it was 3:00 am. I laid down and began to cry. I could not believe this had happened tears ran down my face, the room was dark but just enough light for the ring to sparkle. I pulled it off my finger and threw it across the room. This man did not love me. The very things I had shared with him I went through with my children's father he was now starting to do some of the same stuff.

Jealousy, controlling, physically and verbally abusive. I couldn't do this again. True enough he shared with me his childhood and how he'd been in and out of prison, so maybe he wasn't taught to conduct himself. He did say he saw his Mama being abused, and that his father abused him. He had a crazy life, so this could be why he acted this way. Every time he did something I thought of his childhood and felt sorry for him. I always allowed him back in my presence only to find that he'd do the same thing. I couldn't do this. I couldn't expose my children to this.

The next morning, I got up and the first thing I did was look at my face. Surprisingly I had a very faint purple contusion between my ear and chin. I quickly rambled through the bathroom drawers to find some old concealer and foundation, I hadn't even washed my face, and quickly rubbed it on the spot. I was surprised that it wasn't worse, especially considering how hard he hit me.

My jaw was still making the clicking noise and I could barely open my mouth. I did my regular routine and got the kids ready for school. They were very quiet. I thought maybe they had heard, so I tried to say something to break the silence.

"Hey , you guys want to go to the beach this weekend?" I asked in a cheery voice.

"Not me, Mom. Remember I am doing something with Chris," Alonja said nonchalantly.

"Mom I am spending the night at Sid's, remember you said I could?" De-De said, "But Mama if you don't want to be here by yourself, I will stay." This boy loved his Mama and he could tell I was a little sad no matter how hard I tried to play it off.

"Oh no, I forgot, you guys do your thing. I know you miss your friends. Your Mom will be fine, maybe me and Hakeem will go to the beach or catch a movie," I said

They both looked up with wide eyes and quickly smirked at each other. It was then that I was convinced that if nothing else, they'd heard us arguing. Shit!

"Ok y'all, let's be on time. Rinse your bowls off and place them in the dish washer, brush your teeth and let's roll," I rushed them to get ready.

Hakeem had not tried to call, he left with no clothes, and his prayer rug still neatly rolled up in the corner of the bedroom. The ring I threw last night laid right against the rug, just as sparkly and shiny as ever. I had to wear it, because people at work would start talking if they did not see it on my finger. I picked it up and placed it on my finger.

I finished getting ready for work and I just stood in the hot water crying again. I was so depressed, ashamed, embarrassed and hurt right now. Even though no one knew what happened, my pride and my heart were crushed.

I dropped the kids off at school and  headed to work. Just as my exit came up on Avenue K, I  saw Hakeem's car getting on the freeway, headed back towards my house. I know he saw me too. I waited for my cell phone to ring but it didn't. I refused to call him. I went to work and the day drug by. I wanted to go home to see if he'd gathered his things and left. As I've always done, even in my previous relationships, I smiled so that no one would ever know what was going on underneath my smile. I was hurting, I was injured, bruised and all, but I pretended well. I still laughed and had fun with my coworkers, but every time I went to the bathroom, I cried my eyes out.

When my work day was over I headed straight home. When I hit the corner of my street, I noticed Hakeem's car in the driveway. I sat in the car a while and tried to gather my thoughts. I wanted to make sure when I told him that his actions were out of line and would not be tolerated that I was not confrontational.

I smelled food when I walked through the door. My son was playing a video game. He greeted me, and I asked him if his homework was done. He told me he had and after Hakeem had fixed him and Alonja turkey burgers and fries, he'd given him permission to play the game. He also mentioned that Alonja was at practice and would call when she needed to be picked up.

I took a deep breath and walked into my bedroom.

Hakeem was asleep on the bed. He awakened when he heard the door shut and sat straight up.

"Come here baby," he said softly and motioned for me to come to him.

"Are you fuckin kidding me right now?! You tried to break my jaw Hakeem, what the fuck is wrong with you?!" I said in a low, angry voice. I didn't want DeDe to hear us arguing again.

"Baby ball your fist up as tight as you can and come sock me in my jaw." he smirked, "Let me see your face."

"Do NOT touch me Hakeem, you knocked me out like I was man in the ring with you, have you fuckin lost your mind?" I tried so hard to keep my voice down, it was especially hard because I wanted to go in on his ass so bad.

"I'm sorry baby…I did not mean to do that to you. That shit happened because of Sol. I was angry at him and took it out on you, and when you called my mama a bitch, I blacked out," he said trying to look pitiful.

"You had called me a bitch Hakeem like 5-6 times being totally disrespectful to me and my kids who were trying to sleep." I didn't care what he said, he was way out of order.

"Hit me…hit me baby, with all you got…" he pleaded.

I stared at his face his hazel/green eyes glazed over like he was about to cry, I took a deep breath and went to reach out to hug him and just as he reached out for me, I socked his ass 3 times in his face, busting his lip. He grabbed his mouth and smiled hard. Those hits didn't even phase him.

"You feel better now? Are we even?" he asked

"Hell no, we are not even… this is crazy Hakeem, you say you love me, and you would hit me like that…" I was still hurt by his actions.

"You say you love me, and you just busted my lip" he said sarcastically and giggled.

"Oooh I hate you, why did I ever let you in my life, my home?" I said. By this time, I was crying.

"Adrianne…I made a mistake baby, I love you with all my heart, I have never met a woman like you. From day one you showed me you were down with me," he continued begging.

"Not down for this shit… no way will I go through another abusive relationship, fighting and disrespecting each other I am not doing this," I said firmly.

"Come here girl, even with what has happened, tell me you don't love me" He pulled me into him "…tell me you really want me out of your life…you can't. Me and you baby we together forever, we will get through this and I will never ever put my hands on you, but you gotta let me be a man," he said with emphasis.

"How am I not letting you be a man?" This dude was tripping!

"You go back n forth with me…when you should just remove yourself when you see I am having an issue," he reasoned.

# A. MICHELLE

"Why can't you just control your anger Hakeem…:"

"I will work on that baby, but you need to know your man…and calling his Mama a bitch does not go over well no matter how I feel about the crazy lady," he chuckled.

I did not like how he was making light of what he did. Throwing it back on me.

"I got good news though, I have a job with the concrete company in Lancaster, they are going to pay me $26 an hour. I will still be able to pay the rent here and help as I had been.

"What about the boxing?"

"Unless I get some honest people in my corner that will be placed on hold. My kids and your kids need something consistent and that will be my focus. I need to make ups for lost time with my girls so that my focus now. I start tomorrow 4am, there is a lot of construction going on here and they said as long as I do a good job, I will have a job with them for a very long time."

It sounded good, but I was still upset. I made sure my actions showed just that too. He went to kiss me, but I pulled away. He got up and blocked the door. He grabbed his little remote control and turned on some music. This had always worked the past but not today. He played SWV, Use Your Heart:

*Alone, you and I intertwine*

*Refreshing conversation for the mind*

*As we stare we both seek and hope to find*

*Real love purified*

# STABBED TO LIFE

*Use your heart and not your eyes*

*Baby just relax and ride*

*If you got time, then I got time*

*Yeah, yeah, yeah*

*Free your thoughts and watch them fly*

*Use your heart and not your eyes...*

I did not want to be touched by him, I did not want to slow dance with him and I really did not want to have sex with him. He pulled me close to him and whispered in my ear and apologized again. He started crying. When I first saw the tears, I was like "Whatever."

He kissed my bruised cheek and then the back of my neck and why, oh why, did he lick my ear? I still had my work clothes on, so he reached under my jean skirt and tried to pull my panties down. I would not let him, so he touched me with his fingers instead. Just as I was about to give in my son knocked on the door telling me it was time to pick up Alonja. I yelled that I was on my way.

"He saved you huh…" Hakeem said confidently, "Go pick up your daughter, this dick gone be waiting on you when you get back, so hurry up."

I hated that his sexual advances always seemed to work, and he knew that and used it every time. I stood firm though.

# A. MICHELLE

"I wasn't about to do nothing with you anyway…did you want to make love to me when you socked me in my jaw, did you love me then?" I asked, and I began crying again

"Hey…just hurry up and get back here…I love yo crazy ass and you love me, cut that shit out," he said, dismissing me.

I rushed to get Alonja and then we needed to stop at the store so what would have been 10-minute errand ended up being about 30. When I returned, I fed her and put a load of clothes in the wash before I went back to the room, hoping he was sleep. No such luck. He was wide awake watching T.V.

"Now I gotta be up at 3:am so come over here and let's do this so I get some good sleep. I ain't boxing no more so we can fuck as much as we want to now, right, ain't you happy?" He asked looking like a kid.

I walked into the bathroom and turned on the shower. I let the hot water wash over my body trying to lather off the bullshit from the night before, but before I was ready to get out he came in and got me. Still wet, he led me to the bed and just forced himself on me. A few times holding me tightly around my neck. I noticed he had turned the TV up loudly, I guess so that my kids would not hear. He was so rough and not romantic at all. Almost as if to remind me he was in charge and I belonged to him. He began biting me which often seemed sensual when he had done it before, but he felt like he was literally biting chunks of my skin out. I did not yell, but I groaned a couple of times in pain and finally whispered, "You are hurting me."

"Well you hurt me, when you called my Mama a bitch and when you busted my lip, c'mon stop acting like you don't want this," he said gruffly.

# STABBED TO LIFE

He finally was done, I was sore and wanted to get up and get back in the shower. He held me there and curled up with me till he dozed off to sleep. I got up to shower and he whispered, "I love you babe."

I did not respond, instead, got in the shower. My body stung as I drug the towel and soap across my body. I could see all the areas he had bitten me, nothing like before these bites were very profound and very visible. You could tell they were his teeth marks; even the crooked one at the bottom had pierced my skin. He'd even broken some of the skin. This nigga was a savage.

I put my gown on and went to make sure my kids were getting ready for bed. I turned off all the lights and climbed into bed next to Hakeem. He wrapped his long legs and arms around me. I needed to really figure some shit out. Yes, I loved him, but this was unhealthy. He was crazy, and I was too for continuing this toxic relationship. Maybe I could work with him and teach him that his behaviors were criminal, and he should never force sex on me. That was rape. I didn't dare say that to him though, at least not now, but he was crossing every line and seemed to not care.

His alarm sounded right at 3:15. I got up and fixed him lunch and a small breakfast. He kissed me goodbye and headed out the house to his new job.

We never spoke again about that shenanigans of the previous day. We acted as though it never happened. He was back to his sweet self; acting like a gentleman, thanking me for dinner and saying how appreciative he was that I was in his life. Setting a date for the marriage kept coming up in his conversations. No one really knew we were engaged, I certainly did not mention it to my family or friends, and I would hear him every once and a while share it with people.

He told his P.O. and I never forget the look he gave me when he shook his head like "lady is you crazy?"
I was beginning to think so. Certainly, a sane person would not have stayed with a person that knocked her out cold, with his fist, on purpose. That just sounded crazy.

One night we laid in bed for hours just talking about how he wanted to someday get back into boxing not even for the love of the sport any longer just for the pay. He said he often reflected on his childhood and did not want his children to live in poverty like he did. Or how my children had this small house with very little space, and how he wanted to put his Mom in a better position. It was a sad conversation that had me in tears and later he was in tears too.

 I reminded him that he had an opportunity to make a better life for his children without boxing, he could just work. He was making good money and claimed to be sending them money every chance he got. He knew I loved shopping, but he no longer allowed me to shop for them because Sherry did not like it. He told me she talked shit and I think threw the clothes away or gave them away. She was a little crazy too. He talked and talked and when I dosed off he would wake me up to continue listening. He seemed a little depressed or down, something was off. He motioned for me to scoot really close to him and he whispered, "Hold me babe."

I cuddled up and hugged him tightly and he hugged me back just as tight.

# STABBED TO LIFE

"No woman has ever put up with my shit like you, I know you love me, I don't ever want to lose you...ok?"

"I'm not going anywhere."

We kissed, and he finally let me fall off to sleep, I had work tomorrow and I looked at the clock before going off into a deep sleep and it was 3:36 am. He was up at 4 and insisted that I stay in bed, that he'd fix his own breakfast and lunch and I was able to sleep two more hours.

Hakeem called at 7:15 to say he enjoyed our conversation and he promised to treat me like the queen I was. He told me to go shopping when I got off and he was treating me to a dress and shoes for my mother's 50th birthday that was in 2 weeks.

I was excited, but nervous. My family would be meeting him for the first time. The only person besides my mother and father that had met him was my cousin Tenia. Her husband was currently in prison so she kind of understood when I shared with her some of the stuff I was going through. I never told her about the physical altercations, but she knew some of our issues. I minimized the mood swings but shared in detail about his background. It was good to be able to talk someone that appeared to everyone else they thought we were the perfect couple.

When 5:00 pm came along, Hakeem called me to make sure I was going shopping. He insisted I not buy anything cheap. He really wanted us to look nice. I think he was trying to make a good impression. He would soon find out just how big my family was and how protective they were too.

# A. MICHELLE

I headed straight to Dillard's, because we didn't have many options in the Antelope Valley, so that was closest to high-end retail that we had.

My mother had made it very clear that she wanted us to wear black and gold, so right away I found a very form fitting black dress and some cute, black Steve Madden strappy shoes.

Everything came to $210 because I'd gotten a necklace and earrings too. My entire shopping spree took me only 2 hours.

When I arrived home the house was nice and clean. Everyone had eaten, and the house was cleaned up. They were all watching a movie in the living room.

"Hey Mama," my baby DeDe came over and hugged me

"What did you get?" Hakeem and Alonja asked at the same time.

I started opening the bags and showed them. I explained to the kids that this weekend we were going to go look for their outfits too.

"Let's see the dress," Hakeem said.

I was a little nervous because the dress was a bit revealing up top but out of respect for his religion, it had a very modest length and a furry fancy shrug to cover my shoulders. I went and tried it on and they all were like "Wow!"

Hakeem liked it too, especially with the shoes on. He recognized that I had made my choice based on him and his

# STABBED TO LIFE

religion and out of respect for him. His eyes lit up and he smiled. It was a sexy dress and the length was perfect.

He had a tuxedo that was nearly new that he wore when he went to the several events to promote his boxing. All he needed was a gold bow tie, which I would find the perfect one so that it matched my outfit. We would look cute. Already people would see us together and say we were a cute couple. He was so tall and because of that I could wear my heels, the highest ones. We just complimented each other so well.

I still had to get the tie for Hakeem and my babies' outfits too. My daughter was very picky, and I needed to take her with me, but De-De and I had similar taste in clothing. We both liked clothes that were very trendy and whatever was popular at the time. However, this time no hip-hop gear. We had to be fancy, prim and proper, "Mudder" was very clear about that. I would go the next day and shop for them.

With Hakeem still having a lot of money in the bank and some stashed here and there, even without his boxing we still were doing ok. He made good money pouring concrete and because of the booming housing market in the Antelope Valley, work was plentiful. He was working a lot of hours and was paying the entire rent and most of the bills. He insisted on me keeping my money and doing for my kids and keeping myself up. He emphasized that part of keeping myself up was eating right, working out, and keeping my weight down. I purchased all the groceries and did all the cooking, and it worked. Things were going well. He didn't request anything more from me other than look cute and keep him satisfied.

# A. MICHELLE

The day of my mother's party finally arrived, and we arrived in style and so did my mother. She came by limousine to the Hotel where the party was taking place in the Grand ball room. Over 200 people were invited, and they were all showing up. As they entered the venue they all took their picture with her in front of balloons shaped in the number 50. She was so happy, and my Dad was so proud. She was beautiful and youthful for 50; full of energy with a cute little shape. Hakeem looked nervous, but he was stirring up conversation and laughing and having a good time. I could see people checking us out and probably talking about me, but we looked good and I felt good on his arm.

Family and friends were coming up to me whispering how cute he was and saying things like "you did good." They had no clue these last few months was a vicious, emotional chaotic roller coaster. But tonight, I felt good. Hakeem was being such a gentleman and we got a room at the hotel, so we did not have to rush home to Lancaster. We danced, we laughed, and we had a ball. His mood the entire night was awesome. He was treating me like the Queen he often called me, and it felt so good. The DJ played a song by Jon B, "They Don't Know"

*Don't listen to what people say*

*They don't know about you and me*

*Put it out your mind cause its jealousy*

*They don't know about this here*

*Don't listen to what people say*

*They don't know about you and me*

# STABBED TO LIFE

*Put it out your mind cause its jealousy*

*They don't know about this here*

The minute Hakeem heard the song he reached for my hand and lead me to the dance floor. We looked so cute, and the photographer must have thought so too, because he took picture after picture of us as we danced so romantically across the floor. Although there were a few other couples on the floor with us, it seemed like it was just us in our own little world.

He whispered in my ear, "I love you babe…"

"I love you too" I said… and meant it. Even with all that had occurred, all the fighting, and name calling. I felt like I was leaving it right there on that dance floor and we were going to start fresh.

After the song ended, several family members and close friends came over and said how happy they were for me and I seemed happy and in love. Believe it or not I was. I know that sounded crazy, but I loved this man and it certainly felt like he loved me.

The evening ended shortly after that for us. Certainly, my family and friends stayed up partying and celebrating my Mom's birthday well into the early morning, but Hakeem and I headed to our room. The room was beautiful, and we had danced so much both of our feet were tired. We had drunk a little which neither of us did too much anymore. We showered and before our heads hit the pillow, we were out sound to sleep. Before you know it, the sun was shining through the window.

Hakeem was still snoring and when he felt me try to get out of bed, he reached for me to stay in bed with him. We were

# A. MICHELLE

all supposed to meet-up at the restaurant downstairs for Sunday brunch and it was already 7 am. We were to be there by 10, so we had plenty of time-time for what he loved from me most; we made very passionate love.

We laid in the bed for another hour just talking and laughing, He shared that he had such a good time. He also said how he thought my family really liked him. I felt they were being tolerable and sometimes I caught my mother cutting her eyes and my Daddy speaking with his cousins and friends and did not appear they were saying anything nice. I did not care, last night my baby showed the world he loved me.

When we finally got up to get dressed, we stood next to each other in the mirror. My hair still perfect because I slept like a princess and our morning love making was done strategically to avoid messing up my French roll up-do. We looked at ourselves and smiled. Hakeem placed his cheek on mine.

 "We are a beautiful couple babe…we have to make this work." "You love me, right?" he asked

"I do honey. I love you," we kissed and got ready for brunch.

My kids were at my mother's house which was only 10 minutes away, I called to check on them and they were fine.  They didn't want to come to brunch, So I told them to be ready when we were done. We were going to swoop by and pick them up then head up the hill back to Lancaster.

Brunch went great, but we were ready to head home. I could tell Hakeem was tired, so after we got fat and full off waffles, prime rib, ham, omelets, beef sausage, champagne, etc., we snatched up the kids and headed home. Both of us had work the next day and wanted to get home to prepare for the week. Before leaving though, Hakeem, being a gentleman, went over and wished my mother a very happy birthday and told her he had such a good time.

The look though she had on her face said it all, she really did not care for him. I only prayed she'd warm up to him because I was going to be with him. I couldn't imagine how she'd react if she knew some of the things that had already occurred that no one knew about. My father shook his hand and looked him the eye and said, "Take care of my baby man."

The ride home was quiet. I drove, and Hakeem and the kids were all knocked out asleep. I reflected on the night and only wished that things going forward could remain this way. If so, we would be in good shape, but something just told me we would run into another bad spot. Didn't all relationships go through rough patches?

My first relationship was full of drama and chaos, but like a lot of domestic violence victims, I didn't grow up with that. My ex-husband experienced both physical and sexual abuse and Hakeem had shared often how his father was abusive to his mother and the children. Deep down inside I knew he was a good man. He had the potential to be a great leader for my family once he got past his rough spots. For God's sake, he was an ex-con who I am sure suffered some trauma in prison as well. I just needed to be patient with him, right?

*"Adrianne, that's the thing I was telling you. Since you didn't grow up with domestic violence, it's important to define what repeated the attraction to abusers."*

# A. MICHELLE

*The therapist was determined to get me to recognize, not just the pattern of the offender, but of the victim who continues to allow herself to be re-victimized.*

*"So, what happened when you made it home?"*

When we pulled up to the house, I woke the children and Hakeem and we all gathered the things out of the car. Hakeem had to be at work at 4:00 am so as soon as we settled in, off to sleep he went. I packed his lunch, made sure the kids' laundry was done and prepared them for bed as well. No sooner than my head hit the pillow Hakeem's alarm clock was sounding. I whispered softly that it was time to get up.

"I packed you a lunch don't forget it."

"Thank you, baby," he said trying to get dressed quietly.

My day at work was good. I shared with everyone all the fun that was had at my mother's 50th Birthday Party. Some of my co-workers had gone too and mentioned the dance me and Hakeem had on the dance floor. They said it was so romantic and it seemed at that time we were in another place just he and I and others picked up on it too. Hakeem and I had many issues and even some physical violence, but I felt strongly we were in a better place.

That evening I got home, Hakeem had not made it in yet but later called and said he had some mandatory overtime to do. So, the nice dinner I had prepared sat wrapped in foil on the stove waiting to be heated up whenever he arrived. I sat up till well after midnight and finally went to bed. Around 2:30 am I heard him come in. He came in turned on the tv in the living room and sat on the coach. I laid there for a while to see if he was going to come in the bedroom and say something to me, he never did.

I thought at first maybe he just didn't want to wake me, but I needed to see his face. As I got closer to the living room there was a smell of dirty sweaty working man, but something different. A smell I recognize from the last time he had been accused of smoking meth.

"Hakeem…you made it, they kept you long" I said very nicely. He didn't respond. I could only see the back of his head at this point and the room was dark only lit by the light of the TV and the light on the stove. I turned the light on.

"You ok?" I asked softly

"NO, I'm not ok. Go back to bed," he said roughly.

I could now see his eyes were blood shot red and although the room was cold he was sweating.

"Hakeem…what's wrong," There was a cry in my voice and he could tell I was upset.

"Adrianne just go to bed!" he shouted.

Adrianne? I thought, he only called me Baby, Queen, Beautiful, but never Adrianne. Adrienne was only used when it was something serious.

"What is wrong with you Hakeem, you look high" I yelled, then thinking of my children in the next room I quickly lowered my voice.

"You are high, aren't you???

"Babe, my boss offered me something to stay awake for a few more hours the entire crew did a few lines of that shit, so we could finish our work. It's no big deal. Now take your ass to bed, it ain't something I do all the time," he said in a final, dismissive tone.

I clinched my robe and went back in the bedroom. I laid there and thought about this new job, how good they paid him which was really helping us, and he was able to send his children money on a regular basis, or least that's what he said. All I paid were my cell and house phone bills and the internet bill, and he paid everything else.

I could not sleep, and he was still awake in the next room. I could hear him watching old boxing clips; his own and his idol Muhammed Ali. I knew he missed his boxing. I could only think he was probably feeling like this guy I knew growing up who was a popular football player in high school, scouted by big colleges.

When things did not go as planned, he became an addict. Alcohol, drugs and bad behavior ruined his career and became his lifestyle. Football was his love and it was who he was. Without the football it was as if he felt like he was nothing. With Hakeem's rough upbringing and getting into trouble, I think he felt boxing was going to turn things around for him, his children and maybe even his ex-wife, Sherry.

Around 4 am he came into the bedroom only to turn on the shower, I laid there as if I were sleep. He blew his nose over and over took his shower put on some clean work clothes, reached down and kissed my forehead and left for work again.

I had only slept 2 hours, but I managed to get my kids up, get dressed, and feed AK. Times like this always made me wonder did my kids hear the drama from the night before.

# STABBED TO LIFE

They were mighty quiet this morning as they ate their cereal. I knew they could tell I was sad and sleepy. I loved my babies, but damn I loved Hakeem.

After he left I pulled out the yellow pages to see if there was a rehab locally to help him with the drug issue. Maybe it was an "every now and then thing" maybe he didn't need help, but I was going to make a point to call a few places and see how I could help him.

The kids and I started our day. I dropped them off at school and no sooner than I got on the freeway headed to work, Hakeem called my cell phone.

He sounded sick and asked me to call off work so that we could spend the day together because we needed to talk.

I was not one that called off sick often and I had tons of sick time so part of me really wanted to and the other part of me thought I needed to stop dropping everything to accommodate him, but he was right we needed to talk.

"Ok Hakeem, I'm turning around, I'll meet you at the house…"

10 minutes later we were both pulled up in the driveway. He was still looking like a dusty 'old crack head, not the healthy clear skinned green /hazel eyed chiseled body man I fell in love with. Leaving him when he was going through something did not show loyalty at all right? Damn I was so confused, but I followed my heart.

We went inside, when Hakeem gently grabbed my face and said, "I know you are sick of my bull-shit by now and I don't blame you. I have been tripping, and Allah is not pleased. I am not pleased but you just continue to stick by me. I have never had that before. Sherry certainly did not

171

try to help me, she walked away whenever the money stopped, and she got her trifling ass back on the County. At the time, it was hard to compete with welfare. You could have cut me loose, long time ago, you come from a family that would help you, my family don't care if I live or die Babe, but you got a nigga's back," He took a deep breath and continued, " I have really showed my ass and you encourage and motivate me to keep going. You are my reason for living. Last night I wanted to end it all. How I could start using this shit again, encouraged by the devil, these fuckin white folks. They would love to get a nigga strung out on drugs and back in that cell, but I ain't falling in their trap. They were shocked I showed up this morning to work and no one else that worked with us last night made it in, because of that they told me to take the day off. Not even the foreman showed up. The owner came out and praised me for showing up after only a few hours of sleep…shit ain't been sleep. This shit probably will have me awake till tomorrow. Damn…I fucked up!"

I sat there and listened to him rant, I guess it was the drug. He just went on and on. He even had this crazy twitch he did with his eyes like a fuckin tweeker. I was with a tweeker.

"Hakeem…I heard everything you said. I love you honey but it is one thing after another with you. After the party I thought we were on a new road to change and peace and I thought we wanted the same thing. You are easily influenced by others; your temper is out of control. I think you are hurting because of the boxing thing failing, because of not being involved in your kid's life. This all stems from something that I don't know if I can help you with baby. I don't know what to do…" I started crying. "Looking at you with blood shot eyes and smelling of something I cannot even describe; Hakeem I am afraid for you. You are like a loose cannon. Then when you say you want to end it-your life baby- you are scaring me!"

"Baby just promise me you won't leave me, you all I got!" he explained and reached over and hugged me.

As we embraced I thought about the first time I suspected Hakeem to be using drugs. I'd talked to his mother who confirmed he once had a problem with methamphetamine, and her exact words were, "Whatever you do, keep him down there!" Even his own mother did not want to be bothered with his drug issue, or maybe she was just tired of him getting in trouble over and over again, but she was clear that she did not want to be bothered.

Sherry had also shared with me times before that Hakeem was a drug addict, a woman beater, but I thought she just wanted him back. Truthfully, at one point she did want him back, but everything she'd said was coming to fruition.

Oh my God, I am so confused I loved this man so much and guess what he was doing right now? Putting on his slow music to pull me back in as he did repeatedly. He had that sad puppy dog face; unshaven and scruffy. This was not a good look but the minute he pulled me in to his embrace and gyrated those hips, I was lost.

Usher's mellow voice came from the speakers creating a sexual atmosphere:

*Let me take you to a place nice and quiet*

*There ain't no one there to interrupt*

*Ain't gotta rush*

# A. MICHELLE

*I just want to take it nice and slow*

*Now baby tell what you wanna do with me*

*See I've been waiting for this for so long*

*We'll be makin' love until the sun comes up*

*Baby*

*I just wanna take it nice and slow*

After our dance he looked me in the eyes and stared deep into my soul, much like he did when we first met. It was so hard to look at him, his eyes were all glassy and blood shot red. He took my hand and made me touch his penis. He was very erect and ready to have sex. I pulled away because something about him being on meth and the way he looked was a turn off.

"You don't want me no more?" he asked, genuinely confused.

"Not like this…I can't." I still couldn't look at him.

"Come on baby, you will never ever see me look like this again, I promise" he pleaded.

"You have never kept a promise to me yet Hakeem" I said as he led me to the bedroom.

The house was ice cold because when I left I had turned off the heater and in the Antelope Valley this time of year, late November, the temperature would barely get over 40 degrees in the day, even with the sun shining brightly. This was the type of day it was.

When we got to the bedroom it was dark because it sat on the west side of the house and when the blinds were drawn it would be very dark. Hakeem for whatever reason opened all the blinds to let the sun in. Our house was the last house on the hill, so our backyard was a huge mountain. There were no houses at all behind us, and even though the windows were opened, no one could see inside other than the wildlife that lurked in the hills.

Hakeem took off all his clothes and his erect penis seemed like it was thicker and longer than usual. Could the drugs do that? I stood there still in my work clothes, still wearing my ID badge and heels. I was frozen because a part of me did not want him to touch me yet looking at him stand there totally nude with his sad face, made me feel so torn.

He began removing my blouse, his tall ass towering over me. He began touching me and telling me how he wanted to go to Vegas the next weekend and just get married. I don't know why the talk of marriage and his touch jut mesmerized me. I pictured us walking down the aisle amongst friends and family knowing that would never happen. No matter how cordial they were at my Mom's party, I could feel a vibe from my family they were not feeling him. They were probably hoping this was one of my many mistakes that I would get past.

The seduction continued. Hakeem could feel I was tense and felt reluctant towards his advances, but trust me, he knew the things to do to get me to comply and that is exactly what he did. He pulled me down to him from the back with my back against his chest and he kissed my neck. I took a deep breath and then he licked my ear, and at that point I melted in his arms. I slowly removed every stich of clothing. Once again, this main had seduced me into doing something I did not want to do, nor did I feel he deserved from me. I wasn't sure whether it was due to him still having the drug in his system that the sex went on and on. Hakeem was already able to go long periods of time, but we started at 8:45 a.m. and it was now 9:30.

He tossed me every which way and he was sweating profusely. It was beginning to get very uncomfortable. My insides were raw and irritated. I finally stopped him and said I couldn't go any longer. He found a way to moisten the area and whispered in my ear that he couldn't get enough of me. He told me that if I ever took it away from him, it was going to be BAD. This was his. All his.

Finally, he let out his grizzly bear groan and orgasmed. It was soothing to my insides. From the hours of friction, anything was comforting.

He would not let me get up, I needed a warm towel to put on my sore labia, but when I tried to get up he wrapped his entire body around me.

"So next weekend we will take a ride to Vegas and get married, ok?" he asked.

I pretended not to hear him and acted like I dozed off.

"Baby, you hear me? Next weekend we will go to Vegas and make it official, I think that will help me stay focused on being the good man you need me to be," he reasoned.

If that wasn't the dumbest shit ever said. Really? Just because we'd have a piece of paper that was going to help him with his anger and his drug issues and his "wishy-washy" mood swings and confusion as to what he wanted to do with his life. Even with the long list of dysfunctionalities, as I usually did, I agreed to whatever he said.

# STABBED TO LIFE

"Sure babe," I said hesitantly

"So tomorrow book us a room down there in a really nice place, a suite in the MGM, tell them who you're marrying you might give us a free upgrade or something," he chuckled

I was chuckling too, although I was shocked. So many people often recognized him from the few fights he had, but I was sure no one at MGM would recognize it.

He got up and got me a warm towel and washed me up like a baby. He knew my inners and outers were sore after that massive beating of the coochie, so he laid the hot towel on my vagina and asked if it felt better because he was ready for round 2.

He laughed when he saw the look on my face that said, 'HELL NO' and went off to run a hot bath with Epsom salt. He promised that it would be everything back in its proper place.

The bath was extremely soothing, and while I soaked in the tub he cooked us a little brunch. I must have dozed off while in the tub because he came in with a towel to get me. His eyes were still red, so it was still hard to look at him in his face without getting upset all over again. I found myself avoiding eye contact. I threw on the towel and went in the kitchen and we sat there and laughed and talked.

The laughter was difficult, because a part of me so disappointed all over again. Hakeem still had not been asleep, yet he was still going. Hakeem even wanted to take a ride to the beach. I convinced him that because we'd both had minimal sleep it wasn't a good idea. Surprisingly, he agreed, so instead we curled up on the couch to watch the

# A. MICHELLE

movie "Liar-Liar" featuring Jim Carey. I don't think the movie credits had stopped rolling before I was knocked out and snoring. Hakeem had even closed his eyes briefly till he received a call on his work phone that they had some overtime and wanted to see if he was interested. This was going to be another late night and that scared me. But I also was pleased that he never turned down the opportunity to make some money. He reminded me Christmas was coming and he wanted to help me with Christmas presents even though he really did not celebrate it. He took a shower and got dressed for work.

"Baby thanks for staying home with me today, I know you are worried I will mess around with that shit, I promise I won't," he was trying to convince me, but he saw my face that I didn't believe him. He also knew that I wanted to help him way. I just kissed him and told him to be careful.

When he walked out the door, my eyes filled with tears. I knew in my heart this was not over. I prayed it would be, and because I could not seem to leave him, I felt like God was telling me to stay and help him through this. I had never been more confused in my life.

The job Hakeem had was with a very well know construction company. This company was known throughout the Valley. The building boom had just started in this area, and the company Hakeem worked for got most of the jobs. They poured concrete for the new home foundations as well as the parks, schools, and stores that were going up in the area. They stayed very busy and Hakeem and his family had so much experience in pouring concrete, that he was a licensed contractor with an excellent reputation in the Inland Empire and Los Angeles area.

# STABBED TO LIFE

No doubt this man had skills and was not afraid to work, in fact, he was very willing to work, but had some major issues. I knew I wasn't qualified to help him with all these issues, but even with that information and my doubts about our future, I pressed forward anyway to try and make it work.

That evening once Hakeem was off work, which was rather late, I was already in the bed. I looked over at the clock and it was 11:40 pm.

"Wake up babe, I need to show you something," he whispered with excitement.

I grabbed my robe and he led me by my hand. As we walked, I squinted past the bright lights in the house. It seemed like he had every light on in the house. Before we stepped outside I stopped him to get my vision right so that I could focus on his face. I needed to see if he looked high. His eyes were clear. I smelled him, and he just smelled like hard working man not like the boiled wiener smell that the Meth smelled like. I smiled with approval. He opened the door and pointed to the brand-new work truck that had the company's name and logo printed on the side. He was so excited.

"I got to work, and they offered me a promotion which included a company vehicle!" He was proud and excited like a little kid.

Right then, I concluded based on his excitement which was so childlike, that no one ever really praised his accomplishments. So, I laid it on extra thick. I needed him to really know I was proud of him. I wondered did they know his background-that he was a 2 striker with multiple felons. But hey, maybe they were giving him a chance, he

# A. MICHELLE

had been referred there by the re-entry program, so they had to know his history at least a little bit.

"Oh my God babe this is really good" I said over and over.

"It includes a raise to $30 an hour." He explained.

"Wow" I said, thinking to myself, "they must really trust him if they allowed him to have a company truck."

I was so excited for him, the look on his face was priceless. He looked so happy.

"Baby, no one has ever believed in me, I know I fucked up many times but every time I tried to turn things around my family, Sherry, nobody believed in me babe…only you. That's why my queen I will do anything for you, anything! I love you. I thank Allah for you," He said looking up towards the dark sky. He had tears in his eyes and a cry in his voice.

"I love you too honey, now let's go in the house it's cold out here," I begged and shivered.

He locked the truck and we headed in the house. It was late, and I was tired, but when he got out of the shower he wanted to cuddle and talk. We talked well into the early morning until we fell off to sleep. At the end of the day, I could not deny how this man melted my heart, but no matter how hard he tried, I knew he really didn't deserve another chance. I still felt like I h ad to be there for him. I didn't realize this was part of the manipulation of an abuser.

When I woke up the next morning, he was already up fixing breakfast for me and the kids and reminded me again to call to reserve us a room at the MCM.

# STABBED TO LIFE

Before I jumped in the shower, I got on the phone and called MGM Hotel and surprisingly when I mentioned his name they upgraded us to a Honeymoon suite, the Skyline Terrace suite. The price was $465 a night but for whatever reason the lady didn't ask for a credit card or anything, she just said she would see us Friday evening. We were going to be there two nights and head back Sunday.

I was nervous, I had not shared what I was going to do with my family or my children. I had received paperwork just a month ago that my divorce was final, so I knew I was not in violation, but Hakeem, I was not sure. Oh well, we were getting married Saturday and I was scared shit-less.

*"I bet," the therapist interjected. "How did you feel when he spoiled you with expensive gifts and was known at the MGM?"*

*"Well, I like nice things. That was part of my upbringing," I said slightly defensively.*

*She made a note of it and nodded for me to continue.*

# CHAPTER SEVEN

## THE MARRIAGE

Friday came quickly and the week leading up to this day was very romantic. Hakeem was sweeter than ever. He'd had another home visit from his Parole Officer and everything seem to go ok. The PO was not feeling our relationship at all and he would always look at me and shake his head. He thought I was making a huge mistake in being with him and thought it was insane for me to be considering marrying him. Maybe it was crazy, but I loved this man. He treated me and the kids to dinner this night and he had a long talk with them asking them how they felt about us getting married.

You could tell they didn't know what to say. I knew that they mostly went with whatever I did because I was their Mother and was really all they had. I loved my babies and if it were only me this decision would be easy, but one of the biggest reasons I was afraid and hesitant was because of them.

I'd packed me and Hakeem's bags for the short getaway. This wasn't just a getaway, this was our wedding weekend. I looked down at the ring and let out a huge sigh. "Stop doubting this" I said to myself "This man loves you…and you love him, you can make it work" I thought.

I placed the two overnight bags in the hallway. I had filled one bag with 8 pairs of shoes even though we would only be gone 3 days and 2 nights, but as usual, I had to be fly. My heels, hair and outfits were banging. Of course, I had packed sexy lingerie too for the honeymoon. Although both of us had been married before we both felt it wasn't the same. Our feelings for each other were deeper and real, and not because of kids. This was strictly out of love.

I dropped Alonja and DeDe off to their friends they were staying with for the weekend. The parents knew we were going to Vegas but didn't know we were going to get married. Both parents were awesome and loved my children as their own and took really good care of them. So, I was very comfortable leaving my children in their care.

My family also knew we were heading to Vegas for the weekend but had no clue that I was going to tie the knot. I didn't have the nerve to tell them because I knew they wouldn't approve.

When I returned from dropping off the kids, Hakeem was ready to go. The car was packed, and the house was all locked up. I reminded him he needed his ID and social security card, and the 2-day pass that gave him permission to be out of the state from the Parole Board. He had forgotten them and ran back inside. We got in the car and he grabbed my hand.

"You will soon be what so many women in the world have wanted to be…my wife," we started laughing. "Thank you, my Queen. All this foolishness is over bae, your man is going to take good care of you," he said as he lifted my hand to his lips and kissed it. He closed his eyes and prayed in Arabic. When he finished his eyes filled with tears.

"I love you," he whispered

# A. MICHELLE

"I love you too" I said, wiping the tears from his face, "Now let's go before I change my mind!" we laughed and pulled off.

We always made each other laugh. It was almost unbelievable how we got along when there was no drama or drugs involved. Our relationship was truly beautiful.

He'd made an oldies slow jam CD that we listened to on the 3 ½ hour drive, and of course tried to sing every song to me. Stopping only once at a rest area to pee, he tried to get a quickie in and I strongly objected.

I told him that we could do all that when we checked in. I reached up and kissed him on his cheek. He towered over me in my flipflops. His 6'8 frame made my 5'6 frame look like a midget.

The next stretch of the road trip was quick and within 45 minutes we were pulling up to the MGM Grand hotel. He got valet parking and had a bell boy take our bags to the room. He got out and stretched his long legs and motioned me to come over to him. I walked over, and he reached from under the seat of the car and pulled out a box. I got rather nervous at first because this man was known for always having a gun at his reach, so I was not sure what was going to come from under that seat.

"I got something for you, I hope you like it…" He handed me a slender rectangle box and I opened it. We were still outside of the MGM in the valet area and people were everywhere.

"Open it baby," inside was the most beautiful diamond bracelet.

# STABBED TO LIFE

"Awwwww thank you honey, it's beautiful" I said. I hugged him and kissed him.

"I thought I should give you something for putting up with a part of me you will never ever see again. You deserve a good man that treats you with respect and from this day forward that is exactly what you will have. Ok?" he explained

"Hey baby that's behind us, we are getting a fresh new start tomorrow," I said optimistically as he gently grabbed me by the hand and we headed into the hotel.

The classic smell of cigarettes and ringing of slot machines hit you like a ton of bricks as soon as the doors opened. The temperature was warm outside so when we got inside the casino, although a little stinky, it was cool, and this Hotel was beautiful. Hakeem had done an express check in over the phone so the Bell boy that picked up our luggage also gave us a room key and directions.

We headed for the elevators. We were on one of the upper levels, and I was eager to see the lovely view of the Las Vegas strip. It wasn't quite dark outside, but I knew it was going to be gorgeous with the lights glimmering and flashing from the highest level at the MGM.

We finally found our room. It was beautifully decorated with plush carpet in some areas and fancy shiny tile in the bathroom that had the biggest tub I had ever seen. It was a suite, so there was a separate sleeping area away from everything. There was even a chandelier hanging above the tub and a separate area to shower. The shower was the size of a walk-in closet. It was beautiful, I feltlike royalty. We'd driven for 3 ½ hours and both of us were exhausted, so we tested out the tub.

# A. MICHELLE

There was some fancy bubble bath and oils in a nicely decorated basket and I turned on the tub and dropped in a few drops of the bubble bath. Instantly, the entire room was taken over by the beautiful scent of lavender and sweet pea. I got undressed and eased in to the hot water and bubbles and my soon-to-be husband stood there looking around. He too, was over taken by the fancy room, but eventually undressed and joined me in the tub. We sat there and talked in the hot water until the bubbles disappeared. We decided to jump in the shower to test it out. We were having a ball. We got dressed and went to eat, and later drove around to find the place to get a marriage license. We decided we would do it the following morning after breakfast.

After spending a little time in the casinos, we went back to the room and did what we do best; had some very passionate sex. All the while Hakeem reminded me over and over that I was about to be his wife. We laughed, played and tickled each other and eventually fell asleep. We were awakened a couple times during the night by the flashing lights from the strip, I finally got up and pulled the curtains. That made the room extremely dark, I crawled back in the bed and cuddled with my man who would be my husband in less than 24 hours. All night we held each other and Hakeem every now and then would whisper, "I love you babe."

Again, I struggled with whether I was doing the right thing or not. The morning when we woke up and started getting ready for our day.

Hakeem said to me, "Today is the day I marry a woman that in less than a year has shown me love more than my parents did my entire life, more than my children's mother did in all the years I dealt with her…baby I owe you. You deserve a good husband and I promise to be that."

My eyes filled with tears and at that moment, I felt this was the right thing to do and that I could go through with this. We got dressed, but not too dressy, like dressy-casual. He had on some jeans with a dark blue button-down shirt and I wore a casual summer dress. He gave me the thumbs up and a little wink and grabbed my hand.

We drove off to the Clark County court house in downtown Las Vegas to get the license and then find a chapel to marry us. It was a quick and painless process. Rather than go back to the casinos, we found a little chapel at the end of the strip. It wasn't bad, but it had an old, musty smell. It was run by a husband and wife- an older couple who were so sweet. The wife made me bouquet and she made Hakeem a boutonniere. It was 10:30 a.m. and we had the whole place to ourselves. We didn't get any of the picture packages, but I had a disposable camera and I had the lady snap a few pictures. We picked Ribbon in the Sky by Stevie wonder to walk down the aisle. Hakeem stood at the alter with the sweetest smile on his face as I walked the up the ten steps to the alter as slow as I could so at least most of the song could play. Hakeem had tears in his eyes and had to keep looking up so that he would not cry hard. When I reached him he firmly reached for my hand and sang the last part of the song to me.

*"There's a ribbon in the sky for ooooour loooooove,"* he sniffled and kissed me on the cheek.

"Hey," the officiant said, "It's not time to kiss yet!" We all laughed.

# A. MICHELLE

The old man went through the whole process and the typical vows were said when we said our I do's. Hakeem did not seem to doubt his decision to marry me at all. I, on the other hand, did through the whole process of exchanging vows. I thought of my kids, my parents, my family, and what they would say when they found out. Then I thought, either way I loved him at this moment, right now and nothing could change that.

We were pronounced man and wife and we kissed and hugged, and Hakeem whispered how much he loved me. Of course, I cried a little and said how much I loved him too. The couple wished us well hugged us and thanked up for choosing their little chapel. We signed the paperwork and they had to sign as our witnesses and off we went to start our new life.

Hakeem was not a real gambler at least not as far as casino gambling was concerned, so he was not really interested in hanging out in the casinos. Gambling was also frowned upon in his religion, so we headed to the outlet stores, shopping at the Nike outlet and some of his other favorite stores.

Hakeem was 6'8 which made it sometimes difficult to purchase clothes off the rack. So, the Nike store and sports stores were best for him. Of course, I got my son and daughter some things. It was fun shopping, but we were tired and headed back to the room.

We arrived back to the room, and room service had already come in, opened the blinds, and made the beds. The room was beautiful. We dropped our bags and flopped on the bed for a brief nap. Wrapped in Hakeem's arms as his wife felt different to me. I really felt a sense of commitment, a sense of obligation to be by his side and help him stay on track. He was a good man with potential to be great and I felt responsible to pull the best out of him. While he slept I rubbed his face, stared at him, and reflected on all the stuff he shared with me that happened in his life growing up. The heartbreaking things he shared about his time in prison and his sad relationship with his children made me want to wrap him in my arms and make the hurt go away. I ran my fingers around his neatly groomed goatee and rubbed his eyebrows and then softly kissed him on the lips. This was my husband. Good looking, strong and smart and he was mine. I let out a sigh and it woke him.

He asked me was I ok, I whispered that I was. He teased me saying I just wanted some of his dick! We both laughed.

The room was bright and sunny and warm. He took his flower off his shirt and stuck it in my hair. It was just a white carnation, but the act was sexy and sensual. In a matter of seconds, he was standing in front of me butt naked, his clothes at his feet. Directly in front of the hotel window, he stood completely nude. Normally this was when he would turn on one of his old R&B love songs, but he didn't have that. He pulled me towards him. I was still fully clothed, but I could feel he was ready to make love to his new wife. His muscles were tense, and his breathing was heavy but gentle. He slid the straps on my sun dress down and my cute bra was exposed as he pulled the rest of the sundress off till it hit the floor. We kissed passionately, hugging and touching right in front of the window. Soon we were both naked and the passion began. The room was quiet and only the sound of our lovemaking could be heard. The sun shined on our bodies as if we were outside on the beach right were all this began.

# A. MICHELLE

We didn't even make it back on the bed. We made love right there on the floor next to our clothes. I felt the need to go all out and allow him to have me however he wanted me. I never wanted him to desire anyone else.

I finally took charge and he laid on his back as I took over. In front of that window, I rode him and held his long arms down so that I had full control of everything, and he let me. Our reflection in the window looked like a professional porn movie and it added to the sensuality. He let me have my way for a while but soon rolled me over back on my back and finished it off.

From every angle he touched the deepest, most-erotic parts of my body that resulted in the best orgasm ever. We both seem to reach our climax at the same time. He grunted like a bear and I belted out a moan that was probably heard on our entire floor. We laid there catching our breath covered in sweat that shined and glistened like golden glitter from the sunshine. It was beautiful. I had just made love to my husband and it felt awesome.

"I know what you were trying to do…" Hakeem said, still panting to catch his breath.

"What?" I smiled and giggled

He told me that I didn't have to do all that to prove my love. He told me that I had him…all of him. He looked me in my eyes for a long, serious moment, grabbed my vagina, and told me that nobody was ever going to fuck my pussy because it was HIS. He told me I would make him kill somebody!

We laid there for about 5 more minutes, basking in the sun light, laughing and playing around. Hakeem grabbed my

# STABBED TO LIFE

hand and kissed it and said, "This is a new beginning for us, I hope you can forgive me for all the things prior to today and give me a chance to be a husband and lead our family. Allah has blessed me with a good job and a means to take good care of you. Let me be a man Adrianne. Support your King and I will support my Queen."

I shook my head in agreement, he kissed my hand and helped me to my feet. We showered and hung around the room for a couple of hours before heading out on foot to walk the strip and look for a nice place for dinner. It was our last night in Vegas and because he had just started a new position on his job, it would probably be a while before we got away to do anything again. We were trying to make the best of it.

With the many disposable cameras, I had, we took tons of picture in front of the many fancy hotels that lined the Las Vegas strip; Caesars Palace, The Bellagio, Luxor, Mandalay Bay. With so much construction you would think the strip would look like a dump, but it still looked fabulous and no matter how broke you were financially, here, amongst all those lights with the one you love, you'd feel on top of the world, like a celebrity.

The remainder of the evening was fantastic. We had a great dinner at a seafood restaurant and chowed down on lobster, crab and fish, then made the long walk back to the MGM which by now was about 4-5 miles away. We could have taken a cab back, but we were enjoying holding hands while walking and talking and people watching. It was great. Upon arriving back to the room, we were exhausted from the long walk but packed up our things so that we could make the 4 hour drive back home.

# A. MICHELLE

I admired the big, beautiful suite and took pictures again of the room and bathroom with the huge tub. I even relaxed in the tub one last time. We eventually fell off to sleep wrapped up in each other's arms. I felt good, I really felt good about our future.

When we woke up we made sure all our things were packed and then ordered room service for breakfast. After eating, we called for a bellman to come and pick up our bags and pull the car up for us. It seemed like less than 5 minutes, the bellman arrived. We looked at our beautiful suite one last and headed back out on Highway 15, back to the Antelope Valley.

Hakeem tipped the valet and bellman and homeward bound we went. Seemed as though we were leaving before the other tourist because we did not run into any traffic on the drive back. That was odd, because Sunday heading back to California from Las Vegas was often a nightmare with major traffic jams. Traffic never slowed down, we drove 80mph all the way home.

The drive was cool, we listened to an R&B oldies cd, holding hands the whole ride home. Hakeem occasionally reached over to kiss me on the cheek, on my lips, or on the hand. I could tell he loved his wife. We were pulling up in the driveway about 3 hours and 35 minutes and the sun was still shining. I missed my babies and I wanted to go get them, so as soon as all the luggage and shopping bags were in the house I headed to pick Alonja and DeDe up.

I wasn't sure if I was going to share with them that I had just gotten married, but I sure needed to see their faces and quickly got in the car to pick them up. I know they would be excited about the gifts we brought back for them. DeDe

# STABBED TO LIFE

was into Jordan's and we found him some at the Nike outlet and Alonja, although not into clothes as much as her brother, I still found her some cute things in her favorite color purple.

As soon as I got to them DeDe seemed just as excited as I was to see them, but Alonja, well her enthusiasm was not quite the same, but nevertheless, I got a smile and I was happy with that.

We talked about all the fun they had had as we drove home. DeDe shared vivid details, but Alonja just barely shared anything at all. She just said, "I had fun."

DeDe began asking me what all we did, and I shared about the big tigers in the MGM and the water show at the Bellagio, walking the strip and the beautiful lights. Alonja hurried and changed the subject "I need some paper for school and a new folder, can we stop at the store" she asked very quickly. She wasn't disrespectful, but it was clear she had no interest in the trip me and Hakeem had, nor the details. It was almost as if she knew and was trying to avoid me telling her about the marriage. Maybe she just sensed it.

Alonja was a very smart girl so I wouldn't doubt that she had some sort of idea what was going on. At first, I was excited about telling them, but Alonja's actions and attitude just made me rethink the idea. Something that would have normally been a joyous occasion had to remain a secret because I did not want to upset my kids. Damn can't I be happy for once? I know they were aware of some issues early on, but Hakeem was different now.

After leaving the store and gathering all Alonja's supplies, we headed home.

# A. MICHELLE

By now the sun was beginning to set and as we went up the hill to our house there was glow from the sun shining directly on the house. I felt like it was God's sign that things were about to be different, a change, a big change was on the horizon and our marriage, although a secret, was just what this family needed. I took in a deep breath and headed inside. Hakeem's brand-new work truck sat out front, another sign that made me smile from ear to ear. Once again, I was at a place of new beginnings. Yes, he had disappointed me in the past, but things seemed different this time.

When Hakeem heard us pull up he was standing the door way to greet us.

"As-Salaam-Alaikum" he said as we approached the door, my kids were used to responding appropriately to the greeting and they both said, "Walaikun Salam."

I could tell by the look on Hakeem's face that really made him feel good. As soon as they got in they went straight to their rooms where they saw the items we picked up for them while we were in Vegas.

"Did you tell them?" Hakeem whispered

"No…I thought I'd wait," I said, hoping he wouldn't push the issue.

"Wait for what?" he asked with obvious disappointment.

I shrugged my shoulders like a child caught in a lie. The truth was I was scared to tell them. The look on Hakeem's face was a combination of sadness and anger. I felt bad, I wanted him to feel that I was proud to be his wife and the truth was, although I was excited and happy for us, I just did not want to further disappoint my children.

# STABBED TO LIFE

"Alonja and De…come here, I need to talk to y'all." I just wanted to hurry up and get it over with.

"Yes Mama?" Alonja said

"Mom. I love my shoes thank you and for my Roca Wear shirt, thank you," DeDe said looking around nervously noting that Hakeem and I had very serious looks on our faces.

"Be quiet De-De… Mama what's wrong?" Alonja asked

"While me and Hakeem were in Vegas…" I swallowed hard. "We got married." I looked over at him before even looking for the kid's reaction. He was smiling and then he began to speak, quite honestly, I was afraid of what he was going to say.

"I am honored to be your stepfather and I will never try to take the role of your father, I do hope this will make us a strong family and that you realize you can come to me if you need to. I want apologize we didn't tell you what was happening we probably should have but we just wanted to do it and surprise you, Surprise!" he laughed

The look on Alonja's face spoke volumes. It was a blank, expressionless stare. Finally, she opened her mouth to speak, "I knew it," she said sarcastically, "You can do whatever you want to do, you're the adults, what we feel doesn't really matter."

"I am happy for you Mama. I know you love Hakeem and he makes you happy," DeDe said hopefully, his little face just made me want to cry. I knew my kids very well, and although Alonja never could hide her emotions, it was obvious she was disappointed. My DeDe even though I knew he wasn't exactly happy he sure did not want to hurt my feelings. I loved my children and I was going to work extra hard to make them feel comfortable with this awkward decision I had just thrust upon them.

We all got back into our routine. Hakeem was back at work the kids back in school and our routine was solid and repetitive. I continued to get up early every morning with Hakeem for prayer before he headed out to work. He always left with a big lunch packed and came home every evening to a full course meal every evening. He communicated with the kids well, they made sure to abide by the rules of the home. No shoe wearing inside, every evening mopping the floors, washing the dishes, and keeping their rooms cleaned. Every Friday night was date night and we went to a movie and dinner.

Hakeem and I even had a schedule for our intimacy; every other night whether I wanted to or not. There were occasional disagreements, but I would never allow them to get out of control. I just complied like a "good" wife to avoid drama and chaos.

My daughter, bless her heart, seemed to want to spend more time with her grandparents or friends rather than be home. She always seemed angry with me. She was very active in school and softball, and I supported it all. I went to the games, got her to her practices. Since me and their Dad had broken up, he had stopped all interaction, and more so now that I was married. I wanted so bad for him to still have a relationship with the children, but he just would not cooperate.

Hakeem and I were married, but it was not what I thought it would be. I still felt like some days he was still dibbling and dabbling with drugs, and he continued to be controlling.

However, as far as working, he did work hard and even took side jobs often for extra money. I could not complain much in that area. Where I had problems is that he would often get irritated if I asked about his children, when I asked if he was sending money to assist them. He acted as if that was none of my business. He did talk to Sherry from time to time, but always like it was a secret. Whenever I asked what they were talking about he would say "our kids" yet every time there was a need for me to speak to my children's Dad, he needed to know word for word what was said. There was always a double standard. As always, I remained silent to avoid confrontation.

One day he went to Riverside to visit the children and he called and told me he would be spending the night.

"Hakeem?" I asked "Where will you be spending the night"

"With my children" he said sarcastically

"At Sherry's apartment" I asked

"That's where my kids are."

"Nigga you got me fucked up! You sleep over there, you better get your shit and move in with her, I will not have that, I don't who you think you are!" I shouted.

He knew for the most part I would be very passive, and I would try everything to avoid confrontation, but he knew if he did something extremely disrespectful, I would stand up for myself.

# A. MICHELLE

His nonchalant attitude made me realize he was trying to get a rise out of me and I played right into it. I had reacted just like he wanted me to, aggressively and irate.

He laughed, "Are you mad?"

"Would you be mad if I told you I was gonna spend the night at my ex-husband's home? Why would you think that would be ok?"

"I'm visiting my children, isn't that what you wanted?"

"Yes, and you go right ahead and do what every you feel you should do Hakeem, I am not going to go back and forth with you over this bullshit," I said finally.

I could tell he was unable to respond like he wanted to, not sure if he was in front of the children or Sherry, or someone else for that matter. Either way he was not himself. I was upset and when I slammed the phone down I was in tears. The one thing we tried to do is to not upset the children no matter how heated our arguments got. Even if we had physical altercations, I always tried my best to not scare my children.

I went in to the bathroom so that my kids would not hear me cry. I sat there on the top of the toilet with the shower running and thinking to myself, "he has to be high."

There is no other time he makes this dumb of a decision. Irrational, dumb ass, disrespectful decisions. In my gut, now that I really thought about it, he was high. He never wanted me to see him when he did it. My first thought was to get in the car and drive to Riverside, but for all I knew he could have been right here still in Lancaster or Palmdale, and he was in his work truck. I grabbed my phone and called Sherry.

# STABBED TO LIFE

"Sherry, I am sorry to bother you, Hakeem and I are getting some things for Amina's birthday, what size does she wear?" I asked this way because I did not want to seem like I was calling looking for him, especially if he wasn't there.

"I didn't think he was going to do anything for her because, yesterday I asked him for a little extra to get stuff for her birthday party and he cussed me out." Sherry explained.

"What???? He's been giving you something every month, right?" I asked

"Yes, he does, sometimes…but yesterday he was so rude and nasty it sounded like he was high to me." Sherry said

"Wow…I had my suspicions too," I said but quickly interjected, "I think he may just be worn out from working and may be a little irritable." There I went, making excuses for his ass again. I always kept his secrets for fear that it would get back to him. I knew if he ever thought I talked about someone to him, negative or not, it wouldn't be good.

"Just be careful when he does those drugs he gets really violent," she said, "Are you guys coming to the Birthday Party?"

"I'm not sure, depends on what's going on with him and if he's working, either way I will be sure to send her something from us." I said.

This was the most Sherry and I had talked in a while. Based on her answers, he wasn't there. At least it didn't seem like it. I was shocked we managed to have a 5-10-minute conversation like grown women. I was proud of myself. I looked at the caller ID to see had Hakeem called earlier from his work number or from wherever. It was a shame I had to play detective to figure out where my husband was and praying he was not on a drug binge, but that is certainly what it sounded like.

The number he had called from was not his cell phone number, I knew that by heart. It was a 310-area code which was Compton, LA, area but before I could call it back, the phone rung and the caller ID read Hakeem's number from work. I hurried and answered.

"Hello, this is Jerry I am the Superintendent for Hakeem and just wondering had he made it home, we were really worried about him he left sick." the gentleman on the line explained

"Oh yes, he's fine, he made it home, he's sleeping and feeling better, thanks for calling to check on him. Should I have him to call you when he wakes up?" I asked

"Yes, please do, we really need him on Thursday, if he needs to be off tomorrow that's fine, but we are short staffed for Thursday's job and can really use him, yes have him to call me."

I swear I forever ran interference to keep him from getting in trouble, I need to stop doing that and let him face the consequences. I did it with his parole officers, his parents, Sherry. No one knew half of the craziness he had done. I guess in a way it was me protecting me too. If anyone knew this stuff, I would be so embarrassed, so ashamed. However, it was becoming exhausting.

*"That's not abnormal," the therapist said handing me more tissues. "Victims usually cover for their abusers, even when the evidence of abuse is overwhelming. What did you do next?*

# STABBED TO LIFE

I decided to call the 310 number he called from and it was a pay phone. The person who picked up says it was located outside of the Baldwin Hills Crenshaw plaza, a mall in L.A. I asked the person who answered was there a nearly 7 ft man standing anywhere near and he said no, but he sounded like a crack head too. I tried again to reach Hakeem on his phone and this time I blocked my number, so he didn't know it was me. You know, the *67 just to see if he would answer if he didn't know who it was calling. Sure enough, it worked.

"Hello," he said, sounding like he was just awakened from a deep sleep. His voice very raspy and rough. I wanted to start cussing, but I knew that would probably make him hang up on me.

"Baby are you ok, your job called checking on you"

"What did you say?" He asked quickly.

"I told him you were asleep Hakeem. What is going on"

"Don't act like you don't fuckin know, you like humiliating me," he accused angrily.

"What happened, and where are you?" I asked again

"I'm in my car in Redondo Beach, just sitting here thinking."

"Thinking about what Hakeem? How you are about to fuck off a good job, a relationship, and your relationship with your girls, again. How come you cannot stay off drugs? Is that what you're thinking about? What you are going to do about your drug problem? Because if you're not thinking about that, that is what you need to think about."

"This is why I didn't tell you the truth."

# A. MICHELLE

"I didn't sign up for this drama Hakeem!"

"You said you loved me, so this is me," He said cockily and angrily.

"So, you are a Meth head? That's who you are? You didn't tell me that part, had I known I would have done something else,"

"You knew who I was, you knew my struggles"

"You told me I would never have to deal with this shit again Hakeem, you promised."

I couldn't help it, I began to cry. My voice cracked trying so desperately to hold back the tears. It had been 4 months since we "married" and now we were here again. We had so many good days how is it that we could be here again? Every time Hakeem "fell off" the comeback took a while. I never knew what would exactly throw him into wanting to use again, because the way we dealt with it was we'd fight, we'd argue-he'd apologize, and we would not discuss it again, until the next time. I was tired of NEXT TIME!

I didn't want anymore "next times" Often, I went away thinking it was something I had done, that I drove him to use. Maybe I didn't love him enough, cook enough, pray enough. I was so confused. Here I go blaming myself again, and this was his problem.

"Why are you crying Adrianne?" He asked, and now his voice sounding like he was crying. I didn't answer. I just sat there with the phone wiping tears and holding my breath, so he could not hear I was breaking down.

"Adrianne, I'm sorry baby, I have a problem, these demons keep following me. You know all these white guys I work

# STABBED TO LIFE

with do that shit to stay awake, so we can work all hours these and get that overtime. I wasn't going to do it and Hank, the one guy on my crew snorted a line of that shit and I said fuck it, a little ain't gone hurt, so I hit that shit too. That shit had my heart pounding like I was going to die. I knew I could not come home like that babe. I honestly thought I was going to die."

As he told me what happened I literally had to turn the phone away from my mouth because I was breaking down. What do I do now? What do I say? That I am going to stick by him again? I had to come to grips that I was married to a 2-time felon and drug addict with two strikes. Who was often very violent and put his hands on me when he got angry. *"Wow, Mom and Dad would be proud,"* I thought to myself sardonically. What have I exposed my children too? I was married to an abusive, drug addict who was beginning to show signs of mental illness too. Was I in denial? Was I scared to leave him? I was as confused as ever.

*"Adrianne, when abuse is coupled with alcohol or drugs, it's not something any person not professionally trained can deal with. The abuse is not your fault. His problems were present long before the two of you met. Males who come from homes where violence was witnessed are three times more likely to grow up as abusers."*

*I looked at her in disbelief. I had always thought that he was violent because of his past childhood and prison time, this started making more sense.*

*"So, if he didn't do drugs..." I asked wistfully.*

*"No, Adrianne. Sadly, removing those factors do not end domestic violence.*

# CHAPTER EIGHT

## THE METH

I didn't know if I wanted Hakeem to come home. I didn't know if he even wanted to come home. The rest of the conversation just went completely left. He began speaking about how he no longer wanted to live. That he was a no-good father, and step-father. He talked and cried about how this drug once again was ruining his life. I was sad for him, but I was angry with him at the same time. I knew nothing about Meth and could not understand that if you did not want to use it then why would you?

I had no clue how addiction worked. I had a family member who abused drugs and my father drank a lot, but I had never seen the effects like this drug was having on a man that was healthy physically, hardworking, and had such great potential. I don't get it, I guess that was how addiction worked. It did not matter that you worked out, that you ate healthy, that you had children, or a good wife. I just did not understand how he claimed to love me but would risk it all for the drugs.

After an hour of listening to him rant, and then go to being super paranoid and talking out of his head like a crazy man, he begged me to come home. Although I did not say no, I did put my foot down and say, "not yet."

I remembered the look he had before and the process of him coming down off the drug. I did not want my kids to see that. Hell, I didn't want to see that!

# STABBED TO LIFE

It was a very hurtful, emotional process. My kids knew something was wrong, but I never discussed it with them.

"I have money, I will stay in a motel down here till you let me come home, I promise I will not do no more of that shit babe."

"Your job Hakeem…what about your job?" I asked with disgust.

"What about it? I gotta work on myself, I'm the best worker they got, I will have to be truthful and see if they will allow me some time to get my shit together."

He was right, he was good. His boss praised him often placed him on big contracts and had him train the other guys. His boss often said he did the work of three men. But when they find out he had a drug problem and may have to take time off to go to rehab or something, I wasn't sure how that would go over. It was a good job with good benefits, awesome pay, and lots of overtime, but he was right, he needed to fix his life. He needed to address the demons as he called it, and I needed to set some boundaries and stick to them. This was beginning to take a toll on me and my family, not just my children, but my parents were beginning to get more and more suspicious of Hakeem. They were also very concerned for my children.

"Well, I will talk to you tomorrow, we will need to come up with a plan." I said very sternly but still on the verge of tears. I could not deny it, I loved this man and I was not ready to end it.

"Ok baby…can I call you later to say good night?" he asked in that same pitiful voice he always had when he was trying to get in my good graces.

# A. MICHELLE

"Ummmmm…yes I guess so," I said, knowing good and well I wanted to talk to him. "Gotta go," I said quickly and hung up the phone

Because we had gotten married, I had put him on my insurance and immediately thought maybe through our health coverage he could go to rehab. I would call in the morning to figure what our insurance offered. If not, I planned to look of some resources that may be available in the area.

I got my kids fed and ready for bed, turned on one of Hakeem's CDs and cleaned up the kitchen. After cleaning my room, I noticed it was already 11PM. The phone rang, and it was Hakeem.

"Hey babe, are you getting ready for bed?" he asked sounding all sexy, like he was lying there naked .

"Yes, just getting ready to hop in bed, time went by really fast." I said

"Cause I'm not there huh? You miss me?" he asked as if nothing had happened.

"I miss the sober you, the strong handsome, healthy you…the drug free you…yeah I miss that man, I don't know who this is you are showing me now. It's scary Hakeem. It's like you were a fraud, you tricked me," I said angrily.

"Well I'm going to be different now…" he explained

"Yeah ok."

"I was thinking we move out of California" he said quickly

# STABBED TO LIFE

"Move from California? I don't know about that. Where would we go?" I asked

"Missouri, the "Show me State." That's where I am from, I been talking to my brother and he got a hook upon work out there and we could have a nice new beginning out there" he said with excitement

Bullshit, this fool was so unstable, and I wasn't going to pack me and my kids up and move with him to a place where I knew no one. What if he got out there and went off on a drug binge? Who would help me? Hell no!

"I don't know about that Hakeem" I said

"Well, let's get over this hump and we can talk about it again, I know you don't trust nothing I say right now. I've let you down, but I'll show you better than I can tell you"

"Ok. I better go to sleep I have to be at work at 7am," I said forlornly.

"You don't want to know where I am?"

I really didn't. I was just numb to his bullshit, so it really didn't matter at this moment.

"I'm at Sol's. He's going to let me stay a few days, that way I can get my ass up and go to work."

That was right in Palmdale, much closer than I would have liked because he had a way of sucking me in, but this time I really needed to let him stew a bit.

"Oh ok, you told him what happened" I asked a bit nervously.

"Yeah, this brother knows my issues, he said I can stay for as long as I needed to, and he really is hoping we can work out our thing. He loves you like a sister Adrianne. He says you are good for me," He said proudly.

Keep in mind, Hakeem has bad mouth Sol, accused him of wanting me and they have fallen out over money numerous times, but now they were brothers, homies, best friends again. Crazy!

"Well thank him for me please, hopefully it won't be too long, but that is entirely up to you." I said

"I hate that I continue to allow this drug to disappoint you and damage what we have."

"Hakeem, I am to blame too. I keep allowing you back. I cannot keep doing this. I really need to get to bed. Good night I love you."

"Thank you for loving me babe, Good night" he said in the saddest voice ever.

I felt like a fool that I could even still have feelings for him. I really felt like he loved me, but the addiction was just taking over him. Or maybe I was just being played for a fool. What if he loses his job? Then I am with a drug-addict-broke-bum. The little money he had from the boxing thing was nearly gone. He claimed it was because he was sending money to his children, yet Sherry said she had not received money from him in months.

I really needed answers, I needed to talk to someone, but I couldn't share this embarrassing ass shit with anyone, they would think I am crazy. I could hear my friends now "What the fuck is wrong with you…?" "Drug addict…" "Are you kidding me Adrianne…really?"

# STABBED TO LIFE

Oh God I felt like I was going to have a nervous breakdown. I cried myself to sleep.

*"Stop right here and breathe Adrianne," my counselor said, bringing me back to the present. "I can see you are having a hard time dealing with the fact that you didn't tell your loved ones what was going on. You do know that's all a part of it? The cycle of abuse. Hakeem counted on you being too embarrassed and ashamed to tell anyone. You can continue."*

I woke up, the phone was ringing and of course it was Hakeem saying "Good morning" telling me had went for a run trying to sweat the drugs out of his system. He was in a very upbeat mood, asking how the kids were, saying he prayed that morning that Allah allowed him to be a better example to all the children; mine included.

I sat there and listened rolling my eyes up in my head. I had heard all this before. Yet, something in my silly brain made me feel sorry for him. He sounded so pitiful, yet sweet at the same time. I had to cut him short, for a couple of reasons.

One - I wanted him to know that his sweet talk was not working, and I needed to get ready for work.

Two – I needed to put myself first. I had to get myself back to where my children were the priority. This man and his issues had taken over my life. I wasn't even thinking clearly.

"Hakeem. I have to go," I said abruptly.

"Ok," he replied, "I can tell you are still mad at me."

# A. MICHELLE

"We need to talk Hakeem, there needs to be some rules in place and you need to go to rehab or something before we consider doing this again. This shit is getting old, and me and my kids are suffering."

"I'll go to rehab," he begged. "Find a place, any place. I am willing to go. I don't want to lose you. You're all I got baby. Please don't leave me," his voice broke.

My eyes began to feel with tears. Tears of sadness and anger. He could hit me like I was man and now he was sitting there coming down off the drug and crying like a bitch.

Oooh, I hated him so much right then. Something nagged at me. He sounded for real this time. Maybe this was his rock bottom. Maybe he really wanted to change. We were married, I could not just leave him.

I told him "bye" in my strongest voice, although I knew he could tell I was crying, because my voice cracked.

I slammed down the phone and immediately picked it back up. I kept feeling like maybe I should call him back. I had been rather harsh. Something in my spirit gave me the strength to not call him back, and I even took my phone off the hook so that he couldn't call back.

I needed to force myself to keep moving forward. I needed to be present in my kids' life. I was not being a good parent. They were already suffering because of their own absent father, and this so-called father figure sucked big time.

I got myself and the kids ready for work and school. I checked on the dog and headed to work. I was determined not to let Hakeem and his bullshit issues ruin my day.

# STABBED TO LIFE

I walked into work with the biggest, fakest smile, in the cutest outfit, and of course, my shoes were on point. Inside I was crying, but on the outside, I looked good and everyone let me know it too. I strutted the hallways back and forth listening to people say, "you look nice today" "loving that beautiful smile" Today I felt better than I had in a while.

Part of me was done with Hakeem. So much so that during lunch that day I went to the gas station, and a guy flirted with me. I was tempted to give him my number. There was a huge part of me that wanted to just move forward, that was probably the best thing to do, but there I was, staring at my phone and saw 11 missed calls from Hakeem. Every message on the answering machine. The messages began the same as the first.

"Babe, why you not answering, call me when you can I love you, Bye."

"Assalum Alikum Queen just wanted to say I love you."

"When you get a chance call me. I got some good news"

After 8-9 being sweet and kind the first few calls, because I wasn't answering in the time he thought I should, he began escalating to threatening words.

"Babe… you trying to leave me, I am never going to let that happen, you're *my* wife remember that."

*"Be honest with me, what happened next?" the therapist asked knowingly.*

*I guess she could tell I wanted to make myself sound stronger than I really was.*

# A. MICHELLE

Ok, I gave in, the excuse I gave myself was maybe he was in trouble. There was a part of me that kind of wished he would get a parole violation, so I wouldn't have had to deal with his mess, constant drama and feeling guilty. I was clear he was the problem, but me dealing with this over and over showed I had a problem too. I had lied to my parents, friend's coworkers over and over covering for him and me. I looked just as foolish in this craziness as he did.

So, I called...

"What Hakeem?" I asked rudely when he answered the phone

"Dang babe...that's how you do me...??"

"I'm working..."

"You could have just answered and let me know you're ok"

"I'm ok Hakeem," I said blandly.

"Meet me after work at the gym," he begged.

"Gotta get Lonja to practice, can't go to the gym till tomorrow," I said quickly.

"Meet me at Black Angus for an appetizer, so we can talk, baby we need to talk, I got good news, and I want to share with you in person...please?"

I paused a long time and agreed to meet him at Black Angus Steakhouse after work.

The rest of that day I wondered what this "good news" could be. His surprises could be anything; a piece of jewelry, an outfit he would pick, or another elaborate plan to do something with his life. One never knew.

# STABBED TO LIFE

As soon as 5 PM hit, I rushed to my car to headed over to Black Angus. Sure enough, when I pulled up I saw his car parked out front and he sat there staring at me with this smile on his face holding a bouquet of flowers. He bent his long self out of the car, laid the flowers on the hood of his car, and straightened up clothing that looked like they were straight out of the dry cleaners. Either that or he had spent an hour ironing and starching. He looked so good. He walked over to me and embraced me like he had not seen me in years.

As he held me, he whispered in my ear, "Damn, you look good baby… you got all dressed up for Daddy huh?" he said in his deep sensual voice.

I giggled, but I really wanted to tell him that this was no longer for him and if he only knew, my thoughts earlier were to kick his ass to the curb and be done with him. This man always knew how to get to me. He either made me laugh or managed to get me out of my clothes. Either way he knew what to do and he always did it right in the nick of time.

We walked into the restaurant. Black Angus was a steak house, although it was dimly lit, it wasn't expensive or exclusive. They sat us down and Hakeem waited for me to be seated. I am not sure where he learned all these manners, maybe he did a lot of reading while locked up because he was extremely charming, and chivalry was certainly not dead with him. Based on his upbringing at least what he shared, it didn't appear he would have learned all this from his parents. Whatever the case, I loved it.

"So how was your day?" he asked

"It was good…"

# A. MICHELLE

Hakeem proceeded to tell me how good I looked but he couldn't help but to notice that I rolled my eyes every time he complimented me. He told me that indicated I thought he was full of shit. He told me that he probably acted like shit, and possibly looked like shit, but he DID love me, and that was no lie. He kept saying over and over how he was not going to lose me.

"What's the surprise Hakeem?" I blurted out unexpectantly. I did not want to hear all the bullshit. I just wanted to see what his plans were. I wanted to see if they were plans I could agree with.

"I was accepted to an in-house facility for my drug addiction," he explained. He pulled out a piece of paper that showed he was to report tomorrow to the facility and stay a minimum of 90 days. This was the first time I had ever heard him sound so willing and even a bit committed.

"They had it where I could start a month from now and I told the lady straight up I need to get in today or I will lose my entire family," he said with tears in his eyes.

I had to look away because that was another one of his tactics to reel me in. The tears. He could make them come instantly and of course I was sucker for some tears. I said nothing, I allowed him to finish. I could tell he was expecting my reaction to be different. I was just numb to this stuff now. It was sad that I felt I had to be hard, stern and tough now. I had to protect my heart.

The waitress came with some bread and I dove right in grabbed a roll and butter and started eating. He began to look at me with disgust. I looked up with a questioning look and he changed his look quickly and continued talking.

# STABBED TO LIFE

"I was thinking the entire 90 days I would just stay away, no visits, no contact and come out a new man ready to be what you need me to be. I would leave you all the money I have left. That money is to send my kids something monthly and help you with bills and stuff. I talked with my job and they are willing to allow me this time and they are willing to pay for it for me. I guess they have done this for other employees before. You deserve a husband baby and I have not been that. I am ready to give you what you deserve." He had made his case.

The waitress came again and ask were we ready to order. We ordered appetizers, but the potato wedges could not have bacon and we made sure the oil they used to fry them was not lard. He had all these restrictions and special orders due to his religion, or I guess our religion. He wanted so bad for me to totally conform to be a Muslim and study Islam, but I just could not. I felt like it was saying I no longer believed in Jesus and who he was and what he meant to me. He was my only example of a Muslim and Islam and right now that was not the greatest example.

He did drugs, he hit women, and he barely took care of his children. That and the Muslim religion he practiced did not sit well with me. Although he always looked so good, I could only look at him with utter disgust.

I thought how I had stuck by him dealt with his baby mama, his abuse, and now his addiction. I was tired. I closed my eyes and clinched my chest, took a deep breath and told myself, don't cry. Don't shed one more tear for this shit.

"You okay baby?" Hakeem asked. Even though no tears were flowing from my eyes he knew I was hurting inside.

# A. MICHELLE

I wanted to reach over and sock him dead in his face. My emotions were once again all over the place. One second sad the next pissed off.

I told him I was ok, but that I needed him to be the man he pretended to be in the beginning. I told him I needed him to be a father to his kids and to work and never put his hands on me again. I told him to stop lying to me and to himself. That was what I needed.

I explained sternly, and I even managed to keep my voice down. He knew I was upset, and my fists were clinched. I knew that my behavior would normally result in a physical altercation, but I really did not care. I didn't care one bit at this point if he hit me I was going to give him the fight of his life. Instead he walked over to my side of the booth a motioned for me to scoot over so he could sit right next to me. Still holding back, a flood of tears, he attempted to kiss me on the lips and I turned and gave him my cheek.

"Baby…you hate me?"

"I'm tired" I said in my cracking voice.

By now the waitress came with our food and she was looking at us all crazy. Hakeem was in tears and I was looking like I was ready to chop his and everyone's head off. She sat the platter of food down and told us the plate was hot. She also asked if we wanted anything else.

I was always so easily embarrassed so I didn't want to appear that anything was wrong, so I played it off by saying, "You can come get this big dude away from me…make him sit on his side."

She gave a fake laugh Hakeem and I laughed loudly to play it off. She looked back rather concerned but I tried to give

# STABBED TO LIFE

her a look like everything was ok. She eventually was out of sight and I asked Hakeem in my most serious voice ever when he was going to rehab and had he let his parole officer know.

He told me that he did and because he'd come up dirty on a couple of urine test they were glad that he was going without them having to make it mandatory.

I smirked to myself thinking that was probably the only reason he was going anyway. As soon as I thought it, I told myself to stop being negative.

He kept talking like I was trying to talk him out of going because I had so many questions. Quite the contrary, this was the last draw for me. He had to do it or there was no more us. I had to put my foot down.

We ate our food and I eventually loosened up and laughed a bit with him. He was being sweet, but he still had a junky look about him which made it hard for me to stare at him for too long. His cheeks seemed sunken and his eyes bulging, and the dark rings were there probably due to lack of sleep. Of course, that distinctive smell. That smell of boiled wieners that he always smelled like when he was coming off the drug. I didn't say anything, but he noticed that I would pull away from him and was a bit stand-offish Me knowing just a few nights before he either smoked, snorted, or slammed meth made me sick and annoyed.

He paid the waitress and gave her a hefty tip, he liked to show off. I think some of that came from the fact he didn't want to seem like a drug addict, so throwing around extra money seem to make him feel better about himself. He helped me up and hugged me as if he were holding on for dear life.

# A. MICHELLE

I let him, I knew he needed to feel like he was still loved. His tall body still strong and muscular, thank God his body didn't looked sucked up like his face. When he hugged me this time I could feel him nearly collapse. I was literally holding his body up as he sobbed on my shoulder. It was sad. I even began to cry. He composed himself and we walked out to the parking lot. He kept saying he was sorry and how he hated he had brought so much drama to my life. I tried to encourage him that he could beat this and that he could get past this.

We headed home and there I helped him pack. He had a list of things he could take along with him toiletries a certain amount of underwear and shirts and I just stuffed his duffle bag with all his clothing nice and neat like he liked it. I was sad, but I could not let him see it was getting to me. He kept saying how 90 days was a long time, I tried to re-assure him it would probably go by quick. I prayed that this would be the solution to getting this relationship back on track, but more so, I prayed that he could really beat this drug addiction and rid himself of the pain from his past. His past, that was really attributing to his actions. I even believed Hakeem was dealing with clinical depression or something more severe like bi-polar or worse, Schizophrenia. Things just seemed strange and although part of me wanted to just run and run fast, the other part wanted to be there for him.

We piled all his stuff near the door. He made sure to take his running shoes and workout gear. He called my kids in and said good-bye. He did not tell them he was going to rehab, just that he would be gone for a little while to take care of his health and told them to take care of me. They agreed and gave him a hug and then off to bed they went.

# STABBED TO LIFE

We were left there sitting in the living room in complete silence. We sat on opposite couches and I noticed he had his head hung low. I am sure he was going through a lot of guilt and shame.

"Can I come sit by you babe?" he asked

I scooted over giving him some room to sit, and he laid his head in my lap like a kid.

"Thank you for sticking by me through all my bull-shit baby."

I just rubbed his head, I didn't say one word. Although I was emotional and extremely saddened by the thought of him being gone for so long, it had to be this way. It just had to.

Before long Hakeem fell asleep, his head in my lap and it was hard watching his body twitch and spasm ever so often. I am sure it was still a reaction to his body coming off the drug. Every time I tried to remove his head from my lap, he would hold on tight to my legs. He did not want me to let him go in anyway. Eventually we both fell asleep right there on that couch for hours and when he woke up he whispered.

"I'm gonna need to give you something before I leave baby," he whispered.

He walked to the pile where all his things were located and pulled out his favorite green prayer rug. This is the rug I first saw him make salat on when we very first met, and he always told me it was his favorite and very special to him. I later found out this was also the rug he prayed on while he was incarcerated all those years.

# A. MICHELLE

"I need you to pray for me every day as often as you can on this rug every single day baby, I am embarking on a very mental and physical transformation in the next few days. I will need your help. Not monetarily, not physically, but prayerfully. I am asking for nothing more than your prayers," he said quietly.

As he spoke a chill came over my body. He stood there looking like a chiseled picture of health. His body was strong and cut and his muscles were protruding from every inch of his body. He had on nothing but his boxer briefs. I could help but think for 90 days I would not have this body next to me. Looking at his body, he did not look sick today. His face was almost back to that beautifully healthy glow he often had, and you could see those beautiful green eyes again. The whites of his eyes were no longer blood shot. He was almost back to himself.

"I will certainly pray for you Hakeem, you are my husband and I remain dedicated and loyal to you, and I will support you through this process, as long as you are doing what you agreed to do baby."

We hugged and kissed and before you knew it we were making love as if it were the last time we would be together. It was a very emotional connection. There were tears shed by us both in between some very sensual exchanges. He kept whispering "Thank you babe" and "I love you babe" Could he really love me this much and treat me the way he had in the past? I was so confused, I wanted to believe his words. But he had let me down so many times before.

After we showered and got all his things in the car, we said our goodbyes and off he went.

# STABBED TO LIFE

It was a very emotional goodbye. It was almost as if he were off to fight for his country, but instead, he was off to fight for his life. I reminded him to call me when he made it to the rehabilitation center. His employer was paying for this and they sent their employees to an inpatient treatment facility in Long Beach. The pictures looked like a very plush place near the beach, yet away from the hustle and bustle of the city. Each person roomed with someone and the college-dorm-type rooms each had a balcony and a view of the ocean. I sat there for a minute and just read the brochure. I also noticed the rules, one being no visitors till after 30 days, and no pass to leave the facility till after 60 days. Wow, they were a strict place, but they also had all day groups, physical therapy, rec therapy, and counseling sessions. Sounded like a great place. I was keeping my fingers crossed that he could do it. I sure wanted him to.

I grabbed the prayer rug he had given me, went into my bedroom and prayed as he had shown me. I did my wudu and continued with the prayer as I did so many times. I am not going to lie. I did put Jesus in there. And although that was probably against the rules, I knew Jesus as my savior and I ended the prayer in Jesus' name. I guess it was an Islam /Christian remix prayer.

I got dressed for work and began my day, by the time I arrived to work Hakeem was calling me letting me know he had arrived. He even let me speak to the counselor who was doing his intake. She was very clear that the phone would be with her and from this point on I would not hear from him till he successfully completed 30 days. I was going to miss him.

# A. MICHELLE

The first two weeks was a breeze, no problems. I had been alone with my kids before and did just fine, but by week 3, I was really missing him. I pictured him looking healthy and talking in his group. I am sure that he was helping his peers and taking over as he often did. I was happy for him. I kept reminding myself no news was good news, so I stayed positive. I continued my daily routine and regimen with the gym and healthy eating. I took the kids to their practices and did things with them like shopping and movies. They were happy to have their Mommy back. Alonja was so talkative and laughed and shared.

She was certainly different. She didn't seem to miss Hakeem one bit. My sweet DeDe often asked if Hakeem was ok. He was always concerned. I think it stemmed from that one-time Hakeem too much meth and thought he was having a heart attack and DeDe had to call 911. So awful, a kid had to be placed in that position. He was such a loving boy and always so concerned about others, I always said he had a heart like his Mudder. My Mom who, no matter what, always saw the good in people even the worse ones. Her famous lines were, "Oh they mean well" or "Bless their heart" My baby DeDe was just like her even at this young age. He was so concerned about Hakeem. I told him over and over, that he was fine and that he would be home soon."

*The counselor stopped me once again.*

*"Adrianne, I want you to understand that none of this is to make you feel bad. I do want you to recognize the danger that you put your children in. Not to mention the fact that your son must have been scared out of his mind to have to call an ambulance. Did you know that studies have shown*

*that 50% of abusers are also likely to abuse their children?"*

*"No, I didn't know that at the time, although I should have known better altogether. I constantly made the wrong choice in men," I said quietly.*

*The therapist looked at me with kind eyes, "I know this is painful. Just keep taking deep breaths. You may continue…"*

Well, by the end of the 3rd week Hakeem had mange to sneak and call me somehow. There was a phone in the kitchen of the facility and everyone would take turns sneaking on it. I cut the conversation very short because I did not want him to get in trouble. He sounded so good though. He was talking recovery talk.

"I've been clean and sober for almost 30 days baby; your man is going to do this. I'm running every day and my roommate says I should go back into boxing, he saw me knock this dude out in here." He explained proudly.

"Knocked out?"

"Yeah! This old crack head dude came in here with some drugs after his first pass and came in my room with it. I told his ass, this is a sacred area dude, you see my Quran and rug, don't bring that shit in here. He tried to get smart, so I had to lay the 'ole bum dude out!" He laughed, then immediately said, "I felt bad cause he was literally snoring. I put his ass to sleep."

"Hakeem, I don't want you to get in trouble, I'm hanging up. Please don't do anything to get kicked out or in trouble. It's really good to hear your voice baby," I said in my sweetest kindest voice.

# A. MICHELLE

"Hey before I let you go, I have the Greatest hits of Mary J Blige, and I listen to every night." He knew I loved some Mary and her lyrics always spoke to me.

"That's sweet Hakeem, I'm letting you go I love you." I said and quickly hung up the phone.

After that I told myself I wouldn't be an enabler and I would not take any other calls from him, but I didn't have to. Two days later at about 11:50 pm the doorbell rang. I was scared. I was in this house all alone with my two babies, who could possibly have the audacity to come to my home at this hour to ring the bell and risk waking my kids.

I kept the lights off inside. The porch light was already on. The tall shadow I saw made me instantly realize who it was. I knew it was bad and I wasn't wrong. I looked through the peep hole and sure enough it was Hakeem. I slowly opened the door. He looked a mess. He didn't say a word, he pushed past me and walked to the bedroom very quietly. Still not uttering a word he took all his clothes off and jumped in the shower, he stayed in the shower for almost an hour. While he was in there I went to the driveway and didn't see his car. So, he didn't have his car and obviously had no keys. I am not sure what had happened, but he was high he had certainly relapsed. I took a deep breath and I asked in the calmest voice I could find, "What happened Hakeem?"

Just as I did the shower went off. He came out and grabbed a towel still not saying anything. Wrapped the towel around his waist. Even though he had just got out of the shower he still stunk, and he looked like shit.

"Hakeem, I asked you a question." I said.

# STABBED TO LIFE

He looked possessed, eyes bloodshot He put on some underwear and laid on the bed.

"Hakeem, I'm talking to you!" I yelled, "Who brought you here? What the fuck happened?"

By this time, I was in tears. He sat straight up and reached under the bed and pulled out his gun. It was a 9mm. I knew it was loaded because all the guns were always loaded. He was a felon and wasn't supposed to even have a gun, but he had several allover the house and in his vehicles.

*"So, you eventually went against your original decision and let him have guns in the home?" The therapist asked, making sure she heard me correctly.*

*"Yes. That changed shortly after he moved in permanently," I said quietly.*

*Although I could see the understanding in her eyes, I still felt like I was such a weak-minded person to let him do whatever he wanted in my home and around my kids. I took a deep breath and continued.*

He took the gun and first pointed it to his head, then he looked at me and pointed it to mine. I had stopped crying. I was sitting there numb to the world. I felt like I was having an out of body experience.

"So now you're going to kill me Hakeem?" I asked softly. "All I've done for you and you're going to kill me?"

The gun was still to my head the barrel pressed right above my ear. His hand was shaking.

"You might as well kill me Hakeem because you've killed my spirit. My drive, I died when I met your sorry ass. I fuckin hate you, and I'm sure Allah is pleased" I said

# A. MICHELLE

defiantly and closed my eyes. The only thing on my mind was my kids.

He dropped the gun on the bed.

"Leave me alone bitch and let me sleep." he said in a low voice. He crawled under the covers and pulled the comforter over his head. The gun laid there right next to him where it had fallen.

I turned to leave the room and he said gruffly, "Get over here and lay next to me. I don't trust yo ass."

Eventually when he was snoring and in a deep sleep, I was able to maneuver my way from under him. This massive sleeping giant that reeked of boiled hot dogs. I still didn't know why he smelled like that to me. It wasn't a good smell; like old dirty sweat.

When I got from underneath him and was able to get out of the room, I crept silently into my son's room. I did not want to scare my kids. By then it was only 5:30 in the morning and a little early to wake them for school. I just laid there on the floor of my son's room for another hour.

While I laid there, I thought of getting the gun and doing something awful to Hakeem, but I knew it was only the drugs making him behave that way. Again, I justified his behavior. I felt foolish, yet at the same time this was an opportunity to run right? Instead, I laid there staring in the ceiling. I was now afraid that my alarm scheduled to go off at 6:30 would wake him and something bad would happen. I snuck back in my room and tip toed to the alarm. It was 6:28.

# STABBED TO LIFE

I was able to push the alarm's off button, so it would not go off. I even unplugged it from the wall to be extra sure. Hakeem laid there knocked out. His body jerked every few minutes.

That fucking drug was vicious, but like a fool I still had love for him, this sick monster.

I snuck back to my kids and got them ready for school. I tried hard to act like nothing was going on. I got them breakfast and made sure they were ready. They did ask why I was rushing and asked was I going to work because I was still in my pajamas.

I just told them that I needed to be at work early that day, so let's hurry and get dressed so we could get out of there. They looked at me crazy. I was still running around like a fool.

Still in my pajamas, I drove them to school. My kids knew that I would never leave the house in pajamas, but I needed to get my babies out of that house. I gave them one more look-over to make sure their faces were clean and that they had their backpacks.

I could feel Alonja staring at me and I caught her shaking her head in disapproval. She knew something was up although she couldn't quite put her finger on it. She knew there was a reason for my peculiar behavior.

"Let's go guys," I said quickly.

Mama was in crisis mode. I dropped them off at the school. There were only a few students there, the ones who ate breakfast in the mornings. I kissed them both and rushed back home.

# A. MICHELLE

As I drove up the hill and could see my house, I slowed down. I didn't know what I was going to be walking into. All sorts of stuff went through my head. Is it possible that he'd killed himself? Would he try to kill me? Did he die in the bed from over dosing.? Would he be sitting in the kitchen waiting on me? My thoughts were racing a thousand miles a minute.

I sat in the driveway for a minute trying to figure if I could just run to the neighbors if he tried to attack me or should I walk in with my phone ready to dial 9-11. I was scared, but also concerned. I finally crept in the house slowly and noticed it was eerily quiet. It still smelled like the beef sausage I made for DeDe to go with his breakfast. I slowly turned the corner leading down the hall where my bedroom was. The door was still closed just as I left it. I opened the door and I could still see him lying there and as I always did, I looked to see if his body was moving, checking to see if his back was going up and down to make sure he was breathing. Although I was relieved that he was, I was still scared of what could happen next. Just as I tried to pull the door closed Hakeem sat straight up.

"Come here," Hakeem said in a raspy voice. He looked like the devil. As soon as I saw his face I remembered when his daughter said to me one time "my Daddy is the devil" he certainly looked like it today. I barely pushed the door opened so my head could fit through.

"What did you say?" I asked

"You didn't hear me?" he asked

"No, I didn't hear you Hakeem" I heard his ass just fine, but I wanted him to repeat it, I needed to see his hands from under that comforter before I came anywhere near him.

# STABBED TO LIFE

I needed to make sure I was not going to be ambushed or shot. No one should have to live like this.

"Come over here girl, ain't nobody gonna do nothing to your scary ass," he raised his voice.

I gradually began walking over trying to be tough, but I was scared in the inside. I could hear my heart pounding.

"I look like shit, I know. I fucked up Adrianne," he said flatly.

I hated when he said my real name, that always meant trouble. I was normally "babe" or "Queen" but when he said Adrianne it was about to followed by some major crazy ass bullshit.

"What happened?" I asked with a major attitude. He took a deep breath and went into this extravagant and dramatic explanation.

He told me that the guy he knocked out the second week in rehab for bringing in drugs brought it in again and how they thought they wouldn't get caught.

"I was missing you babe and was kind of down, so I fell for it. I got weak and did it. That shit had me so messed up. I was all over the place," he said pitifully.

"You mean were tweeking," I muttered under my breath. I thought I'd said it low enough that he could not hear me, but the fool heard me.

"Oh, now I am a tweeker?"

He was all pissed off. How could he get pissed off at the truth? I had to remember I was talking to a known fool. A fool with a gun just a few feet away.

# A. MICHELLE

"I guess I had that coming," he relented and continued his ridiculous ass story. He said that the guy had drawn the attention of the night attendant because of his tweeking. The night attendant then wanted to test them both for drug use. He felt that if he left as if he were on a visitation pass, he could just go back on Monday.

"So, let me make sure I understand," I said with major attitude. "You left without a pass to come home, you came without your car, you are currently high, and you think they are going to allow you to go back on Monday?"

I felt as though I was speaking to a 10-year-old child rather than a grown ass man. I looked him dead in his blood shot, crusty eyes, and again felt that I was looking at the devil.

He couldn't even respond, he knew what he said made no sense. I think that is what I hated about Hakeem the most. He thought he was smarter than me. He thought that I was dumb and stupid as he often referred to his baby-Mama, but I wasn't the one.

I could no longer take this ridiculous story that I didn't believe half of.

I told him to get some rest and that I was going to work. He acted like he couldn't believe I was leaving him in that condition. I closed the door and sat in the living room for what seemed like hours just reflecting on the story, what happened, how he looked, and asking myself WHY? Why was I still in this?

I used my kids' bathroom and showered and dressed for work. I was going to be late, so I called and let them know. This was being coming the norm and it was always behind Hakeem's bullshit.

# STABBED TO LIFE

Just as I'd pulled into work my cell phone rung. I answered, and it was the rehabilitation center asking had I seem Hakeem. I lied and said no and hung up. Just as I opened my car door something said "Call back and tell them the truth" I didn't want to be a snitch, but I needed to not be an enabler I had been doing that far too long.

I called back and told the lady that Hakeem was at my house sleeping and I knew he was high. She confirmed what he said in his ridiculous story. The other guys were allowed back but he would not because he stayed gone over 24 hours and they found massive drug paraphernalia in his belongings. She told me his things were packed up and waiting for him. She did say they would not report him to the police, but he cannot come back on the premises since he also had pushed the female night attendant down while trying to escape. She had a minor injury.

I shook my head and told her I would relay the message. I apologized and thanked her for trying to help him. My first intention was to call him and let him know. I thought it could wait till I got home. Given his history, he was probably going to sleep all day today anyway.

*"Adrianne. I want you to take a moment to acknowledge what you did there. In that moment, you courageously made a huge step towards your survival by calling the rehab center back and being honest about the situation. So often victims beat themselves up for their lack of action, they forget about the actions they did take to help themselves best they could."*

*I smiled faintly, thinking maybe she was right. My voice was a little stronger as I resumed my story.*

# A. MICHELLE

The day seemed to speed by, and there were no calls from Hakeem while I worked, but as soon as 4:30 hit he began blowing me up. Apparently, my kids had arrived from school and they were making too much noise.

"Babe, please call your kids and tell them to keep it down," Hakeem said half sleep.

I figured they had no idea he was there. His car wasn't there, and he was shut in the room in silence.

I called, and my daughter answered, I asked her to be sure to keep it down because Hakeem was there. She instantly got an attitude but said "Ok."

My kids were sick of this mess too. I cleaned up my desk and as soon as 5:00 hit I was out of there and heading home. My fear was that he would say something crazy to my kids and I knew it would get ugly. Not just with me but possibly their father who I desperately tried not to involve or make him aware of any of this.

When I arrived home, my kids were doing their homework. The house smelled like Alonja had made them some grilled cheese sandwiches. She was good for feeding herself and her brother for me. She could tell I was frantic, and said sarcastically, "We've been quiet."

The TV was on but was on mute with subtitles. No kids should have to live like that.

I thanked her and went into the bedroom. To my surprise Hakeem was awake and getting dressed. I told him the rehab place called and said he could not go back and that his things were waiting to be picked up.

"So, you happy about that?" he asked.

# STABBED TO LIFE

"No Hakeem I am actually extremely disappointed, you knew this was the last chance and you fucked it all up."

"Babe, we should move to Missouri" he said smiling, as if this was the best idea ever.

Missouri was where his parents were from and his brother was living there and was doing well according to him. His brother and his wife had a nice home and great jobs. But what did that have to do with us?

"Babe, while I was lying here I said to myself, you are going to lose the love of your life messing with this drug and being violent and making bad decisions. I think if I move to Missouri where I don't know where the drug is I can get clean and we can start fresh. There are plenty jobs there and the cost of living is way less." He explained

I just shook my head. I was not moving my children and away from my parents to be with his unstable ass. I could not see myself doing that.

Especially since he was becoming more and more abusive. A few weeks after that, the thing I feared the most happened. Hakeem made the mistake of saying something ugly to my children.

I had always said if he ever so much as spoke negatively about them, it would be on. Our fights were escalating to the point to where I would go toe to toe with him, fighting him back with everything I had.

On this day he told my kids to shut the fuck up. I lost it. I socked him in his ear as hard as I could and busted his ear drum. He blanked out and hit me so hard in my forehead that it required 12 stitches to repair.

# A. MICHELLE

I couldn't believe it. I don't think I'd ever been hit that hard by anyone in my life. Both my eyes were blackened immediately, and I had a huge knot in the middle of my forehead.

You would think he'd feel remorseful, but instead, he was pissed because he had to take me to the hospital. He fussed and talked shit all the way there, saying, "If you wouldn't have made me hit you, we wouldn't be going through this."

I had become so numb to the abuse. My head was gaping open from the gash and I had no tears to shed. I rode to the hospital in shock.

I made up some lame excuse to tell the doctors and nurses who cared for me. At one point the nurse got me to myself and asked me if Hakeem had done this to me. Even she could tell I was married to a lunatic.

I was so pathetic. I told her no and even got an attitude that she'd insinuated that he had something to do with my injury.

For weeks afterward, I looked like the elephant man. I swooped my bangs down to cover my bruised forehead and tried to wear sunglasses, but it was impossible to cover up all the damage he'd done this time. Everyone around me at work noticed but was too afraid to say anything...

*The therapist allowed me to stand up and stretch my legs. My eyes were puffy and swollen as I struggled to make it through my story.*

*"Adrianne are you ok to continue?" She asked, bringing me back to the present.*

# STABBED TO LIFE

*I wanted to tell her that I wasn't ok and how stupid I felt for allowing myself to go through all of this.*

*I felt like a failure. I felt like I'd let my children down. I felt like I'd chosen a man over them, and that was the last thing I ever wanted to do.*

*Somehow, I had to find the strength to keep going. I had been holding on to all these secrets far too long. I knew that if I wanted to be completely healthy that I needed to continue this process, so I straightened my blouse and said, "No, I'm fine. I'll pick up where I left off..."*

# A. MICHELLE

# CHAPTER NINE

## THE MOVE

### (TO KANSAS CITY AND BACK)

Ok, call me foolish but I did go and visit Kansas City, Missouri with him and he was right jobs; were plentiful. I was offered 4 jobs just while there visiting. I met his family who were all very nice, but it became awkward because some of the women cousins and aunts pulled me aside and asked me why was I with him? One even told me do not ruin your life sweetie, that Hakeem was nothing but trouble. I could not believe it. I don't know why it was so difficult for me to comprehend, hell even his own mother told me something similar. She didn't even like dealing with him and his crazy mood swings. I loved him though and I really felt like I could help him get healthy and then we would be happy. My parents were not on board with the idea of me moving there either but told me they would be supportive.

I did my homework though, especially when it came to my children. I verified the schools and neighborhoods. I found out that I had to go to court to get approval to move them out of state. Their father, even though not active in their lives, was giving me a hard time about letting them move out of the state. I kept explaining to everyone that I was just thinking about it even though my mind was pretty made up once I knew I could get a job.

# STABBED TO LIFE

Hakeem was offered a construction job and was going to start within 2 weeks. He was excited about getting a fresh new start.

I had been on my Government job for over 15 years at this point and I would have to resign, that part was scary. I was a good employee though and people loved me. I did not want to leave on bad terms, but my boss was very clear that I best be sure this is what I wanted because the likely hood of me being hired back was minimal. Nevertheless, I gave notice and started trying to plan for the big move.

Leading up to the move Hakeem was already in KC, so we ran up huge phone bills talking all the time. He flew me down a few times to come visit and it seemed good. He always seemed very happy to see me and then one day, two weeks prior to the move, he had me come down. I had scheduled a job interview for this time also with a company named Kaiser Permanente. They were a very well know Medical Group also popular in Southern California. I was applying for a receptionist/cashier position.

We had secured our new tri-level home right outside of the big city in a town called Raytown, Missouri. Upon my arrival this time he seemed different. This time he was a little distant even though he had a bouquet of flowers. When he greeted me, his mood was somber and dry. I only had a carryon bag, so we headed straight to the Hotel we were staying at. Even though the house was secured our move in date was not till 2 weeks later. We had to stay in a hotel since Hakeem had been staying in his Aunt's basement. He didn't want me staying there, so he got a Hotel.

"Are you ok honey?" I asked very sweetly

# A. MICHELLE

"I am good, just thinking about when you come how you draw a lot of attention with your look. The way you dress and with your flossy cars. I don't want any negativity down here with these people. I want to leave all the drama in California. I've been talking to my Muslim brothers down here and they know how women from California can be and you'll have me catching a case. I was watching these dudes look at you as you came off the plane, see I can't have that. I need you to dress modest and cover up. You know how I like it." he explained sternly.

By the time he finished his long rant we were in the room and I never got to say a word. It was 10:30 pm and I told him I needed to call my parents and let them know I made it. He became angry.

"That's another thing you don't need to call them every day for everything." he said angrily.

'Well I am calling them right now because I told them I would call when I arrived." I called and quickly told my Mom I had made it and the name of the hotel we were staying. I look over at him. I could tell he was getting frustrated with my conversation, especially because I shared with her where I was staying.

Once off the phone I calmly asked Hakeem, why he was being so mean and nasty? I didn't want to think it, but it was almost like he had been high, or was high, but no… it couldn't be. He said he would never get high out here.

He didn't even answer me, instead he said, "Go get in the shower," very abruptly.

I grabbed my toiletries and got in the shower. He was on edge and being mean, and I didn't understand.

# STABBED TO LIFE

Over the phone he was so cool and seemed excited about my visit. Even though it would be brief, he said he could not wait to see me. He was so damned moody and when he acted this way it always seemed to be after he had gotten high or wanted to get high. I was confused.

I was covered in soap when he got in the shower with me. It did not seem like the normal romantic encounter we'd had several times in the shower before. This time his eyes were evil, and his body language was different. He got behind me and from the reflection in the shower door I could see he was washing himself. Out of nowhere, he grabbed me very forceably covering my mouth. For a minute I could barely breathe. His hand covered my mouth and my nose.

He bent me over and forcefully sodomized me. I was in pain and crying begging for him to stop. He just continued. Then he picked my wet body up and carried me to the bed where he continued. He bit me all the while pinning me down, so I could not get up.

Finally, after what seemed like eternity he stopped. He whispered in my ear "Anytime you think about fuckin somebody else, you remember this… you are my wife, you belong to me. Your body, your mind and your thoughts better stayed focused on me…You understand?" He growled.

From all the fighting and wrestling and trying to resist him, I was out of breath and so was he. I didn't answer fast enough. He asked again…

"Do you understand?" he yelled and grabbed my face.

# A. MICHELLE

I nodded yes and closed my eyes. Tears rolled down my face and he laid on top of me till he completely caught his breath. When he got up, he used my chest to push himself up as if I was a part of the bed, pressing all his weight on my breast and ribcage. He walked back into the bathroom and started the shower.

I laid there frozen. As I gained my bearings, I slowly ran my hand up and down my body smearing blood on my skin. I was bleeding from every area on my body he bit. He'd bitten me before, but this time was more aggressive than ever.

I felt like I had been raped. I was shaking because I was wet, cold, and bleeding, but I could not move. I was frozen in time. I couldn't understand what had just happened to me. Was this some type of fantasy he had or was he trying to teach me a lesson. My thoughts were all over the place.

I heard the water turn off and he slid next to me, held me tight, and whispered in my ear.

"I hope I didn't hurt you... but the thought of you being with someone else makes me crazy, I love you."

I couldn't say anything. I just clinched my eyes shut tightly. The room was dark, and the only light was from the bathroom. As soon as he was off to sleep I got up to see my wounds. I was bitten from head to toe and had searing pain in my butt. He had violated me, he had raped me, and this was like Deja-vu because he had done this before.

I cleaned myself up and got in bed. In a few hours I needed to be at a job interview. Or should I even go? I would be too embarrassed to call this move off. My parents had paid for the moving van; over $1500 dollars.

# STABBED TO LIFE

My brother had agreed to help me drive everything down and had to rent a tow dolly to pully my little car. I would look like such a fool to call this move off.

I closed my eyes to try to get a little sleep and no sooner than I closed my eyes the alarm was sounding. It was time to get up. I prayed that God gave me clarity on what I should do. I figured I would go through with the interview and if I got the job, it was meant for me to go through with the move. Of course, Mr. Mood Swing woke up like a totally different person. He was so loving and insisted on taking me to breakfast. So, I got dressed and put my make up on. Despite the chaos and drama from the night before I looked nice and of course Hakeem agreed and made a point of saying over and over, "look at my wife."

Apparently, the hotel we were staying was not far at all from the Hospital where the interview was taking place. We had time to grab a bite to eat and still make it in plenty time for the interview.

"You nervous?" Hakeem asked

"Not really" I said very quietly.

He knew I was still feeling upset about his actions the night before. I did not want to bring it up right then, but my plan was to address it after the interview was over and I was at the airport just in case this fool tried to trip and make me miss my flight.

Once at the hospital for the interview I took one last look at myself, took a deep breath and in I went. My resume was on point. I was over qualified for the position, but out of all the other jobs I was offered this one paid the most and had the best benefits.

# A. MICHELLE

It was in the Oncology Department, so I would be dealing with Cancer patients; scheduling their appointments, checking them in, and assisting them and their families when they came for chemo treatments. It sounded interesting and I loved helping people. They offered me the job right then and there and I told them I still needed two weeks to move here from California. They were willing to wait for me. So, the move was on. I could not speak about what happened to anyone. They would think I was crazy even if they knew half the stuff I had dealt with thus far with this man.

I never addressed it. I decided to go ahead with the move and make the very best of it. So, two weeks later, my kids and I made the move.

After a couple of days, we finally got settled in the beautiful house nestled in on the quiet cul-de-sac. The back yard sat flushed against the forest where deer walked through and at night fire flies lit the yard. It was a new environment for me and my kids. We had never experienced anything like it.

I looked at my babies and thought to myself, "this better work." I had them keeping secrets from my parents, constantly threatening them they'd better not discuss the arguments and fights they may have heard between me and Hakeem.

I owed them a better life. They already had a deadbeat father and sadly their Mom was not making the brightest decisions. Hopefully we could make new memories. They loved me, that's for sure because they were given an option to stay, but they chose to be with their Mama. Now I wondered if it was to protect me and watch over me?

# STABBED TO LIFE

Alonja had her own room on the first level right off a huge formal living room and the second level was a kitchen, DeDe's room, a dining room, and an entertainment area. The third floor was where me and Hakeem shared a huge master suite with a balcony looking into the forest. It was beautiful.

Every day I came from work and fixed dinner and then shortly after Hakeem would arrive and we would all sit down and have dinner together. He still got pissed off because I spoke to my parents daily. It got to where he would secretly take the phone off the hook, so I would not know they had called.

*The therapist looked over her tortoise shell glasses and nodded her head in understanding. She told me that many abusers isolated their victims from friends and family. This was not only a form of control, this was part of the manipulation that the victim had no where to turn. I nodded my head in agreement and continued.*

Even with that, it seemed we were getting into a great routine and everyone seemed happy. My kids became good friends with some of his younger cousins and would hang out from time-to-time. I was loving my new job, they loved me too, and I enjoyed helping the cancer patients.

Things were too good to be true, because a little over a month of being there Hakeem came home angry. I mean pissed off because I was still driving with California License plates. He accused me of purposely trying to get attention. He was so paranoid. I looked at him closely and there was no doubt in my mind he was high. He smelled like it, the boiled wiener smell. His eyes were blood shot and he looked like he was possessed by demons. Thank God my children were not there.

"I told you over a week ago Adrianne where to go to get the plates changed and what you had to do, you just will not listen huh?" he said in his demonic voice.

"Hmmm…I see you found the dope man" I said sarcastically and turned my face in disgust.

I braced myself because I just knew he was going to hit me. He stopped and stared at me a long time and I did not flinch one bit. I stared right back at him, deep into his eyes. I was beginning to come numb to his hits, to his words and his threats. I never challenged him, but I was tired. How dare he have me move all the way down here from my comfort zone, away from my family and friends who loved me, to be with a fuckin dope-fiend. I was so angry. He could not deny it. He could not say one word.

The coldest part about this time, he was not in his work clothes, you know, jeans t-shirts work boots. He was in is Muslim garb. Kufi cap and Taub which is the long cotton shirt he usually wore to Jumma prayer on Fridays.

This was an all-time low for Hakeem because he respected his religion so much and would never be on drugs and representing Islam. So, me saying something about this was going to hurt him to his core. I had to though…

"So, you do drugs now dressed this way…you are such a fake. Is Allah pleased?"

I said it loud too. I knew it was going to hurt him and that's just what I wanted. I braced myself again just knowing that some blows were about to be exchanged. I had convinced myself if he hit me this time it was on.

# STABBED TO LIFE

I was full of rage at this point, and I was going to fight his ass back. He stopped dead in his tracks and turned around slowly and stared me up and down. I knew I had struck a nerve. I am sure he could also see that I was trying to be tough but inside I was afraid of what was coming next.

I knew this though, whatever he was coming with I was prepared to fight with all I had. Today was not the day. How dare he do exactly what he said he would never do. He promised.

He looked back at me one last time and out the door he went. I stood there still for a few minutes and finally heard him screech off in his truck. I took a deep breath and began preparing for my kids to come home.

As night came and went with no word from Hakeem, I wasn't sure if I should be worried or not, or if I even cared. By the time the sun rose I still hadn't heard from him and I did not call him either. I was in a foreign place but knew my way around now. I was still a little nervous but for my kids' sake I put on a brave face. The weather was beginning to change in Missouri and I was a California girl. I woke up to a light blanket of snow and deer running through the backyard. It was beautiful no doubt, but I was nervous about driving in the snow. And scared that I did not have proper attire for my children. I layered them up and pulled out there California winter coats and hoped for the best.

As we continued preparing for our day and was ready to walk out the house, the phone rang, and it was Hakeem, I saw his number pop up on the caller id.

"Hello" I said very nonchalantly.

# A. MICHELLE

"Hey," he said in his coming-down-off-drugs voice. Yes, there was a voice for that too.

There was a long pause and I said hello again to ensure he was still there. Clearly my tone was very matter-of-fact no extra sweetness, just a tone that said, "what is it this time…what line of bullshit are you going to come with now?"

"I've been at one of the brothers houses from the Mosque, I told him what happened, and he and his wife allowed me to stay for a few days." Hakeem explained

I still said nothing, not one word. He began stammering and stuttering over his words, voice cracking like he was going to cry.

"I fucked up Baby…I'm sorry. I really wanted to put this 45 to my head last night and just end it. I am tired of this shit." he said holding back tears.

I still said nothing.

"I know you hate me and have every right to, I had no business bringing you out here to this, I was not a man of my word. The brother that is letting me sober up over here is a counselor and will give us a few free sessions if you are open to it." Hakeem asked.

I still said nothing. "Are you there?" he asked.

I waited again before answering and finally said, "Yeah, I am here. I'll think about the counseling and let you know."

I said and hung up. I didn't want him to hear the tears in my voice. I was tired of being emotionally played and manipulated by Hakeem. He knew what to say and when to say it, and I was finally catching on.

# STABBED TO LIFE

I wanted to believe he loved me, but he had a very crazy way of showing it. Being counseled by an Imam or Islamic leader or counselor just seemed a bit bias to me. Especially in a religion where it seemed women were not a priority. Men and women were even separated during church/ Jumma prayer. Maybe this was just my perception, but it certainly seemed that way.

I think based on how quickly I hung up he knew I was in no hurry to talk to nor see him. I was just really frustrated. Even the subtle "I want to kill myself" was no longer effective. I just let that go in one ear and out the other. Why did I even care? Why couldn't I just pack my shit and go back to California? My Mom and Dad would allow me back, no questions asked, but I loved this man. This may even sound sick, but I had this feeling that as soon as I left him he would get it together and turn back to the man I fell in love with.

Well I agreed to the counseling and that really did not go well, I guess I was too out spoken, and during the meeting was told several times to stay in my place. Both the counselor and Hakeem stated that a woman was to obey her husband. Every now and then the counselor would tell Hakeem he should never resort to violence to keep his wife in check, but still.

The man was very nice, and he and his wife were both present, but they weren't ready for our type of problems, this was too much for them. The wife afterwards hugged me and slid me her number and she shook her head. She mouthed to me "Go home…go home…" At least she understood, but she really looked like she was scared for me.

# A. MICHELLE

Hakeem barely admitted to his drug addiction, how was anything ever going to change if he was not going to be completely honest. I felt so defeated. So unheard and so alone. The ride home was even worse. Hakeem was upset that I was telling about how he forced sex on me, that he did Meth and didn't properly care for his children, so I got a massive ear full on the way home. He was trying to be calm, but I already knew the minute we got home we would probably get into some physical altercation. So, I just prepared myself. I wasn't even scared. I just prayed he waited till my children were asleep.

We got to the traffic light just a block from the house and he grabbed me by my hair.

"You like making me look bad huh? You are my wife; did you hear what the brother said? I can do whatever I need to do to keep you in check," He said it with his teeth clinched and his jaw tight.

He was mad because his cover was blown. The men at the Mosque thought very highly of him, but he was exposed now. They didn't even know about his prison stays and I didn't even tell that part he did, but he was mad at me now. I didn't even care.

"Let my hair go Hakeem," I said in a stern voice. Surprisingly he let go of my hair and pulled up in the driveway of the house.

I knew the pattern, it wasn't over. He went in the house, and half ass spoke to my children. They even knew by his greeting there was a problem. Out of respect they still greeted him as he liked with "Walikum Salam."

# STABBED TO LIFE

I motioned for them to go to their rooms and they gathered their homework and went directly to their rooms. Hakeem went up to our room, this was his first time he'd been in the house in about 4-5 days. He had been staying with the counselor from the mosque and his wife. I followed him up, part of me just wanted to get it over with. Let's fucking do this.

"Why are you following me? Something or someone up here you don't want me to see?" Hakeem asked in his paranoid tone. I didn't even respond.

Hakeem looked in the closet and under the bed, and finally looked out on the balcony. Of course, nothing was there. He was a meth addict and part of that was paranoia and hallucinating. I just looked at him and shook my head. Look at my "husband" Wow girl, you should be proud. I laughed in my head. He went through my dirty clothes hamper sniffing my clothes. He went in the bathroom just inspecting everything. I sat on the bed and just watched the foolishness.

My room was immaculate, everything in its proper place super clean the carpet was freshly vacuumed with the lines all going the same way just like he liked it. The bathroom was spotless and smelled like pine-sol. In the past we would get into heated arguments about how the house was kept. He liked that I was clean, but he just had a certain way he liked things done. Never forgetting the number one thing - absolutely no shoes in the house. I continued to sit there on the side of the bed watching him frantically look for something, but I knew he wouldn't find anything.

"Are you done?" I asked rather sarcastically.

# A. MICHELLE

Of course, he didn't say anything because he probably realized he looked like a damn fool. But then again, I was staying with him dealing with this foolishness, so it was I who was the biggest fool. He the shower, so I went down to check on my babies. They were both in their rooms doing their homework. My son always just kept a straight face and never let me see that he was bothered by all this craziness, but my daughter did not hide her expressions. It was very clear she was thinking, "here we go again with this bullshit." Her face said it all, she did not have to utter a word.

I rushed back upstairs, and Hakeem was in his underwear sitting on the edge of the bed. His behavior was becoming more and more unpredictable. I looked to see what his mood was, he had a puzzled look on his face like he wanted to have a discussion but was not sure how to say it.

Finally, I said, "What's up?" I asked in a way that was not kind but not disrespectful either.

"I know you have stuck by me, you have been the most loyal to me, you have been by my side. I have treated you bad, I can't shake these drugs for shit man. I look at your kids and think damn her kids love her and she is dealing with my bullshit. The brother Amir says I am wrong for what I am putting you through, that Allah is not pleased. I want to apologize for bringing you way out here and still not doing right by you" Hakeem explained

I didn't want to be mean, but his apology did not seem sincere, it was almost as if Amir the counselor from the Masjid/Mosque had suggested he do this. Then again maybe he just did not know how to express himself maybe he was embarrassed of his behavior and did not know how to express himself.

"Ok, apology accepted," I said, and I went and took a shower to get ready for bed. When I got out he was still in the same place on the edge of the bed sitting in his underwear, kind of stuck and staring into space.

"Have you met someone since you've been out here?" Hakeem asked in a very low voice.

What? He just apologized for his bad behavior and now this. I didn't get this dude. He knew my every move and knew that I didn't know anyone out here other than my coworkers. I went to Walmart and to Jumma prayer on Fridays. I had to stop going to the gym because he saw people looking at me and he accused me of flirting with people. He said I smiled too much. So where was I going to meet someone?

"No Hakeem, I have not met anyone, why do you ask that?" I said in a very upset tone.

"I don't understand why you stay with me Adrianne. I don't deserve you and because of how bad I've hurt you sometimes I don't think I deserve this life, if Allah did not frown on suicide I would be gone from here," he said with big tears in his eyes. "You deserve better than this."

As mad as I was at Hakeem I hated seeing him down and hurting. The night we spoke with the counselor Amir, he said he thought Hakeem might be Bipolar and suffering depression and the drugs were his way of self-medicating. This was not the first time I heard this Bipolar thing before. Sherry, his children's mother had said the same thing many times, but Hakeem never acknowledged it.

# A. MICHELLE

Amir said that in Islam mental illness was hardly ever talked about and he was trying to get more people to understand that Mental illness was like anything else, if treated you can have a close to normal life.

I reached over and hugged him, and he cried like a baby. He finally laid his head in my lap and sobbed for what seemed like an hour.

"You cannot ever leave me baby. I am going to make all this shit up to you, I promise. I just need you to remember, you're MY WIFE and I will never let you go. Nobody and nothing will ever keep me away from you, do you understand?" he said with a cry in his voice at first, but the end of the sentence was very firm and very clear. He made sure I heard him again.

"Do you understand the love I have for you baby? It's some sick shit," he said again this time making sure we made eye contact with me. "Hey?" he gently grabbed my chin and pulled my face so close to his, our noses touched. "I have 2 strikes Adrianne. I go to prison for 25 to life no matter what I do next." He explained and made sure I understood. He had said this to me before, but this was like another reminder that I'd better think twice about whatever I was going to do. Without saying it aloud, that was a very real threat that said, "I will kill you or hurt you really bad if you ever try to do anything crazy." Since he still held my chin and cheeks he kissed me on the lips.

"I love you." he said.

After that awkward conversation I really did not want to respond to his I love you, but I was afraid not to. He needed me to respond too, so he said it again.

# STABBED TO LIFE

"I love you Hakeem," I said reluctantly, but there was still a huge part of me just as sick as the man I loved. It was weird, and it seemed wrong.

With the way our tri-level house was designed, the kids could barely hear anything going on in our room which was on the top level. Hakeem was in the mood for dancing, as he usually was after an abusive episode. He turned on the stereo, not real loud, but just enough to try and change the mood.

He played Tony Terry's song "When I'm with You" which was a very romantic song. I was not feeling quite romantic right now, but I played a long for the sake of peace and hopefully a restful night. The song played:

**When I'm with you, I wonder why**

**People do stop and stare and smile at us**

**When I'm with you, the sun shines my way**

**Baby, our love reflects its rays of light on everyone in the world**

**When I'm with you**

**It's for real [It's for real]**

**What I feel [What I feel]**

**When I'm with you [You], Hey, hey, hey**

**Uh-huh [Special touch, a warm embrace]**

**A sweet and tender, your smile, whoa**

**Body warm my heart, so pure**

**Chills when I look, look in your eyes**

# A. MICHELLE

Of course, he knew every word to the song and quietly sang along as he danced with me. It would have been beautiful had we not just had the threatening conversation and the fact he was coming down off a drug binge. It felt kind of good to have him hold me in this way. I knew deep down inside he was a kind, gentle soul. He was just plagued with these demons from his past and the addiction. There seemed to be nothing I could do to help him.

The room was dark, and the curtains were open to the deck. The full moon shone so brightly that it lit the room just enough for us to see one another. I also saw the handle of the gun from under the bed. It got to where seeing the guns no longer scared me. When the song was over we laid down and just talked more. He shared that he thought this move to Missouri was not properly thought out. That he came for all the wrong reasons. He told me his plans to stack some money and try to get custody of his kids. He was full of ideas, but this was his pattern. He would come down off the drugs feeling energized and ready to do all this stuff, only now he was doing it so more frequently. There used to be a long period in between each episode, not anymore, they were closer and closer together.

As the conversation went on, the topic of us sending money to his children came up. Keep in mind, I had always told him the importance of this. He was not happy that I said he wasn't doing enough in my opinion. He said he couldn't because he was caring for my kids.

What??? He wasn't doing shit for my kids. My child support still came even though we were in another state. Of course, not willingly, but nevertheless the County garnished the kids' fathers' wages and sent me a check. That money is what I brought clothes and food with.

# STABBED TO LIFE

We had not even been there a whole month yet and I had already received two checks because their Dad was in arrears. So, I wasn't sure where he came up with that one. He was not taking care of my children. Of course, an argument ensued and before you knew it , we were going back and forth. He named the things he did for my kids, I named the things I did for his. It went on for about 45 minutes and next thing he was in my face. So much for the dance and calm conversation. We were now in a heated conversation. That's the one thing I would not tolerate. No one could talk about my kids or my parents.

 I told him he'd better hope and pray that those little girls did not end up like their trifling Mama. I knew I shouldn't have said, but my mouth was vicious once someone said something about my children. This crazy dude picked me up like a rag doll and threw me down the stairs. I ended up in the area a little way from the kitchen and I just stayed there. I mean I stayed there till the sun came up and I heard him leave for work at 4 am.

I gathered all I could fit in my little Honda Accord and got my kids dressed. They thought they were going to school. I said nothing let them get dressed like that's what we were doing. They had their back packs and then they saw all the stuff piled in the car.

"Mama, where are we going?" my son asked

"We're going home baby" I explained. I looked in the rear-view mirror and of course my daughter rolled her eyes and shook her head, but then she smiled. My babies did not want to be there. I really feel they only went to protect and watch over me. They knew things were bad before we left and probably just feared me being in Missouri alone.

# A. MICHELLE

All I remembered was highway 70 to Highway 40 would take us to California. I charged my cell phone pulled out my AAA maps and got on the road. There was only enough room in the back seat for one person, the other side was piled with clothes and other items and the trunk was packed too. I knew I had to go. I was starting to have thoughts of doing something to him, especially when I saw the handle of that gun from under the bed. It was getting bad and I did not need my kids to witness some horrific exchange between us that would traumatize them for life.

The drive would take two days and we would have to get a motel and sleep for the next stretch, at least that was the way I remembered it from my drive there. Me and my brother took turns driving the U-Haul and we made it in a little over 48 hours. I wasn't scared with him, but with it being just me and my babies on this often-pitch-black road, it was a bit scary. Thank God I had a case full of cd's to keep us occupied and my little Honda ran like a champ. It handled that road just fine. I was nervous, but I could not let my kids see it. It was funny yet sad. They began singing a song that they made up when me and their Dad broke up and it was often to subtly remind me, we were going to be ok.

**"Just the 3 of Us…**

**We can make it we try,**

**Just the 3 of us…YOU AND I"**

The song said, "Just the 2 of Us," but they made it fit our situation. It was by Bill Withers and Grover Washington Jr. In between cd's and while filling up with gas they would just break out in song. My babies wanted to go home.

# STABBED TO LIFE

They felt safest around my parents and I had just uprooted them from where they felt the safest. How selfish of me. I also constantly threatened them to not speak on what they heard or witnessed in our home. I was feeling terrible for that because I knew they were often scared for me, even with their father and his abusive ways.

As night fell I looked at my phone to see if Hakeem had tried to call. He hadn't. Maybe he had worked overtime, he often did. Or maybe he just didn't care that we had left. I pulled into a Motel 6 right off Highway 40, close to Texas and got us a room. It was only $39.99 with two Queen beds. It was clean and only 4 cars were in the parking lot. We grabbed our things, and I could not wait to get a shower. Across the way was a burger stand chain that I had never heard of and that too was basically empty. We got showered and went over there and ate. My kids played around, they did not seem upset or anything. Then my phone rang. It was a Missouri phone number, but not Hakeem's.

"Hello," I said in a very low nervous tone.

"Hi Adrianne, this is Aunt Hazel honey, are you and your kids ok?" Aunt Hazel was one of Hakeem's Aunts that had been in Missouri almost all her life. She sounded upset.

"Yes, we are fine Aunt Hazel, what's wrong?" I asked

She explained that the kids' school called her, and she called Hakeem because she did not have my number and at that point, he had realized we had left, and he was distraught and crying. He was in the background asking to talk to me. I refused and told Aunt Hazel to tell him we were fine and heading back to California. She begged me to talk to him and I was proud of myself, because I refused.

# A. MICHELLE

I respectfully told her good-bye. Aunt Hazel was one who told me I should have never left California and drug my kids there when Hakeem was so unstable. I liked her because she always kept it real. Too bad I didn't listen.

I turned the phone off to save the charge and we headed back to the room. We all fell asleep quickly. The room was quiet and peaceful, you could still hear the traffic since we were so close to the highway. The occasional honk of a horn from the big 18 wheelers would make me open my eyes briefly. I thought of Hakeem, I was worried about him. I was concerned that he probably did not take the news of me leaving well, but I was not turning around, not this time.

The next morning, we were up bright and early and back on the road. I was determined to make it back to my parent's house sometime that same day. They were not expecting me, but even when I was at my worse doing the dumbest stuff ever, they never turned their back on me. I knew they would allow me back there, especially with my kids. They adored them. I wasn't sure what I was going to tell them about why I was back. I didn't want to tell them the truth; that Hakeem was on drugs and was physically abusive, that he had thrown me down a flight of stairs. I didn't dare want to say that. I didn't know how long I could keep lying about it.

The drive seemed never ending. In between stopping for snacks, stopping minor disagreements with the kids, we were all getting tired, and then finally we saw a familiar sign that read WELCOME TO CALIFORNIA. For some strange reason LL Cool J's song "Going Back to Cali" was playing in my head.

# STABBED TO LIFE

Finally, another sign that read LOS ANGELES, then COMPTON and finally CARSON. We were almost at my parents' home, and the entire time the cell phone had been turned off. I reached over and turned it on and there had been numerous calls. Hakeem had called, and also my parents. They had pretty much been banned from calling the house, so the cell phone was how they communicated with me. I thought I'd better call them and let them know I was really close by.

"Mom, it's me," I said as soon as she picked up the phone. I could hear the concern in her voice. By now I was sure they thought for sure their daughter had a mental problem.

"Are you ok, where are the kids?" she asked frantically.

"We are right here about to pull up in your driveway," I said in a normal voice, so she would not be too concerned. I really wanted to just break out in tears. I was tired and frustrated. I'd left behind all my stuff besides what I had packed in my car; clothes and other items.

She could not believe we had just come all that way. Just up and left. If she knew the real story she would understand, but instead I made up another lie as to why we abruptly came back. I was tired of lying I swear I was, but I didn't want to look this stupid…again.

My Mom told me Hakeem had been calling all concerned, she said she had asked him had anything happened between us and he said no. He told her "I think she just didn't like it here." He told her my job was calling and concerned and my Mom said he sounded as if he had been everywhere looking for me. Another one of his attempts to make it seem like I was the crazy one, yet through it all I took the blame and said it was me, so he wouldn't look crazy.

259

# A. MICHELLE

Of course, I had to come in and minimize the situation and make it look like it was me to my Dad too. Thank God this time I had no visible marks. The bruises from the fall were under my clothes and every time I breathed, it felt like my ribs were broken. So, I just took shallow breathes to minimize the pain.

I unloaded my clothes and items from the car and while I did that I thought the first thing I better do is call L.A. County about getting my job back. There was no way I was going back to Missouri. I needed to be near family, I needed to be where people loved me, and I needed my kids to comfortable. Although they had only been in Missouri a few weeks, I had been there a few months and it probably would have been nice had I been with a sane, drug-free individual, but with Hakeem it was far too much chaos and drama.

I could tell every time I entered the house or room where my parents were, my Mom was trying to encourage my father not to talk about the situation. She was giving him the evil eye. The look on his face said he had questions, but I guess they were trying not to upset me. However, my father made it perfectly clear, if I went back, I could not take my kids… "over his dead body" and I totally understood.

# CHAPTER TEN

## THE NEW START

Thank God I was allowed my job back, this did not happen often where you were granted a reinstatement with Los Angeles County, but I left on good terms and in good standings, so I was blessed with another chance. I had a friend Rick who had just purchased some income property and needed to rent out a very nice house which was in range with what I needed. He didn't even require a 1st and last rental payment. Left and right I was being blessed to start over again. The only thing I was missing was furniture. All my furniture had been left back in Missouri and me a Hakeem were not on good terms. I had not spoken to him in weeks. When he tried to call, I did not accept the call, or I would just not answer.

The day me and my kids moved in the new house we took a few pots and pans from my mother, some blankets and all our clothes and made pallets on the floor. My plan was to purchase one item at a time. My parents offered to help me, but they had already spent so much on helping me get to Missouri, I dared not ask for or accept more help. I refused and figured I would find a way.

Probably another week had went by and by this time I was tired of living like savage in that nice house without simple amenities. It was hard. Hakeem called, and I answered, he was happy that I answered and started with how sorry he was. He shared that he had to leave the house in Missouri and placed all my things in storage. He asked was I still staying with my Mom and Dad and I explained I had my own place back in the Antelope Valley, but I had no furniture.

"I can bring it to you," Hakeem said quickly. Instantly silence came over the phone. I really did not want to see him. I was too scared to have him around me. I knew him by now and he was so manipulative, he would try to weasel his way back in somehow. I noticed he was like a drug to me. He was addicted to Meth, but I was addicted to him, and codependent. It was not a good idea.

"No, let me call some movers and see what it would cost to have the items shipped back," I said very calmly.

I called 4 to 5 places and all were well over $1000 to move it and I could not afford that. I called Hakeem back and he said he could get the items to me in 3 to 4 days, he was going to rent a U-Haul and bring everything. My kids were glad we would have our things back but was not happy that he was coming to bring them.

I tried to assure them he would only be dropping our things off. Their little faces just instantly became sad. I certainly did not want to upset my children, but I wanted to get my things back. Honestly, I was a little nervous that he would do something to pay me back for just up and leaving him; no warning, just left. I am sure he was furious about that.

We manage to push through a few more days and then on a Friday evening right before it got dark, Hakeem pulled up in a big U-hall truck. He said 3 to 4 days and he arrived on the 4th day. I did not want to look at him, but he jumped out the truck and ran to embrace me.

# STABBED TO LIFE

"I missed you Queen," he whispered in a soft tone his voice cracking like he wanted to cry. My kids stared at him and Alonja gave me the look of death, as if to say don't fall for the bull-shit.

I swallowed hard and gently pulled away from him and smiled. I did miss him. His warm comforting hugs and gentle caress, his slow dances and off-key singing when he was trying to get romantic. But the bad defiantly outweighed the good at this point. We had far more bad days than good. He'd had way too many "high" days than sober days. I knew I should be focusing on that, but he looked pitiful and I felt sorry for him.

We all started unloading the truck. It was all neatly packed as he did everything, neat and organized. All my things together and the kids' stuff was separated and placed where it needed to go. We had the truck unloaded just short of two hours and he set up beds and dressers for everyone. By now it was close to 10 pm.

After we'd finished, Hakeem told me to follow him over to a U-Haul place, any U-Haul place. There was one on Sierra Hwy not too far and he parked the truck and dropped the keys in a slot on the door. He quickly jumped in the car with me and told me to hurry and drive off.

I knew something did not feel right. He told me that he paid for a local truck 3 days ago in Missouri and was supposed to return it to that same location. He paid $27.99 and filled the tank up once. So, I was sure in Missouri they were looking for the truck. I asked if had he used my address or anything connecting me to that truck he looked at me crazy and said no.

# A. MICHELLE

I guess with the truck being dropped off at another U-Haul place it wasn't like he'd stolen it, but he certainly had not paid for it. Oh well, I had my stuff back and that was important. Even more so, my children had their things.

When we got home I explained to the kids that Hakeem would be staying the night, but the next morning I would take him to the airport to go back to Missouri. The kids didn't seem to mind. My son had his PlayStation back and Alonja was getting her room in order. They both thanked Hakeem for bringing their things and said good night. Hakeem's flight was leaving at 9:30 am, so we had to get up super early.

The night was long, we spent hours talking, he was in a very calm state. He was very apologetic as he usually was after every incident. Thank God the stereo was not hooked up or I am sure we would have danced and ended up doing more, but he was very respectful and saw I was not feeling him in that way. However, he still asked.

"So, you gone let me hit that before I go back? " he said comically. "You're still my wife," he said.

"Well I was your wife when you threw me down the stairs too," I smirked.

"Hey baby, I am sorry about that, really I am. That's why I brought your stuff down here, you didn't deserve that, and your kids really didn't need that," he explained

I was over the excuses, I just wanted him to realize I had not forgotten, and I was pissed.

We finally fell off to sleep which seemed like just a few minutes then we were up headed to the airport. He had nothing but a "carry-on" which made it easy to get in the airport. He insisted I waited with him till he boarded the flight.

So, while we waited he pleaded his case all over again. He was sorry, and he wanted to come back. I was his wife. I meant everything to him. I was all he had. I was a good woman. All the bull-shit he had said time and time again after he messed up. I told him my kids no longer needed or wanted this and what they felt mattered.

I also explained I was blessed to get my job back and God had given me another chance I could not mess up. My parents would be so disappointed, again, if I let him come back.

"Babe, at the end of the day this is our life, you've got to do what makes you happy and I know you hate me sometimes, but I also know you love me, and you want me back." He explained

Just as he said that they called his flight number to start boarding his plane. We hugged and embraced for a long time. He went to bite my neck and shoulder and I quickly pulled away. I shook my head no. I needed to make better decisions and place healthy boundaries. I had no clue what those were, but I sure had better learn quick.

"I love you Queen," he kissed my hand. "I'll be back," he said.

I stood there and watched his tall, handsome body disappear onto the plane; watching how he had to duck to avoid hitting his head as he walked.

Damn I wish I could just get over this dude. My entire ride home I thought about him how I wish we could make the relationship work.

# A. MICHELLE

More than anything, I wished he could be forever free and clean from drugs. I knew his thoughts would be more rational and without the drugs it would rid his head of the demons. I even began to think was he still dealing with his baby's mama. How he constantly reminded me I was his wife. As if I had no say in anything. Oh, how he was in my head. But really, I just kept going back to the beginning how he treated me nice and spoiled me and all the flowers. Did he ever mean any of that?

When I finally made it back up the hill, my house looked like a real house with couches and beds and lamps. We had lived without those things for almost 3 weeks. While I was gone the kids tried to get everything in order and it looked nice. The cable guy was coming in a few days to hook up the cable and the internet and in the mean time we watched movies and of course my son played his PlayStation. The block we lived on was pleasant and there was a nice family across the street with kids my kids age. The father was a Probation Officer and the wife was a hair stylist. They were both so sweet. My next-door neighbor had teenagers too. We were only at the point of waiving and short conversation, but I could tell we were going to be ok here.

I noticed some mail was on the counter. A lot of the mail had been forwarded from Missouri and my old address. In the stack of mail was something from DMV indicating my driver's licenses was suspended. I needed to go to court to rectify some outstanding tickets that I had failed to appear for. In addition, something from my finance company for my Honda and Hakeem's truck that I cosigned for. Thank God my job had not found out about all this before rehiring me back, things may have looked much different.

# STABBED TO LIFE

As I opened each piece of mail I was depressed and was trying to figure out how I could I make this right. I got behind on my car  payment because listening to this genius Hakeem I was no longer in California. "Let them find you!"

He'd said that about the tickets too and like a fool I listened to him. Well they found me and was threatening to garnish my little wages and take my car.  How foolish I was to do that. My first thought was to call Hakeem and go off on him, but I needed to own my shit. I knew better but chose to trust him and let him lead our family since he was the man.

I had tons of things to straighten out, I needed to get my life in order. I needed to be a better example to my children. Part of me missed Hakeem and part of me wished he'd just go away, stay in Missouri and leave me alone. But who was I fooling, he was not going to leave me alone, and he'd made that perfectly clear.

Later that evening once we were all in bed, I was lying there watching the 11:00 news and the phone rang. It was Hakeem letting me know he made it back safely.  It had to be well after midnight there and I thanked him again for bringing our things back. He seemed sober, he seemed like he was in a good mood, but for how long?

We talked briefly and of course his last question was, "I love the house, what do you think about me coming back to help you?"

# A. MICHELLE

I paused for a while I started to act like we had a bad connection. I answered, "We'd have to really talk about that and see what that would look like Hakeem, you really would need to show me you have changed. I cannot keep going through this. You take my kindness for weakness and I am tired of that." I said very calmly, yet very stern.

"Well get some sleep, let's talk about it tomorrow. I love you," he said so sweetly as he often did when he was trying to get back in my good graces.

I just hung up the phone. With all the bills laying on the bed with me, tickets and repo threats spread across my comforter, I had way more things to worry about than if he was coming back. At this moment that was the last thing on my mind. I needed to figure out a way to keep my car, I needed to figure out a way to get these bills paid without going to my parents. I could not ask them for anything else.

Just a few months away, I thought, tax time I could pay everything. We were already in November-Thanksgiving was in a few days and Christmas was right around the corner. I knew my parents would make sure my kids had things, but I had better apply for another job. I had done it before. With the holidays it should be easy to pick up some extra work at the mall after my main job with the County. There was always some seasonal employment and I had worked retail before when my kids father slacked on paying child support.

Of course, Hakeem called me like 10 times the next day. I answered twice and let him know I was busy and would call him back. The other times I just ignored the call. I was so frustrated, and he knew I was drowning and had not offered to help with anything.

# STABBED TO LIFE

Why would I want him back? He couldn't give me anything towards this debt some which was his! I was supposed to be eager about him coming back to California? Finally, on the 11th call, I heard him out. It was as if he was in my head and heard everything I was thinking.

"Hey, I wanted to send you a little money to help you with all those bills, I can wire you a couple hundred dollars, it isn't much, but it will help a little. When I get paid on Saturday for this other gig I'll send you some more." Hakeem explained.

I was happy, but I would not allow myself to completely feel it till I had some money in my hand. He asked for the information to send it Western Union which I quickly provided. As soon as I was off the phone with him, I went and picked it up and he sent $300. It was a drop in the bucket to what I owed out, but it was a help. I called my finance company for my car and they said it was too far behind they just needed to know where it was, so they could pick it up. I didn't know what to say. I lied to buy me time and said I was still in St. Louise Missouri.

I was sick, having to be at work hiding my car from the repo man, it was just a matter of time before they would find the car. I took the $300 and put some towards my tickets and signed up for community service to get the amount owed down. Meanwhile driving every day on suspended license. I was able to get a part time job at a boutique in the mall from 6 to closing. I barely got to spend time with my babies and again my daughter was placed with major responsibility no 13-year-old child should be subjected to.

# A. MICHELLE

But Alonja willingly helped without hesitation the best she could with her brother and keeping the house in order. I hadn't shared with my parents all the debt I was in, but they knew I was working my ass off.

Hakeem and I talked daily, but very briefly. I explained that although there was nothing I could do to save my car, his was back in good standing, he was only behind two payments, I was behind four and they were not willing to work with me because I took the care out of the state as if I were running from them.

It was a month since he had brought our things and he did try to help me on a weekly basis which I appreciated, but I was still not wanting him back. Then one Monday evening I was in the garage putting laundry in the dryer and I heard a truck pulling up in the driveway. I knew that truck sound anywhere. Even the distinctive squeak the driver's door made when it was opening and closing.

Hakeem had come, without letting me know, without us discussing further, he just showed up. I took a deep breath and wanted to meet him outside before my kids had to face him. Thank God they were upstairs. I ran outside and there he was. I saw his huge shadow first on the wall near the porch and I turned the corner there he stood smiling with a bouquet of flowers. I put my finger to my lips to tell him to be quiet.

"Shhhhh…" I motioned

"Surprise" he whispered, with this huge grin.

He looked full faced and healthy. He didn't look like he had done any drugs in a long time. Of course, his body was banging.

# STABBED TO LIFE

Even with his coat on you could tell he was back in the gym, but he always did this clean up to mess up. He handed me the flowers and hugged me he held me so tight. I felt so small in his arms. He smelled like he'd been traveling. That old truck had an exhaust leak and he smelled like exhaust. The bed of the truck was full of his stuff and the back of the truck had more of his belongings. He was back, I guess. As I hugged him before we headed in the house I said a quick prayer:

"God you obviously want me to be here for this man, you keep sending him back to me, please let him act right." I silently prayed. As we walked into the house my kids were upstairs and had no idea he was here yet. He took his shoes off at the door and I snuck him up the stairs to my room. Still not revealing to my kids he was there, I yelled to them that I was going to bed and closed my door.

As you can probably imagine the night was very erotic and exotic. It had been a few months since we had been intimate, and if nothing else, I certainly was missing that. He was gentle and loving; no biting or pinning me down as he had done at times, especially if he was under the influence. It was just very romantic and sensual. Gentle forehead kisses and caressing my body like he really loved and missed me.

The next morning the kids knew he was there by then, and although my son did not show whether it bothered him, my daughter was clearly disgusted. We walked down the stairs in robes and Hakeem greeted them both with his Muslim greeting. DeDe returned the greeting, and Alonja did too, barely.

# A. MICHELLE

Later that day when I was alone in the kitchen she looked at me and said, "Mama, please don't let him come back" she pleaded.

My selfish response was, "Look girl, I'm the Mama, if I want him back here he can be here, you just do what you're supposed to do."

Alonja was smart, much smarter than I was at 14, in fact, she was smarter than me then and I was 30 at this point. In my mind I knew something else was going to happen, but at this very moment I was smitten by his overly affectionate ass. His sweet words had me caught up in a romantic fantasy and again his body had me mesmerized. Never had I seen such a chiseled physique, especially on a man that had a drug problem. He always knew how to pull me back in. He was my drug and Meth was his.

Alonja rolled her eyes and headed to her room where she shut the door rather hard and then yelled down "Sorry, I didn't mean to slam it."

She knew I did not play that, slamming doors in my house prohibited. Yet allowing a drug addict to stay was acceptable. Damn I was really screwed up.

Hakeem spent the weeks ahead looking for work and had a couple of side gigs he was able to pick up immediately. In the area we lived construction was booming and since he was a licensed contractor, he always found work quickly. We were back in the gym and back in a cool routine. In the extra bedroom we had was where we made salat (prayer) every morning, I had memorized the call to Adhan (Islamic call to prayer)

# STABBED TO LIFE

Allahu Akbar

God is Great

(said four times)

Ashhadu an la ilaha illa Allah

I bear witness that there is no god except the One God.

(said two times)

Ashadu anna Muhammadan Rasool Allah

I bear witness that Muhammad is the messenger of God.

(said two times)

Hayya 'ala-s-Salah

Hurry to the prayer (Rise up for prayer)

(said two times)

Hayya 'ala-l-Falah

Hurry to success (Rise up for Salvation)

(said two times)

Allahu Akbar

God is Great

[said two times]

La ilaha illa Allah

There is no god except the One God

# A. MICHELLE

Keep in mind all my life I was raised Christian, so when my family had heard I had pretty much converted my religion to Islam, that did not sit well with them at all.

I think this is the point when my family truly felt like I was losing my mind behind this man. They felt that I was being brainwashed. I was covering my head (wearing hijab) only when we went to prayer on Friday's, even though Hakeem would have much preferred, I wear it 24/7. He seemed to be ok with what I was willing to do. I did not wear it to work.

It only took the finance company another month to find my little Honda, and sure enough one day I looked out the window at work and it was being placed on the repo truck. I was so embarrassed. This was the second time a vehicle had been taken from me at work. I made up some lie to my coworkers that I was having it picked up because the transmission was going out. Thank God I had been preparing and stashing some money aside and when I got off work, we went to a private seller that was selling a very clean Cadillac that I paid cash for.

I was back on the road in no time. This car was beautiful. It was a canary yellow Fleetwood Brougham with peanut butter leather interior and woodgrain. Just a pristine vehicle. I loved it and it floated on the road like smooth sailing ship. It was weird because Hakeem acted a little jealous of the car.

Over all, me and Hakeem were doing well, but every day I was looking and anticipating for the bottom to fall out. He had been there almost two months, seemed clean and sober, and back in the gym we had a very strenuous workout regimen to stay in shape.

# STABBED TO LIFE

He was friends with Sol again and they were hanging out from time to time. I guess they had resolved their finance issues. We would even hook up and have dinner with Sol and his new girlfriend from time to time. After our frequent double dinner dates Sol would always give me this look that said, "Sis be careful" It was crazy how everyone had this fear for me, but me. Hakeem's aunt in Missouri would call discreetly to check on me and encourage me to leave Hakeem alone, but I didn't listen.

Although Hakeem seemed sober, he still had this possessive quality about him. He had me weighing in weekly to make sure I stayed between 165 and 170 and if I ever weighed more than that he would belittle me and remind me how he really preferred petite women. He had said that often but always said it in a funny sarcastic way, but I knew he was very serious.

One evening in the gym a man got on a treadmill that was directly next to me, even though there was a row of unused treadmills further down. I instantly looked over where Hakeem was lifting weights and saw him look over at me and the man standing next to me. I knew he did not like the fact that the man was standing next to me. I froze and probably should have moved, but I kept exercising.

Hakeem walked over and wiped sweat as he approached the man. "Hey nigga, you don't see all these fucking treadmills… you got to get on the one next to my wife? Take your disrespectful ass on somewhere," he said gruffly.

The man grabbed his things apologized and moved completely away from the treadmills. I think he even left the building. I was so embarrassed. Hakeem went back to the weights and completed his work out.

# A. MICHELLE

Of course, the ride home he told me that I should have moved away; that I should have known the dude was trying to flirt or get at me. I was beginning to question his whole religious persona. Islam was about love and a lot of the things Hakeem did were not loving at all.

Later that week as I had expected, Hakeem had gotten high. He called me while I was at work and told me to come and get him, that some Mexican's were following him, and they had Sombreros on. He said they were walking on the roof of the buildings. He was so paranoid that he parked his truck and got out and walked. He told me where he was, and I left work looking for him. Just as I expected the red eyes, the smell of hot dogs (meth) let me know immediately he was high.

I calmly asked, "What's wrong?"

He literally pointed to the top of the Post Office on the boulevard and asked me did I see them? He said it was at least 10 Mexican's walking on the roofs of the buildings. He got so enraged that I did not see them that he punched me.

"You fuckin see them, you are trying to make it seem like I am crazy, you are plotting with them" he said. I grabbed the side of my face where he hit me, and I looked at him, I glanced quickly at the back seat to see if there was anything I could crack him across the head with. When I didn't see anything, I just remained quiet and still.

"I thought you was done with that shit." I said, never allowing a tear to fall from my face.

"Take me home!" he yelled.

# STABBED TO LIFE

The ride home he repeatedly accused me of trying to get him caught up and sent back to prison. He was on a good one. I never uttered a word. I pulled up at the house, and he got out, then I turned around and headed back to work. His truck was left on the Boulevard and I didn't care.

I didn't know what to expect when I got home. But when I arrived my dog AK was gone, and Hakeem was not there either. My kids both had had after school things going on, so they were not there. As I walked in the house, I just felt an uneasiness.

I knew I fucked up letting him come back here. I should have refused to let him come and disturb me and my children's peace. Where was my dog? Had he gotten out? I couldn't imagine him being with Hakeem, he didn't even like Hakeem. This poor dog had witnessed do much he was squeamish around Hakeem. Hakeem knew I loved that dog. We'd had him since he was a puppy and believe it or not, he was jealous of the dog too.

I called Hakeem on his cell phone and he didn't answer, I called back to back like 10 times and still no answer. I left a message asking where the dog was, and he didn't call back. The kids were arriving home and still no Hakeem. I fixed dinner we ate cleaned the kitchen and got ready for bed still no Hakeem. I quit calling and could only imagine he was out there doing his thang. It was typical behavior when he was using, not to show up, not to call and acting just weird.

About 2 am I was awakened out of a deep sleep. I heard the front door open because the alarm I had installed had a chiming beep whenever the door was opened.

# A. MICHELLE

It had gotten to where I could tell by the sounds of his footsteps if Hakeem was in a bad mood, if we were going to be fighting, or if it was a pleasant romantic night. These footsteps said fight and danger. It was cold, so I was in bed under a few comforters and I pretended to be sleep. His smell told me even more, he was using.

He walked to the side of the bed and went under the mattress. There he kept one gun that I knew of and then he went under the bed, not sure what he was doing. I continued playing possum but had one eye opened.

"You ain't, sleep get up," he said low but very demanding.

"What?" I replied as if I didn't understand him.

"You trying to make a fool out of me. I think you are in on this conspiracy to get me locked back up," he said.

Since his ex-wife Sherry and other members of Hakeem's family told me he was more than likely bipolar, I had been doing some research on the subject, and sure enough he seemed to have the classic signs of the mental illness and using drugs to self-medicate.

He told me to get up again only this time with the gun pointed at me. When I stood up he saw all I had on was a gown nothing underneath and some socks.

"Go get in the car" he demanded

I was scared. He kept telling me I was his wife and I had better do what he said. He told me he would hurt my kids and kill my parents. He was high. It looked like he had a busted blood vessel in his eye and his lips were chapped. I was trying to distract him and said the only thing that came to mind.

# STABBED TO LIFE

"Where is my dog Hakeem? Did you hurt my dog?" I asked. Probably not the best question to ask but it was the first thing out of my mouth. All I thought about at that moment was getting him out of the house far away from my kids.

He followed me down the steps the gun still pointed at me. It was dark, but I could see the silhouette of the barrel of the gun pointed directly at me. I swallowed hard and moved faster down the steps and out the door. He made me get in the car. The whole time we drove he had the gun in his hand. He was taking me to the middle of nowhere.

On 50th Street East is where we turned, and it was pitch black. It was an area where several farmers grew alfalfa and green onions. He drove in the dirt and then directly in the middle of the crops of onions. The strong smell of onions was almost overpowering.

"Get out bitch.," he said.

I didn't move, so he leaned his long body over me, opened my door and pushed, then kicked me out. Instantly my feet were soaked through to my socks, it was wet, muddy and reeked of onions. He pulled the door closed and sped off leaving me smack dead in the middle of this enormous onion field. I began to try and walk to the paved street which seemed forever.

50th Street East was a street that many used to take as a short cut from Palmdale to Lancaster to avoid traffic, but at 2 am not many cars were traveling down the two-lane road. I was so scared. Was he going home to do something to my children? I'd finally made it to the pavement and was walking toward oncoming traffic. I was on the dirt shoulder flagging people down, but no one would stop.

# A. MICHELLE

I couldn't blame them. I was muddy wet and had only a gown on. I was bare footed and probably looked like a crazy woman. I walked for what seemed like well over an hour and then finally Hakeem pulled up laughing.

"Nobody would help you huh?" he asked with an evil grin on his face. I was shivering and had no feeling in my feet or hands.

"Nobody's ever going to help you, nobody's ever going to want you, just my dumb ass and remember I got 2 strikes, what I got to lose?" Hakeem explained

At that very moment I realized getting away from him was going to be hard and dangerous. I was in love with a man who was mentally ill, a drug addict and a 2-time felon with 2 strikes. He also reminded me that I was all he had. He knew that his family was done with him, so he didn't have anything to lose. He constantly threatened that I had better abide by the rules or I would die, my parents would die, and worse than anything, my children would die. He was very far gone. I needed to end this somehow some way.

He drove me home only to drop me off at the curb and sped off. I felt like I had just been in a dream. It didn't seem real. By now it was close to 4 o'clock in the morning. My kids were sound asleep, I opened each of their doors and made sure their backs were moving so I knew they were breathing. I jumped in the shower quickly washed up and just sat on the edge of the bed wrapped in a towel trying to figure what to do next. Even though I had just bathed I could still smell the onions on me. My whole room smelled of onions. It was awful.

# STABBED TO LIFE

That day, once the kids were up and dressed, I had placed them on the Metro Link which was the train that took you from the Antelope Valley where we lived to L.A. Union station. They were going to spend the Christmas vacation with my parents as they always did. My parents would pick them up at the train station. It could have not come at a better time because I needed to figure some stuff out.

I kissed my babies goodbye and reminded them, as I often did, that they were not to discuss with their grandparents anything that goes on in our house. They were so used to that statement that they finished the sentence before I could get it out. Part of me wanted them to say something but I could help but remember what Hakeem had said… "Nobody will ever help you." That played repeatedly in my head off and on all that day.

While at work I'd never had really confessed to anyone just how bad things were, but today I looked for spiritual guidance from one of my dearest friends Mag. My other friend, Windy was the friend who was like "Let's get this motherfucker!" I appreciated them both.

On this day the only thing I told them was, "If ever one day I do not show up to work, come to my house and check on my kids. I think Hakeem is going to kill me." I calmly explained.

Both were a bit hysterical, but I looked at them both and with tears in my eyes I said very seriously again, "He is going to try to kill me." They began asking a bunch of questions and I just walked away.

I was embarrassed for several reasons. One, was that I was tolerated this bullshit, and the other because I fuckin still smelled like green onions.

# A. MICHELLE

I received a call from Sol and he said Hakeem was staying there and he really wanted him to leave. Sol said he was brandishing guns and constantly walking by the window thinking someone was after him. He told me that he had dropped AK, my dog, at some junk yard and he gave me the address.

I went by there later that day and met the guy that ran the junkyard. I explained to him that. that was my dog. AK's paws were bloody because the area he was in was covered glass, so he had no way of getting around without going through the glass. I told him I was going to call the police if he didn't give me the dog. After some convincing he handed the dog over. Apparently while I was talking to guy running the junk yard someone called Hakeem, and next thing I know Hakeem was there. He pulled up with some white girl. I didn't even care at that point. I assisted AK in the car and drove off.

The white girl and Hakeem started following me. I pulled up in AM/PM, the gas station a few blocks from my house, and the they pulled in right behind me. The white girl got out looking like a hot mess, both tweeking like crazy. The white girl walked right up on me and asked, "Are y'all married?"

"Hell no," I said, looking at Hakeem who looked worse than I'd ever seen him. He was good about his hygiene and grooming, even if he was using, but this day he had on dirty clothes, needed a haircut and a shave, and smelled horrendous.

I just shook my head. He was at an all-time low. He didn't even seem embarrassed about it and the white girl was covered in meth sores. Both looked awfully disgusting.

# STABBED TO LIFE

My dog was barking like crazy. He could sense something was going down. He was so upset he was drooling. Part of me wanted let him out to bite them both but I didn't. Knowing Hakeem, I was sure he was strapped and would have shot my dog.

"I should have a check at the house," Hakeem said.

Then the white girls yelled out "We gonna go get it?"

I didn't have to say a word. Hakeem went in on that ass.

"Look bitch, don't disrespect my wife," he said very aggressively.

The woman was quiet. While I pumped the gas, he got out and sat in the passenger seat of my car. My dog was really going off by then. I calmed him down while I sat there for the longest convincing Hakeem he should leave with the girl, that it was best he stays wherever he was. He said he was leaving with me. He remembered my kids were gone.

"I need to stay at the house and watch you, you can't be home alone." he said sarcastically. I had to leave with him because the white girl pulled off and left him.

When we arrived at the house I thought if I just handed him his mail he would want to leave even if it meant me taking him somewhere. He got comfortable removed his shoes and started doing his paranoid investigation of the house.

Oh my God what was I going to do. I felt so trapped with this man. He sniffed me from head to toe trying to see if I smelled like someone. Did his inspection of the dirty clothes, looking to see if there was traces of any other man, but of course, he was unsuccessful.

# A. MICHELLE

I told myself, I needed to be very nice to him and do everything like he asked so I could be safe. As he got undressed and removed his heavy Carhart jacket, I noticed he had a gun in his waistband and another in the pocket of the jacket. He laid them both down on the dresser then he jumped in the shower, shaved and cut his hair.

I knew the routine now. He was going to try and sex me and dance with me and all that romantic shit and I was supposed to forget about all the stuff he had done. He looked like shit. Sadly, even with his shower, he still stank. Only thing that hadn't changed was the Anaconda, his huge penis. It did absolutely nothing for me today. It didn't arouse me or make me horny and want to jump on him. Instead I went down stairs while he got himself together.

I sat on the couch downstairs watching TV trying to figure out how I could get away. Listening to every move that was going on upstairs. I could tell when he walked in around in the bathroom, I could hear when he sat on the bed. Finally, there was no more movement and I assumed he was asleep. I was certainly hoping so. Anytime he went on a drug binge he slept for days afterwards. I tipped toed upstairs and just as I thought, he was passed out snoring with his hand on the gun.

# CHAPTER ELEVEN

## THE PLOTS, LIES & NIGHTMARES

At this point the longest Hakeem was staying sober was about a week. My kids were only going to be in L.A. for another week, and I wanted him gone before they returned. I knew that was not going to happen. He had pretty much kept me and Sol hostage. He stayed over there some nights or posted upon me other nights.

One night, I happened to be watching TV and there was an infomercial for Crime Stoppers where you could call and anonymously repot a crime. It was on a recording and you were not required to leave a name or any information. On their commercial they claimed that they would investigate all calls. So, I called. I gave them Sols address and told them that there was a man living there that was obsessed with guns, he was schizophrenic and was hearing voices. I reported that he had threated to kill me and my family, I told them occasionally he stayed with me, but I would not leave my address. I shared so much that the recording cut me off, but it said on the recording that it would be forwarded to an officer to investigate. I thought for sure a few days later when he was over there he would be arrested and taken to jail if for nothing else a felon with a gun charge, In his case several guns.

My kids had returned, and Hakeem was still there. I was now without a vehicle. Another one of his ways of controlling me.

# A. MICHELLE

He'd forged my name on my pink slip for the Cadillac and sold it. I was totally dependent on him taking me to and from work or calling a cab which I had to do many times. I was still working, and working an extra job, so thank God one of my coworkers that lived in Palmdale would drop me off at the mall after work. I just had to figure out a way home every night. Usually a coworker on my extra job that lived near me would drop me off. I was lying again about why I had no car not wanting to disclose this fool had sold my vehicle.

One day out of the clear blue Hakeem came to me apologizing. "Babe I am sorry I have caused you and your kids so much drama, we should go to counseling, I think I am finally ready to get my life right and get off these drugs." He said. It sounded like the 15 other times he had apologized. I got to where I no longer argued with him, I shook my head in agreement to everything he said. He was a ticking time bomb and I had no clue when he would explode. I had to keep cool for my kids.

"I know I have said all this before, but during my prayer today Allah spoke to me and said I am not a good Muslim if I was doing drugs and tormenting my wife," Hakeem explained.

In my mind I was thinking what a hypocrite he was, how he was making salat (prayer) 5 times a day, so he claimed, and sometimes under the influence of methamphetamine. To keep the peace, I still went to Jumma every Friday. Even still participated in the intimacy part of this dead-end relationship. I did that too, even when I didn't want him anywhere near me. I no longer liked it and when he was high it was just brutal, long, sick and painful.

# STABBED TO LIFE

I told him I would call Kaiser and try to set up some counseling for him. He insisted it be couples counseling. I agreed to call and set up an appointment.

Before we could even make it to the first appointment, we had to cancel because and argument ensued. I needed a ride to the store which he gave me, allowed me to grocery shop for over $200 dollars' worth of groceries, and never came back to get us. I had me and my kids pushing two full carts of groceries for 8 blocks. When I arrived home, he was asleep, and I assumed he slept through my 20 calls. I waited to address the issue after my kids were down for the night.

"Hakeem you forgot we were getting groceries and didn't come back and get us? We ended up walking home with all those groceries," I said it calmly but clearly, I was upset.

"Well, all of you can use the exercise," he said sarcastically and giggled

"Please don't put me, and especially my kids, in that position ever again," I said as nicely as I could considering I was pissed off even though hours had passed since we'd arrived home. How dare he sell my vehicle, have me solely dependent on him, and then leave me and my kids stranded. He had pulled the same type thing at the Gym, left while I was working out and never came back to pick me up. Just some dope fiend shit. I had to have my landlord come pick me up. Of course, I had to make up some lie as to how I ended up stranded at the gym. I think I told him Hakeem had broken down and had no way to come get me. My landlord never liked Hakeem and like many people always whispered or got me in private and asked, "why do you deal with this mess?"

# A. MICHELLE

So, the argument about the leaving us at the grocery store got heated and he yelled, "Yo muthafuckin kids needed to walk and so did you, so shut up about that shit!"

Before I knew it out of my lips came, "Fuck you , you crack head!"

He socked me so hard it knocked me out. There was literally a period of darkness and I didn't even remember hitting the ground. When I came to, he was standing over me telling me to get my punk ass up. My nose was bleeding, and my lip was busted. I wanted to take off on him and hit him as hard as I could, but I knew that would make matters even worse.

In the beginning I had always fought back, but I had no fight in me any longer. His obsession with the guns and the many times he said he would kill me just forced me to try and keep the peace and take his shit.

It took me a week to heal from that incident. I had gotten so good with being able to camouflage my wounds. Cheap make up and lies got me through questions at work when people suspected something. All I wanted now was to get him out of my life. There had to be some way. I needed to lure him out of my home, away from my children. I needed him gone. I began having an ongoing dream some might call a nightmare where I killed Hakeem.

*The counselor stopped me and suggested I get up and take a break. I had to admit, sitting down and sharing my entire story was having a traumatic effect on me. I went to the restroom, washed my face, and brushed my hair into place. I stopped at the vending machine for a bottle of water and felt much better when I sat back down. I continued....*

# STABBED TO LIFE

In one of my dreams, I somehow poisoned Hakeem and cut his body up in several pieces and buried him all over the desert. Nobody ever found out and I lived happily ever after. I dreamed this dream so often that one day I am not sure if I had said something out loud, but I woke up to Hakeem over me saying, "You know you could never kill me, right? You bet not ever try that shit either." He said this as if he could hear the thoughts in my head.

This dude had me spooked and going crazy. He was in my head so badly. I was beginning to be paranoid too. My friends got to where they no longer felt comfortable going to lunch with me because we would leave the restaurant and he'd be lurking in the parking lot or drive through real fast like he was trying to hit me, then he'd laugh.

This dude was getting sicker by the day and I had this fool around my kids daily. I was starting to get so scared that I called his mother, who I barely spoke with and I told her some of the things going on. She said well he's probably not on his meds and self-medicating. Again, I was hearing this description of mental illness and yet no one enlightened me or told me much more than that. His mother's words were menacing and insensitive.

"That is your husband, handle it... but don't let him come back out here, I do not want to deal with that."

She knew something was wrong with her son. She knew he had a drug problem. She knew he had some childhood demons and traumas and she just let him destroy other people's lives as well as his? She was just turning her back on him? I could not get over the fact that she was just so cold about it.

# A. MICHELLE

Then again, he was grown ass man and had probably burned every bridge with everyone in his family. It certainly seemed that way. Sherry, his ex-wife, was the only one who acted as if she cared about him and that was just so strange to me since he was so abusive to her. I won't lie, in the beginning, I felt like she just wanted my man, but the way I felt today, I wish she'd just come get him.

Every day was scary. I was literally walking on egg shells. Somedays he was kind and decent, others he was just a demon-possessed, paranoid, addict who thought people were out to destroy him or take him for all he had. He was now reduced to nothing but a work truck and firearms. His looks had faded. His beautiful green eyes were almost always accompanied by bloodshot sclera. The part that was supposed to be white was always red which made him look so evil. I found out that this happened when meth was snorted. If he smoked it, that did not seem to happen. His face was sunken in. He kept a hat on all the time because he would not shave, and you could see his cowlicks and balding head. His clothes that he used to be so particular about, ensuring they were ironed or pressed, were just thrown on with no effort to look presentable.

I had no clue what he did all day. Somedays I would leave, and he would be digging in the back yard. I'd come home 8 hours later he'd still be digging and messing around in the backyard, but nothing ever looked any different. Just weird stuff.

I came home one day, and he had literally moved out of our bedroom and into the prayer room. He had a mattress set up in there and that was where he slept. Since the onion field incident, I no longer slept without having on a sweat suit and shoes and socks. I slept fully clothed.

# STABBED TO LIFE

I just never knew what to expect. I was tired of living like this, and even worse the dreams and thoughts of doing something to him was in my head way too much.

One day my Mom called, and she was upset like she had never been before.

"I need to talk to you about my grandkids Adrianne!!!" she said very harshly. This tone from my mother was not common, she always remained calm even in the most trying times. Her demeanor was way different. She was angry, she was pissed.

"Yes Mom, what's wrong?" I asked.

"I need you to get my grandkids out of that bullshit or I am calling CPS on you!!!"

Silence came over the phone. I had heard her, but I had to let it sink in. My Mom was going to call CPS on me? I still said nothing. I was crying by now and apparently based on her tone, my children had told her something. These last few years I had been threatening them that they better not mentioned anything that was going on in my home, but someone had said something. I could not be mad. My children were tired of the craziness too. They wanted this to come to an end.

"Did you hear what I said Adrianne? " she asked again in a very stern voice.

"Yes, Mama, I heard you," I said in a very low, respectful voice. I knew it was time to end this. I was just scared. She slammed the phone down and said nothing more and did not call back.

# A. MICHELLE

My kids acted funny and nervous the rest of the night. I did not lead on that I knew they'd said something to their grandmother whom they absolutely adored. They loved their Mudder and PawPaw. They were the most stable example they had in their lives. My poor babies were trying to save me, from myself and from Hakeem. They must have known I felt trapped and stuck.

I made up my mind I was going to talk to Hakeem and insist that he leave, so I would not lose my children. He was out in the garage sitting with the garage door up. It was weird because as I sat next to him the street light directly across the street began to flicker on and off. It was almost like a sign from God.

I had misinterpreted God's signs before thinking I was supposed to stay with Hakeem when I knew God meant the opposite. I was trying to make it fit my agenda. God did not want me trying to fix this man. That was his and Hakeem's job, and this is where I finally got to step off. Although very reluctant and fearful of the outcome, I just said what I needed to say.

"Hakeem, this is not working anymore. I can no longer expose my kids to this. My mother knows everything and is threatening to report me for child endangerment. We need to end this. You have to go in the morning." I said very calmly.

Part of me wanted to cry. I had never meant something so much in my life, and although I was blaming it solely on my mother's call, truth be told, I'd been needing to do this for a very long time.

He did not respond immediately. Two or three minutes went by before he uttered a word.

# STABBED TO LIFE

He just kept sipping on his water bottle. Finally, a "Hmmmm" came from his body and he looked at me so hard with his lips tightly clinched. His eyes felt like they were staring deep into my soul.

"I ain't going nowhere" he said very calmly making direct eye contact, "I've told you that time and time again.'

Firmly I said, "You've got to go in the morning."

I got up and went in the house. I thought he was going to be right on my heels following me in the house. Instead, he sat there calmly and did not move. An hour passed by and I peeped out there and he was still there in the same spot.

I got ready for bed, in my grey sweats, sports bra and t-shirt and sat my Nike air max tennis shoes right next to the bed preparing for a physical altercation that never happened, at least not right then.

I finally heard him come in and close the garage and go in his room and close the door. It was way past his normal prayer time, but I heard him praying. I tried hard to go to sleep but I was scared.

Before long the sun was coming up and it was a work day for me. It was late August, so we often woke up to sunny blue skies in the high desert. This day was just like that. I heard no movement in Hakeem's room. Apparently, I had slept through his 1st prayer because it was complete silence. His room was right across the hall from our normal room, so any movement most of the time I could hear.

I did not know what to expect today, so I did like I always did. I made his breakfast 3 sausage, 3 pancakes and three over easy eggs and took up to the room.

# A. MICHELLE

I knocked first, and he told me to come in. I handed him his plate and before leaving I said, "Remember what we talked about last night. You must leave today Hakeem." I said it softly and my voice cracked and trembled in fear. I had never been this firm before, but I had to do it.

He continued to eat his food, paused briefly and looked up at me with the scariest smirk on his face.

My kids were out of school this day, still on summer vacation, so I had not awakened them. I finished getting dressed for work and went down stairs putting a few dishes in the dishwasher when Hakeem handed me his breakfast plate. It startled me because normally I could hear him come down the stairs , but this time, he just popped up. I swallowed hard and I didn't want to say it again, but I had to let him know I meant business. Up till now he said very little, so I didn't know if he took me seriously or not, but either way, he had to go today.

"Hakeem, when you drop me off to work you're welcome to take whatever you want, just please let's get this over with and be gone when I get back, please." I pleaded.

"I told you, I ain't going no muthafuckin where, so quit talking about that shit. You in a hurry to move somebody up in here or what?" he asked, by now his voice was raised and he'd become very irritated.

"Hakeem you got to go," I said as I walked over to the phone. I could see his eyes get big. He wasn't sure what I was doing. He had not seen this side of me. I had never called the police and he had always reminded me of his 3 strikes and involving the police could send him to prison for 25 years to life.

# STABBED TO LIFE

So, I asked him. "Are going to get out of here today, or, do I have to have the police to help me?"

The police had not helped me in my first marriage even when they had been called by neighbors. My experience with the police and abusive relationships was that they never did anything.

I grabbed the phone and pretended to call 911, Hakeem grabbed me in my throat to strangle me, but I had no one on the phone. I could feel he was trying to make me pass out as he had done several times. He squeezed harder and my eyes began to roll back in my head. This time I did dial 9-11 and he heard the dispatcher say, " 911 what's your emergency?"

He let go of my throat and grabbed for the phone. He got a hold of the phone from me and thought he hung it up, but he didn't the line was still open, and the dispatcher was still on the line. I tried to run from Hakeem and his long arms caught me. I thought he was punching me in my sides but as I flailed and thrashed trying to get out of his grasp, I saw my own blood spurting onto the refrigerator on the floor where we almost were slipping in it.

This was when I realized he was stabbing me. I felt short of breath but managed to bellow out a scream for my daughter. "Alonja help me…he's stabbing me!" I screamed with all I had. I saw the knife going directly for my face and held my hand up.

I could see the blade of the knife come all the way through my hand and out the other side. He sliced my neck and hit my carotid artery. Every time I took a breath blood just squirted everywhere.

# A. MICHELLE

My daughter made it down the stairs and saw the horrific scene and she started screaming for Hakeem to stop. Then Alonja literally started hitting him and then placed her body in front of his to shield me and make him stop. All while screaming, "Leave my Mama alone!!"

He finally stopped. He went out the door and all I could think of was that he was going to get one of the many guns he had around the house and kill us all, so I staggered out the door to try and protect my children. I was covered in blood and felt as though I was drowning, I could not breathe. I looked across the street and my neighbor who was the Probation officer was mowing his lawn and could not hear me screaming.

I think he saw me collapse on the front lawn and rushed over to help me. By then I was going in and out of consciousness. Alonja stayed on the phone with 911 explaining to them what was going on. They instructed her on how to help me. The neighbors were also on the phone with 911. I could hear the commotion, but it was like I wasn't there. Every time I closed my eyes I felt like if I just relaxed, I was going to die.

One time as I opened my eyes I said to my daughter who was covered in my blood. "Alonja, I'm dying…"

I remember everyone kept telling me to stay awake, but I could not keep my eyes open. This time when I closed my eyes I felt like I was in a black tunnel or hole and I could vividly see my life going in slow motion. I could especially see my kids' lives playing in my head. I was literally fighting to stay alive. I remember begging God silently to let me live. I remember making a deal, a pact that if he'd let me live I promised to help others.

# STABBED TO LIFE

I knew God had the final say. He had given me many opportunities to leave the situation and I chose not to. I felt a tugging on my body much like the many physical altercations I had been in, but I was not just going to give in. If it were just me maybe, but I had to fight for my kids. I was all they had.

The sun shined so warmly and brightly that whenever I opened my eyes, I was blinded by the rays of sunshine. They were directly in my face like the light others have always described when they are dying. This must be that light, but I didn't want to go.

They landed a helicopter in the parking lot of the school down the street which was out for the summer session. The EMT's, paramedics, firemen and police officers rushed me aboard the Life Flight and they finally carted me off to a Trauma center in the San Fernando Valley.

I remember feeling a cold breeze on my body and looking down in the bottom of the helicopter. I could see my own blood starting to puddle in the bottom of the helicopter. They were still desperately trying to get me to stay awake.

While I was being flown to the hospital my children were being cared for by helpful neighbors, friends, coworkers, police and paramedics, but they were hysterical and afraid.

My Dad called to tell us good morning unbeknownst to the tragedy that had just unfolded. Just as my son answered, the police screamed for him to get out of the house.

"Paw-Paw the police are making us get out of the house, Hakeem just stabbed Mama and they took her to the hospital!"

# A. MICHELLE

My parents lived in L.A. and we were in the Antelope Valley which meant we were about one hour and 30 minutes apart. I was told my Father hysterically explained to my Mother what had happened, and that Hakeem had taken his knife and rinsed it off at the neighbor's house and sat on the curb. He calmly waited for the police to arrive. He was immediately arrested and placed in the back of the police car.

My children were photographed, and our house, which was covered in blood, was now a crime scene wrapped in yellow crime scene tape. Had I never mentioned to my best coworker friends Wendy and Maggie that my life was in danger, I may not be alive today.

I am glad I told them that if there were eve a time I did not show up to work for them to call the police and check on my children, because I'd probably be dead.

Being the loyal friends, they were they did just that. They later told me they hit the corner on two wheels and lost it when the yellow tape was everywhere. They were told by police that it wasn't likely I'd survive. I had been flown to a Trauma center by helicopter fighting for my life.

I can only imagine the chaos. My family members all the way in Los Angeles finding out the way they did, were probably nervous wrecks, I felt so bad for them. All my thoughts were foggy because I was in and out of consciousness.

I recall the helicopter landing and from the corner of my eye I could see mountainous terrain, and the loud sound of the Medi-Vac. Everything was moving so fast. Then suddenly, there were huge bright lights, people talking, and I could hear a heart monitor. The beeping noises were

# STABBED TO LIFE

inconsistent as my heart struggled to beat. The beeps sometimes went from fast and strong to faint and slow.

Then a searing pain that would wake the dead came over me. Both my lungs had been punctured when Hakeem stabbed me, and it caused both my lungs to collapse. When I laid in the grass earlier, the feeling of drowning was because I was literally drowning on my own blood.

The only way to fix this issue was the doctors and trauma team had to use chest tubes to drain the blood and fluid off my lungs. This was probably the procedure that brought me back to life because it literally felt like someone was ripping through my flesh and reaching through my rib cage.

Shortly after that everything went black again. I wasn't sure if I had passed out, but the next time I opened my eyes, a Nun was standing over me praying. The trauma center they had taken me to I later found out was a catholic hospital called Holly Cross Providence Hospital in Mission Hills. Mission Hills is a part of the San Fernando Valley a northern portion of Los Angeles County.

This hospital was a well-known Level II trauma center and the only place really equipped to handle my situation. The tendons in my right hand had all been severed. I could not move any fingers because nothing no longer connected them to my wrist. I remember the doctors yelling to me "Adrianne move your hand…can you move your hand?"

I tried must nothing moved. I felt weak and like I was dying. I remember asking one of the paramedics on the ride was I going to die, and she said we are going to do everything we can to help you, but you must stay awake. I felt like I was fighting to stay alive. Although my body was still and immobile, my insides were rushing and fighting to not be taken away from my children, to not hurt my parents yet again. So, I fought with all my might.

I woke up from a very deep sleep not even realizing where I was. I could hear the beeping sound again and I realized it was a heart monitor. This time it sounded stronger and steadier. I looked around the dimly lit room and down at my arm. I had a cast on my arm from my shoulder to my wrist. My arm felt weird and my hand ached. The nurse later came in and told me I was in recovery. I had to have surgery on my neck to repair the carotid artery and a surgery to repair the severed tendons in my hand. The room felt cold and the nurse came in with warm blankets.

Tears formed in my eyes as the morning's events came rushing back to my mind.

"How did I get here? I played back my relationship with Hakeem in my mind from start to finish. He loved me, how could he do this to me? In front of my babies?

*I was crying and shaking as I recounted waking up in the hospital after being nearly stabbed to death by Hakeem. The counselor allowed me to sob silently for a moment, before handing me more tissue.*

*"We have about 15 minutes left, Adrianne. Would you like to finish your story, or would you feel better coming back next week and maybe picking up where you left off?*

*I shook my head vehemently. I was determined to get this out....*

# CHAPTER TWELVE

## THE HEALING PROCESS

## & THE EMOTIONAL ROLLERCOASTER

I still was in shock that this had happened, even more in shock that my parenting was being questioned by Child Protective Service (CPS/ DCFS). They had opened a case and sent a social worker to investigate me and interviewed my children. I guess they thought I was a bad parent. I felt like my children were well behaved, dressed nice, clean and had everything they needed. Why were they questioning if I can care for my children? Apparently, the conversation did not go in my favor when they spoke to my kids. The lies were all coming to the surface, everyone now knew the craziness going on in my home. I was embarrassed and ashamed and had the nerve to have an attitude. They were trying to help me, and I was not being completely honest nor cooperative. It was as if they could see through my story, no matter how much I lied or still tried to minimize what Hakeem had done over the years.

I was transferred to another hospital closer to my parents' home. I had had surgeries and chest tubes removed and my hair was shaved off on one side because I had been stabbed in the head too. I was stapled and stitched in so many places, I looked like the bride of Frankenstein. The arm with cast that I had on barely had feeling in. The doctor said I was going to need extensive physical therapy and possible plastic surgery for some of the areas I had been cut especially on my neck.

With all this going on I was still thinking about what was happening with Hakeem. I knew he was in jail and I knew that he was initially under the impression I had died, and he thought he was going to be charged with murder. The detective that was assigned to the case was a very nice man who explained everything to me. He shared how the initial interrogation went, and he said when he told Hakeem that doctors thought I wasn't going to make it he cried hysterically and nearly passed out.

Hakeem told the detectives that he "blacked- out" and he just could not imagine me being with someone else, so he snapped. He was upset that I was trying to end the relationship. He was honest and told him about his drug use.

The entire time the detective was telling me this I was not sure why, but I felt sorry for Hakeem. Here I was recovering from him trying to kill me and I was feeling sorry for this fool. I went through a range of emotions from one minute to the next. From angry to sad to guilty. I was all over the place. When I finally saw myself in the mirror I went into a deep depression. I had no hair on the right side, my scalp stapled together, and it was swollen and puffy. I cried and never asked to look in the mirror again while I was hospitalized.

The look on everyone's face that came to visit me in the hospital was horrific. I guess I appeared to be a combination of unbelievable, pitiful and shame. I was happy God saved me as I asked, but I was so embarrassed. There were days I wanted to refuse visitors because I just felt like a freak show. Every day I asked myself "what now?" "Where do I go from here?" and sadly "Was Hakeem ok?"

I ended up hospitalized a little short of a month and then was released to my parents' home. My children were also in my parents' custody till CPS completed their investigation. They were concerned mainly that I had my children in a home with a known felon who had an arsenal of weapons which included guns some that were military assault rifles. I also allowed him to stay in my home knowing he was addicted to methamphetamine and would get extremely violent. How was I going to care for them properly when I could not keep myself safe?

I was constantly consumed with what was going on with Hakeem. The detectives kept me abreast of what was happening the entire case.

Hakeem was being charged with attempted murder, corporal injury on a spouse, felon with fire arms, assault with a deadly weapon, felony domestic violence amongst other charges. I believe there were 12 in all.

It had been a little over a month and I hadn't heard from any one of his family members, not even Sol. The day had finally arrived for me to go home. I had no car and had to be driven back up to Lancaster by my mother. I felt bad because it was tough right now for my Mom. Right before I was stabbed my father had been diagnosed with congestive heart failure. My time at her house she was playing nurse to both of us. I felt she could not wait for me to go home, but truthfully, she loved catering to the both of us, but I could still tell she was tired.

# A. MICHELLE

When we arrived at the house, I did not know what to expect. The detectives told me a bio hazardous team/crime scene cleanup crew came in and cleaned up the bloody mess and my coworker friend Gladys came and finished.

The house was spotless when we arrived. Hakeem had sold so much out of the house due to his addiction and his paranoia of me taking his things, the house just seemed eerie and empty. A nervousness came over me when I entered. There was a skylight at the top of the stairs and the sun had to be directly over it at that time because the bright light just blindly shined through it. It reminded me of the way the sun shined on me when I laid in the middle of the grass fighting to stay alive. The house was so quiet, clean and empty. My Mom kept looking at me to see how I was handling this all.

I whispered to reassure her, "I'm ok Mom," I said softly.

I went upstairs, and it felt as if strangers had been all through my things. The room Hakeem was occupying was empty except for a few things in the closet. All his papers, letters, bills, etc. were gone. The detective had let me know to expect things to look a little different because it was a crime scene they had to go through a lot of things in the entire house. I ran to my room to see if the knife I had always kept between my mattress was there and it was gone. I guess things would never feel the same again in this house, but at least I could relax knowing he was in jail.

My mother was tired, and she needed to get back to my father. She called him to check on him several times and although he was glad she could come with me, he needed her and depended on her so much.

# STABBED TO LIFE

Seeing the way my Mother catered to my Father gave me a glimpse of where I'd gotten my sense of what a woman was supposed to do for her man. She waited on him hand and foot.

Before we had left to take me back home my Dad offered to buy me a car again. Hakeem had taken both my vehicles and sold them. My Father didn't want me without a vehicle, but I refused. I was in debt to my parents so much as it was. The move to Missouri had cost a pretty penny and all the many other things I needed help with during this horrific ordeal with Hakeem. I figured between my friends, buses and trains I'd make a way. I just could not ask them for anything else. My pride would not allow me. I felt like I got myself in this craziness and I needed to figure it out.

I walked my Mom to her car, she had tears in her eyes, and I am sure it hurt her to leave me in that house where all that shit had occurred. I hugged and kissed her and thanked her for everything. I stood there and watched her drive off. I couldn't help but look at the spot in the grass where just a month ago I laid fighting for my life. I walked along the sidewalk and could see the dried blood. I wondered at that moment was that why tears filled my Mom's eyes, maybe she had saw the blood too.

I followed the blood trail each drip up the driveway, down the driveway and down the sidewalk again ending in my next-door neighbor's yard. Just following that trail, I began to shake and sweat, I felt like I was having what people described as a panic attack. I could hear my heart beating fast, and I had to stop and go back in the house. I sat at the bottom of the stairs still in disbelief that this all had occurred. I felt like I was in a dream or as if I'd just been in a horror movie, it was unbelievable. The silence in the house was killing me. My kids were staying with friends and were being dropped off later today.

There was complete silence in the house, I even did something I never allowed. I opened the door to the backyard and let AK my Pitbull come inside. He hesitated at first because him coming in the house was forbidden, but he was so happy to see me, it was as if he knew something was different. He sniffed my cast and tried to lick my face he was so happy to see me. I hugged his neck and he wagged his tail and his whole body wiggled with excitement.

Just as I got him calmed down the phone rang. I saw the phone blinking from many messages that had been stored. I am sure so many people had been calling to check on me or to see what had happened, but when I got close to the phone the caller ID read "Los Angeles County Jail."

Now I was nervous. I was curious as to what Hakeem had to say. Surely, he was sorry for what he did, especially from what the detectives had shared, that he nearly fainted and cried like a baby when he thought I was dead. I had to answer it.

"Hello" I said in a very soft voice, the operator asking if I would accept a collect call from and inmate from County Jail…I reluctantly accepted.

"Adrianne?" Hakeem said as if he were shocked to hear my voice. His voice sounded raspy and dry.

"Yes, this is me Hakeem," I said still in a soft quiet voice. It seemed weird to be talking to him and it seemed wrong, just wrong.

# STABBED TO LIFE

"They are trying to strike me out for this shit , I might go to prison for the rest of my life. You should have just taken your ass to work that day and none of this shit would have happened!" he yelled.

He said much more, but I did not pay attention. I was just shocked that he came at me like that. No remorse, no concern about my children, only concerned about the time he would get for almost killing me. I let him rant and continue to talk crazy and finally I just hung up. How dare him, fuckin crack head bitch. Ooooh God help me. I was livid.

All I had done for this man, I tried to help him. I tried to be a good wife and a friend. I tried to give him good advice. I tried to guide him in the right direction. I tried…To FIX HIM. After I hung that phone up I sat there for a minute staring at it hoping it would ring again, thinking he may call right back and apologize. I took a deep breath after about 10 minutes and just started cleaning my house.

After about an hour my children came home. They were so happy to see me, and we sat down and watched a movie and made some popcorn. They seemed at peace, so relaxed not all tensed up. It was weird, they seem to always be whispering before to avoid waking or disturbing Hakeem. Now they could be themselves. I couldn't help but think they did all that to protect me. To avoid Hakeem from yelling at me about them being too loud. What a jacked-up way to live. What had I done to my children?

Hakeem did try calling again, and I'd be lying if I said I didn't accept his calls. I did listen to his cries and lies and whines. He finally did say he was sorry and said all he could think about was me being with someone else.

He kept telling me I didn't have to testify against him because I was his wife and I should just refuse when it was time for court. He had his mother call me and she had the nerve to ask me to help her pay her phone bill which Hakeem ran up with the constant collect calls.

She said, "Your husband ran up my phone bill and I am going to need help with it." She said this in the funkiest, nastiest tone ever. She never once asked about my children either, nor did she ask how I was recovering.

I was back at work, but I had to go to Downey which was an hour away every other week for treatment by the plastic surgeons who were trying to help me get rid of the massive keloids that had formed on some of my injuries. It was a very tedious painful process that required them to inject every wound and I had over 18 of them. Not all developed keloids but most did, and this process was painful. I couldn't drive because my hand didn't work, nor did I have a car, so I took the Metro Link train and would meet my mother to take me the rest of the way to the appointments. I was lucky to have the weekly physical therapy sessions up in the Antelope Valley where I lived.

This issue had turned my life completely upside down. Me and my children constantly relied on rides, public transportation, and walking to and from the grocery store. I finally took my parents' offer and accepted the help for a car. I paid the monthly payments and they financed it in their name till I was in a better position. I so appreciated my parents.

# STABBED TO LIFE

I had found a used 95 Impala SS, which was my dream car. It had low miles, pristine condition and the seller made me promise I would take good care of it.

He had already had 3 of them and his wife insisted he get rid of one. I loved that car, it was beautiful and fast.

I knew it was wrong for me to talk to Hakeem. I didn't let anyone know I spoke to him. I was embarrassed that part of me felt responsible for him being in jail. I constantly played back in my head that day and maybe I should have just gone to work. I questioned everything I did, but nothing justified him stabbing me, right? I was so confused.

The story had made headlines on the front of the Valley Press our local newspaper and on the news. The Montel Williams Show contacted us, they were doing a show titled "Heroic things Children Do" They wanted to meet my daughter and have her share the story of how she saved my life that day.

During this same time the District Attorney was preparing for court and after accepting the invite to New York to be on the Montel Williams Show, she advised me that it might not be a good idea to go but kept saying, "It's up to you." Well the show told me my daughter would get scholarship money, so I agreed.

Everything was happening at once. Preparing for court and preparing for New York to film the Montel show. I remember preparing my suit case and still taking clothes like I was practicing Islam;  long skirts and turtle necks. The turtle neck covered my worse scar though. The forecast for New York was chilly so we packed accordingly.

# A. MICHELLE

The more I looked at my daughter, the more I realized I needed to testify against Hakeem. I don't know how I even 2nd guessed it. She had risked her life to help me and how could I even consider not testifying? He was still all in my head.

His letters were syrupy sweet and said all the familiar things he said when he was trying to get back in good standings with me. I was almost allowing this even from jail. I had to stop the contact. I needed to put a complete end to the craziness and the manipulation and the mind games. His letters were talking about how he was so mesmerized by the sexual relationship that it made him crazy.

He began sending explicit drawing of what he said was me and him drawn in very detailed positions and graphic details of explicit sexual positions. It was a little uncomfortable, but I did reflect a bit and had to shake that out of my mind as well.

He knew what he was doing, and he knew how to draw me back in, even from jail. I felt sick that I was so easily manipulated and controlled by him. I was like a damn puppet. I had to fight the thoughts. How could I even almost dismiss what he had done to me, my family and my poor children? I was sick too and I needed to heal. I needed to recognize this was just a part of his sick game to get over on me, to get me to not testify. I had to literally keep talking to myself. Someone on the outside looking in would think " Damn…he tried to kill you, what's so hard ?" But it was hard.

# STABBED TO LIFE

He'd misrepresented himself, he'd betrayed me and the more I think it about it, it started early. I thought of this song by Stevie Wonder called Rocket Love:

**You took me riding in your rocket, gave me a star**

**But at a half a mile from heaven you dropped me back**

**down to this cold, cold world.**

He made me feel he was coming into my life to make things better, when in fact he made it way worse, He knew I had just gotten out of an abusive relationship, he knew my kids had suffered and look what had happened. Now, they really have suffered. At the end of Stevie Wonder song, Stevie says **"I would not do that to a dog."** This man, who I thought was my Knight in shining Armor, that had come to protect me, did just the opposite. But like a drug that I knew was bad for me I kept chasing him, hoping to feel like I did in the very beginning.

The Montel Show was awful in my opinion. It made me look foolish. I was being honest, but when I finally saw the episode air, I looked so dumb. Montel drilled me with questions and even without trying, I was still making excuses for Hakeem. It turned from honoring my child for her saving my life to "lady you need help and we are going to connect you to some therapist in your hometown to help you."

I was hesitant in answering questions truthfully still trying to avoid Hakeem from looking like an evil villain. Why??? My entire family and friends watched that episode when it aired. As if I hadn't embarrassed my family already enough. I was happy though, that they recognized Alonja. She also received an award from Los Angeles County

# A. MICHELLE

Board of Supervisors and from the Mayor of Lancaster, California. My baby was my hero and she deserved the recognition, because I really had failed them and placed them in harm's way, and she saved my life.

The District Attorney was a young woman named Jasmine Taylor. She was African American with a short pixie hair cut like Haley Barry and she dressed sharp.

She wore precisely tailored suits that fit her like a glove. She could have used my help her with her shoe game, but other than that she was pulled together very professionally. Whenever she called me she had such a strong voice. You could tell she was trying to toughen me up and prepare me for court. She spoke with a very stern voice, explaining to me what to expect in court. She told me Hakeem would try to intimidate and scare me. She was not worried about Hakeem at all. She knew she would eat him alive, especially since he had decided to defend himself.

She obviously knew he was not that bright and could not handle the pressures of court. She told me that he would not make it through the first hearing and will certainly bow out from the pressure. She stayed in constant contact with me because she was preparing her game plan for trial and wanted me to be well prepared. I think a part of her thought I would try and avoid court to protect Hakeem. I had made up my mind at this point I had to be honest and let him pay for what he had done to me.

Hakeem's mother called me a few days before court asking for money again and asking me why I was testifying against him. She had been made aware of a deal he was contemplating taking to try and avoid a long sentence, I knew nothing about it. She claimed he was offered a 17-

# STABBED TO LIFE

year deal to avoid a lengthy trail and because of his background a jury would try to send him away for life.

She told me that was far too much because in her words "you didn't die… people get that kind of time for murder." I was shocked at her words. I would never disrespect his mother but at that moment it was on the tip of my tongue to call her out her name. How dare she, not even ask about my kids, but was going to defend her son to the bitter end.

I quickly ended the call with her because it was making me so upset. Her lack of compassion for me, her dry demeanor was just awful, and I did not want to say something bad to her.

The day had finally arrived to go to court. It was just me and my children. No family, no friends just me and my babies… just as it was when this horrific incident occurred. Not even my mother because my Dad was in the hospital and she needed to be there for him.

Because the case was such a high-profile case, it was moved to downtown Los Angeles in the Criminal Courts Building. Quite frankly, because of all the details that were going to come out, I was a little relieved. I was still so embarrassed and ashamed.

I was also made aware Hakeem decided to let the Public Defender help him. Someone must have told him representing himself was a foolish idea. Ms. Taylor the DA had warned me that the question of why I took Hakeem back and let him stay so many times may come up. She told me they may ask if I was also on drugs, or why else would I allow a known addict to be around my children? It could come up that I knew he was a felon with firearms. She just told me "be honest" and that was just what I did.

# A. MICHELLE

No more hiding or lying. I couldn't help me or my children by sugar coating this mess. As ugly as it was, and even though I felt like I was the only one going through this, I knew there were others just like me. I had to be a voice for them also.

My children were placed on the stand first, and I was not in the court room to hear their testimony, but by the sad look on their faces when it was over, I could tell it was traumatizing. My son was in tears, and my daughter was trying to be strong, but I could tell it was a grueling experience. I didn't want to make it harder by asking them to share with me what had happened. I just hugged and comforted them.

It was now my turn and as I walked in to the court room, it felt like all eyes were on me. I felt like I was moving in slow-motion down a never-ending hall. I saw people whispering to one another. Hakeem's mother and father were there and what appeared to be some other family members. I was escorted to the witness stand. The room seemed so cold and old. The floors were super shiny as if they had just been waxed for this special occasion. The judge who had on reading glasses, pulled his glasses down to get a good look at me.

I was wearing a pair dress slacks with a blouse buttoned all the way to the top and my hair pulled back in a ponytail. The Domestic Violence Advocate assigned to me was so sweet and she whispered to me before I went up, "Just stay focused on me honey, don't look at him, just look at me."

God, I wished I would have done that because no sooner than she said it, me and Hakeem made eye contact. He first gave me a smirk; almost a smile until the DA started asking questions. Then his looks were evil and mean. As we say where I'm from, he was "mean mugging" me, just staring me down trying to intimidate me and make me afraid. But I kept thinking of my children what they had been through, and what they had witnessed.

I had to be strong for them.

The questions began and just as I was warned, the DA. Ms. Taylor asked, "Adrianne, what made you stay so long in this relationship?"

You could've heard a pin drop in the court room. It seemed like my lips were glued together, I couldn't utter a word. I closed my eyes, took a deep breath, turned away from Hakeem and I asked God to help me do this.

"I loved him," I began slowly, "he kept telling me he was going to get better and believed if I stuck by him maybe he would. Toward the end though when the drug use got so bad I feared for my life." I explained with tears in my eyes. The judge passed me the box of tissue.

"Why were you so afraid Adrianne?" Ms. Taylor asked her eyes looking over at Hakeem and she almost rolled them, she did not like him, and it was obvious.

I looked over at Hakeem with his nostrils flared and his jaws clinched tight. He stared at me so hard and looked me up and down. "Come on God" I said to myself while staring back at Hakeem just as angrily. The domestic violence advocate was desperately trying to get my eyes focused back on her. We were having an evil staring match. I regained my composure and finally answered Ms. Taylor.

"I was scared because he had threatened to kill me and my family. He constantly reminded me that he had two strikes and whether he simply caught a petty theft or murder case he was going to prison for 25 to life, so I had better watch what I did." I explained

Ms. Taylor surprised me and told the judge that she had evidence that I was afraid and played the We Tip Hotline call I had made. This was the anonymous crime stopper tip line where you could call in a crime and the County would investigate. There playing over the court room speakers was my voice clear as day. I had said on the recording that Hakeem had threatened to kill me. That he had guns and was on drugs, I gave Sol's address, but nothing ever happened. Ms. Taylor made a point of bring up the County's negligence on not following up on the call and how it could have possibly avoided all of this from happening.

I looked over at Hakeem who was now whispering to his attorney. They appeared to be arguing. Ms. Taylor said to the judge, "I have no further questions for now your honor," she grabbed her folder and sat down and began to write. She looked up at me and smiled and winked as if to say "you're e doing good" well I did just what she suggested, I was just being honest.

Hakeem's attorney seemed unprepared and his turn was up to question me next, but he was scrambling through his paperwork , finally he came up and said, "Good morning, I just have a few questions for you ma'am…there was a knife found between your mattress on the side of the bed where you slept, was there a reason for that?" he asked.

It was like he had a list of questions prepared and now after the recording played, he was all discombobulated and thrown off.

# STABBED TO LIFE

After being asked this question I was thrown off as well. I'd forgotten about the knife I had there. He was correct. I did have a knife in between the mattress and I placed it there shortly after Hakeem started threatening to kill me.

"I placed the knife under the mattress after Hakeem repeatedly threated to kill me, the meth had him acting irrational and unpredictable and I was afraid, I could no longer tell what he would do while under the influence," I said as my voice cracked, fighting back tears.

I looked over and Hakeem who was rolling his eyes and shaking his head.

"Did you pull the knife on the defendant the day of the incident?" his attorney asked.

"No, I did not." I answered truthfully.

"Do you still love the defendant? I have records here from County jail that you accepted several calls from him even after the incident occurred." He asked holding up a stack of papers and waving them towards me.

"I did, and I thought he would show remorse for what he had done, instead he continued to blame me. I did take his calls a few times and later realized this was not good, especially after all my daughter did to save me from him. I know it was foolish and I am not sure why after being treated so badly I still had love for him, but I know now, he never loved me." I started crying uncontrollably. The advocate had to come up and console me.

Once I had myself together the judge was so kind to ask, "Will you be able to continue ma'am?"

# A. MICHELLE

"Yes, your honor, I will be fine," I said. I looked over nodded and smiled at the judge took a deep breath, "I'm ready" I said.

"Last question ma'am, the defendant stands to serve 25 to life for this issue that occurred. According to information I have obtained you were aware he was suffering from mental illness, Bipolar disorder to be exact. Do you feel your actions the morning of the incident provoked what happened to you?" he asked sarcastically.

"Objection your honor!" The DA Ms. Taylor said angrily. "Your honor that is speculation, the witness was in fear of her life and his mental illness whatever it was, was not a reason to do meth nor attempt murder!"

"Sustained…" the judge said quickly and shook his head at the attorney.

Lastly Ms. Taylor stood up and said she had one final thing to share with the court, another recording, she submitted as evidence and the judge approved of her to play in court. It was the 911 tapes. There were 3. The one I made, the neighbors and a cab that was called. The one that played where you could hear me scream, brought everyone in the court to tears. It was horrific because as the tape played a slide show of my daughter covered in my blood, the house and refrigerator covered in blood, the knife as it laid in the flower bed, the area in the grass where the administered aid and lastly my son crying. Those tapes were powerful, and I was convinced at that moment he was going to prison for a long time.

The judge just shook his head and said with emotion, "We are in recess till March 3, court will resume, and sentencing will take place then. Thank you all." he hit his gavel and we were dismissed.

Ms. Taylor met me in the hall and told me to write a letter to read in court, sharing how this has changed me and the impact it has had on my children. She hugged me and the kids and said how well we did.

I figured we had waited long enough to avoid Hakeem's family, but we all ended up on the elevator at the same time. It was awkward, and I made no eye contact with any of them. Right as we walked out, Hakeem's mother said, "Take care of yourself Adrianne."

I think his mother knew I tried hard to help her son, more than anyone had. I think in her heart she also knew I did not deserve what he had done to me and after witnessing what occurred in court, all the evidence, her outlook was a little different.

We walked to the car and headed to the hospital to check on my Dad. I shared just a little of what happened, and they were happy. My Aunt was there, and everyone apologized for not being there to support me, but it was probably for the best. I don't think anyone could have handled seeing all the gruesome pictures and the detailed explanation of what had occurred.

I was ready to move forward with my life. I did still think of Hakeem from time to time. He had started sending inappropriate letters to my family, talking badly about me. Sharing very detailed information about our relationship no parent should ever be privy too. Finally, my mother reported the explicit letters to the Prison Warden and the letters were stopped.

# A. MICHELLE

On March 3rd Hakeem was sentenced initially to 17 years but later more time was added to his sentence.

He found ways to write me and be nasty and he did that for well over a year. He even stayed in my head with this "333" thing. He told me anytime the clock said 333 that was him thinking of me, so all his letters had 333 on them as a reminder. It was eerie and creepy.

I began to have a new hobby of donating blood, my way of giving back since I had benefitted from so many blood transfusions when I was stabbed. Whenever they called, I showed up. I ended up donating several gallons before becoming anemic. The promise I had made to help others when I was dying was never clear to me.

I knew it had to be more than just donating blood. I talked to my daughter about it often asking her what I should do. I thought of going back to school to counsel other women who had experienced this type of torture and abuse, but I was scared.

Life was getting back to some normalcy. My children were back into their regular routine and bouncing back like kids do. Their resilience with all that had happened was so shocking. My daughter Alonja was doing exceptionally well in school and my son was back to hanging with his friends. I had become really close with my neighbors across the street who had helped me so much the day of the incident. This family became my bonus family and they always included me and my children in all they did. I will forever be grateful to the Moore's.

One day while at work I was introduced to a lady named LaToyia. I had seen around numerous times but never really conversed other than hello when passing down the hallways. She was a very sweet woman and very bubbly personality. She reminded me a lot of myself. She would walk the halls greeting people and stop for an occasional hug. She was not directly an employee of L.A. County, but a contracted employee through one of our local drug treatment facilities. I had the pleasure of finally talking with her. Instantly I felt a connection she shared with me all she did with the drug treatment facility. She not only helped women get sober, but she helped victims of domestic violence. She apparently had heard about what had happened to me and asked if I would be willing to come and share my story with the ladies she mentored. I was a little taken back because I certainly did not feel I was ready for all that. She shared with me how empowering it would be and how it would help in the healing process.

"Think about it ," she said in the warmest loving motherly voice. She then reached over and gave the biggest heartfelt hug I had ever received.

I did think about it, I even went home and shared it with my daughter who also encouraged me. But I was scared. I was afraid of judgment. It was bad enough I had gone on the Montel Williams show and looked like a complete idiot, but now in front of people in the small city I lived in. I had already been in Walmart and a couple said to me "Hey weren't you on Montel?" I almost wanted to lie. I just nodded and smiled. The wife hugged me and said she was praying for me and my kids.

Maybe 8 months after Hakeem's sentencing I started talking to men that were pursuing me. I had dropped a friend of mine off at the airport and met a Detroit Fireman, seemed cool but after a few dates it was clear he was not

# A. MICHELLE

for me. Then a journalist from Canada that I met while in New York.

Oddly enough, during the filming of the Montel show in Inglewood, CA, I even dated a police officer who was Montel's security. Once I was back home in California, he took me to see the R&B singer Tena Marie. All these men had issues, as did I. Either that or I was just not ready. Maybe it was just way too soon and sadly enough, even with all the crap Hakeem had done to me and the pain he had caused me and my family, I constantly thought about him. A lot of it was the guilt of feeling like I was the reason he was going to spend most of his life in prison. I could not get that out of my head.

One day while on my break at work I ran into a guy I had seen many times in Lancaster. He, much like me liked cars, this time when I saw him, he was doing donuts showing out in the parking lot of our neighborhood gas station / convenience store, AM/PM. We had similar vehicles, except mine was slightly better and faster. Of course, I swooped up and busted a few donuts too, we left tire smoke all in the air. I ran in the store to pay for gas and when I came out, he was sitting there with a friend smoking a cigarette and asked for my number. I smiled and told him I was running late getting back to work so I didn't have time. As I drove off, I showed out again; speeding off tires screeching and a cloud of smoke lingering behind me.

That was fun, and when I got off work that day he had left a piece of paper on the windshield clipped there by the wiper blades. I grabbed and read it. It was cute, it read "Call me when you can Speed Racer, we should hang out." It was signed Bart with his phone number. I looked around and got in my car, smiling from ear to ear. I was flattered,

# STABBED TO LIFE

he was a tall, Hispanic looking guy who wore oversized baggy hip hop clothing.

He appeared to have been a little younger than me, but the way he was trying to connect with me was flattering and sweet. He didn't give up either, even after the first few times I ignored his advances. After the 3rd note left on my car, I called.

He seemed a little "stalkerish", but it was harmless and cute. I hung out with him and went to a few of his car shows. He was the president of a car club and it was fun going to their lowrider hang outs and cruising Crenshaw on Sundays. Crenshaw was a popular street in Los Angeles where the car enthusiasts hung out to show off their cars. We were just having fun.

I did start noticing Bart drank quite a bit. I was beginning to drink right along with him as well as smoke a little weed from time-to-time. Nothing too crazy. My neighbors across the street grew very fond of us, and some days Bart would have his car club meetings at our house. It was fun, and the neighbors would come over too. We became very close with the Moore's and would plan events together and support each other's events as well. They loved my children and I cared for theirs too. Life was looking up.

After watching Bart and really paying attention to his drinking, my smoking, and thinking about how I just had gotten rid of a drug addict, I certainly did not need an alcoholic in my life. I had begun my same pattern of enabling and was buying gallons of alcohol every time I went to Costco and a carton of cigarettes.

I was happy that I could now identify patterns of codependency and now knew how to address it.

# A. MICHELLE

Bart and I were getting closer and about 9 months after we started our relationship, we talked about moving in together.

I was somewhat reluctant because of the drinking. My kids adored him. He helped my daughter get her 1st car and was close with my son, but I had concerns. I finally just talked to him and said, "Look Bart, I love you, you came in my life when I needed someone the most and we have had a ball getting to know each other. My parents like you and my kids do too, but the drinking and the smoking is a problem for me. I have already had a drug addict around my kids, I cannot do that anymore." I said nicely. His eyes were big and almost looked like he wanted to cry.

"I understand," he shook his head and the next day he was sucking on mints trying to stop smoking. He got rid of all the cigarettes and all the brandy. It was rough, but he did it. I felt like he loved me enough to honor my wishes.

Some weeks had past I ran into LaToyia at work again and she asked me would I be willing to share my story at her event she was having at the drug treatment facility. She said it would be all women and I was going to be her main speaker, and all I had to do was to share what occurred and how it affected me and my children. She told me it was going to give someone hope and help me heal. I wanted to say no, but when she said it would give someone hope, I thought what the heck, do it.

She gave me the date and address of where I needed to be. It was less than a week away, so I knew I had better start preparing myself. When the time came for me to speak, I was so nervous.

# STABBED TO LIFE

I had rehearsed what I was going to say at home in the mirror a few times, ran it by my daughter even, but when that day came I was sick to my stomach. I took a deep breath and just did it. Two minutes in I was already fighting back tears, especially the parts when it came to how I hurt my children. LaToyia was right though, it did help the ladies.

After the event, one by one, each one of the women came to me and hugged me and was also in tears and shared how their situations were similar. They kept saying how strong I was, and I showed them that they can get through it. I was in tears for weeks after that. I had discovered my calling, my God given assignment was to mentor and advocate for women.

After that I was called on to speak, I jumped at the opportunity. Me and LaToyia created a bond and planned more events where we were able to reach out and help our community. We both had a passion for helping women and a desire to make a difference. She asked me to help her start a non-profit she had always dreamed about I was honored that she had chosen me to help her. This was an amazing opportunity to help families affected by abuse. We gave classes, spoke at engagements, talked to the youth. It was amazing.

My life was finally getting back on track. I was in a new healthy relationship, and my children were thriving. My son was doing well in school and my daughter was ready to go off to the University of Santa Barbara.

I discovered my passion and was pursuing it full force. I was assisting families affected by abuse.

# A. MICHELLE

I used my ugly story to help women to identify the red flags of abuse, to keep themselves and their children safe, and helping them to create a safety plan to escape. Most of all, I was teaching women to love themselves.

I was not the example of the correct way to do it, my example was the wrong way, but I realized people can learn what NOT to do from my experience as well, and I am ok with that.

My children have had to work through there issues, triggers, and nightmares too. From time to time I have flashbacks. Sometimes simply brushing my teeth, if my gum bleeds even slightly and I taste blood in my mouth, it freaks me out. It reminds me of when I was coughing up blood. Also, someone standing too close behind me can preempt a panic attack, but I am here, and I am alive.

Hakeem is still in prison due to be released in 2026. He caught several other charges while incarcerated. His family never again reached out to me.

My father passed away but was able to see me get my life together. I miss him tremendously. I am grateful that my Mom continues to be my biggest cheerleader, so supportive and the true matriarch of our family.

*The counselor had tears in her eyes as I finished up the story. She set my appointment for the next week and shook my hand as I got up to leave. I thanked her for her kindness and said one last thing before walking out....*

I could have died that hot August morning, I was stabbed over 18 times. He could have stabbed me to death…instead, I was STABBED TO LIFE.

# AUTHOR BIO

A Michelle also known as Adrianne was born and raised in California. Her primary upbringing took place in the beautiful city of Carson, a part of Los Angeles County; 13 miles South of Los Angeles nestled between Long Beach, Compton and Torrance.

Adrianne is the eldest child born to Lee Ethel and John Anderson. Both she and her younger brother had a great middle-class upbringing with loving caring parents who raised them to be respectful, law abiding, and charitable with love for everyone.

# A. MICHELLE

After High School Adrianne began working for Los Angeles County, where she is currently still employed after 30 plus years.

During her years with LA County she has met so many amazing people; some who she is still very close to today.

After the trauma she endured in her life she committed herself to assisting other women by mentoring, counseling and facilitating classes such as Parenting, Anger Management, and Domestic Violence, at an agency called Two-Lifestyles Women Empowerment Programs (TLS).

The organization's CEO, LaToyia Conway Hampton, is one of Adrianne's closest friends who took her under her wing and poured into her and encouraged her to help others with her story.

Both LaToyia and Adrianne are passionate about the work they do in the community and have vowed to do this work for as long as they live.

Adrianne became a reader later in life and always had a strong desire to write. She has written curriculum for TLS which often includes handouts and scenarios, so the client / students can practice what they are learning with detailed story examples.

Adrianne is determined to put other books out accompanied by workbooks to use as a teaching tool in agencies that do the work of educating people on domestic violence and sexual assault.

# ACKNOWLEDGEMENTS

I would like to take a moment to acknowledge all the people who loved me even when they knew I was making some horrible decisions. Those that stuck by me and helped me when I was at my worst. Please note that if I don't mention you by name, you are forever engraved in my heart.

The Moore's, my neighbors on Arnica Lane. The first responders who showed up to help save my life, thanks for the helicopter ride. Every time I hear a helicopter, I thank God for you all. The Trauma team at Holy Cross Hospital - San Fernando Valley who performed lifesaving procedures. I appreciate you.

My family, especially my mother Lee Ethel Anderson and father John "Big John" Anderson who had my back no matter what. They helped me raise some very well-rounded children. I can never thank you enough. My brother, one of the first faces I remember seeing when I woke up in the hospital. I love you Maria, Cooper & Ian.

My entire family was there then and continue to be now. They have supported all my events, encouraged me to write this book, and continue donate to the cause every chance they can. I love you guys and especially my cousin Vertenia who I confided in many times during this crazy roller-coaster ride.

To Bart, thanks for showing me that healthy relationships do exist.

# A. MICHELLE

Finally, my babies Alonja and Darrell (DeDe).

Mama made so many mistakes but I'm trying my best to turn it around. I love you two for never giving up on me. You guys were with me every step of the way good, bad or indifferent. Alonja you are forever my hero. Thanks for allowing us to rebuild something I messed up; a strong trusting mother-daughter relationship.

We're getting that back slowly but surely and it means the world to me.

Made in the USA
San Bernardino, CA
17 May 2020